The Complete Guide to
Point-and-Figure Charting

The Complete Guide to Point-and-Figure Charting

by

Heinrich Weber and Kermit Zieg

HARRIMAN HOUSE LTD

43 Chapel Street
Petersfield
Hampshire
GU32 3DY
GREAT BRITAIN

Tel: +44 (0)1730 233870
Fax: +44 (0)1730 233880

email: enquiries@harriman-house.com
web site: www.harriman-house.com

———————————————————

First published in Great Britain in 2003

Copyright Harriman House Ltd

The right of Kermit Zieg and Heinrich Weber to be identified as Authors has been
asserted in accordance with the Copyright, Design and Patents Act 1988.

ISBN 1-8975-9728-2

British Library Cataloguing in Publication Data
A CIP catalogue record for this book can be obtained from the British Library.

Printed and bound by Ashford Colour Press

Contents

About the authors

Heinrich A. Weber

Heinrich A. Weber was co-founder and managing director of the market-making firm, Servisen Trading/QT Optec. He learned technical analysis while working with one of the early exponents, Ed Hargitt. In a joint venture operation with HSBC-James Capel, he directed the development of one of the first trading systems using the Hurst coefficient.

He is a partner and risk manager of the active Eurex member firm, DeTraCo. As a partner, he develops risk models and financial forecasting applications with AleaSoft,[1] the European leader in the use of neural networks for the prediction of energy prices. Occasionally he does specific consulting in the securities area, some of which is conducted jointly with Dr. Zieg.

Heinrich studied at Swiss Federal Institute of Technology (EPFL) at Lausanne, Switzerland, and has a PhD and an MBA from Rushmore University.

He lives with his wife and two young daughters in Geneva, Switzerland.

Kermit C. Zieg, Jr., Ph.D.

Being an avid investor since age 12, Dr. Zieg has a BS with a Finance Major from Indiana University, an MA in Investments from Ohio State University, and a Ph.D. in Finance and Investments also from Ohio State. Based upon over 40 years of personal investing experience and academic research, he has written nine books and numerous articles on many of the most successful investment strategies. He is a Full Professor of Finance and Investments at Florida Institute of Technology's National Capital Region campus in Alexandria, Virginia, where he keeps his finger on the pulse of the markets through active trading. He travels extensively, training, lecturing, consulting and serving as an expert witness.

Dr Zieg's research and writing is unbiased. He is not a broker, and does not manage money, other than his own. He doesn't publish a newsletter, and is not an investment advisor. His two major areas of trading and research interest are point-and-figure charting and options. In his study of point-and-figure charting conducted continuously since 1961, he has run thousands of tests (back tested and live), and numerous what-if simulations.

Dr. Zieg is active in trading options and fully utilizes point-and-figure in all of his decision-making. He lives in Vienna, Virginia.

---

[1] www.aleasoft.com

Preface

Who this book is for

Point-and-figure is the best of all technical analysis methods. That's our firm conviction. The aim of this book is to explain point-and-figure to European investors and traders, and we have therefore used European securities in all the examples given. But because p&f is universal, exactly the same concepts and techniques apply equally well to US securities. Prior to this European-focused work, the authors have written books applying p&f trading techniques to commodities and US equities.[2]

This book covers every aspect of point-and-figure from the basic concepts to advanced technical information, because the book is meant for the novice as well as the experienced trader. We have included all the relevant information, from drawing your own charts manually to the computerisation of p&f, so the book can also serve the committed independent trader who controls his own computer environment.

What the book covers

We have put every effort into writing a book which is based on facts, research, and genuine market situations, in contrast to many technical analysis books which list all sorts of hypothetical buy or sell situations. This was done because we are professional traders, market makers and academics, so we understand the need for an approach that is academically sound, based upon rigorous testing and analysis, but which is also of practical use to active traders. Our book is a manual, not a compilation of anecdotal evidence. We are convinced that when you have studied it, you will understand:

- point-and-figure charting
- point-and-figure trading tactics
- the essence of optimisation
- the application of all this to real trading

The purpose of the book is thus to cover all material aspects of point-and-figure charting. Whether you are a novice or an experienced trader, you should find answers to all p&f-related questions. We explain the concepts thoroughly, though in a way that is easy to understand.

---

[2] Kermit C. Zieg, *Point & Figure Commodity and Stock Trading Techniques,* Traders Press, 1997

In this book, we use simple charts for illustrative purposes, but also real charts of the kind we rely on in our daily analysis and trading. We have mainly chosen charts of stocks from the FTSE 100, EuroSTOXX 50 and Techmark index. We also use some other interesting examples, such as the impact of the 1987 crash on the S&P 500 index or the decline of the Nikkei 225.

The book is structured in such a way that it can be used by readers of all levels of trading and investing knowledge from the novice to the experienced trader.

Structure of the book

The book makes use of many real and recent charts to illustrate the points made in the text. But in some instances, especially in the first part of the book, we use small excerpts of charts in order to illustrate a specific idea with the utmost clarity.

The book is divided into six sections, which are summarized below.

Section summary

Introduction

The uniqueness of point-and-figure is explained, and as a contrast some other types of price charts are presented. The advantages of p&f are listed explicitly, and the method by which investment decisions are reached is briefly touched upon.

Drawing point-and-figure charts

In this chapter we explain how to draw a point-and-figure chart, with pencil and paper and also with computers.

Interpreting the charts

We explain the basic buy and sell signals, then more complex signals, and finally show how trend lines are incorporated into a chart.

Trading applications

Horizontal and vertical count methods are used to estimate the size of upcoming price moves. Stop-orders are used to protect positions and to enter into the market. Pyramiding is used to concentrate capital in the trending positions. The subject of risks relating to point-and-figure trading is dealt with. Swing trading is a trading style that profits from mid-term swings in the market and can be implemented well by adapting the point-and-figure parameters. Trading styles that generate a high number of transactions are analysed with point-and-figure. Other investments than stocks are briefly mentioned. And finally we list tips and strategies of experienced traders.

New optimisation techniques

Optimisation and simulation are explained in detail. We show you how to do it and how to avoid the most common trap – 'over-fitting'. Then we list our most conclusive results and show you how to profit best from those techniques.

Profitability analysis

Here we summarize the original Davis, Davis-Thiel and Zieg studies, and also summarise the results of our most recent research regarding the profitability of point-and-figure trading.

Technical notes

Research in quantitative finance is explained. Technical details regarding scaling and optimising are clarified, and we show in detail how we have programmed our p&f computer program. Computer-related issues such as databases and data feeds are covered.

At the end of the book, you will find a bibliography, a glossary, an index of websites and a general index.

The structure of the book reflects a top-down approach, whereby we start with the two fundamental concepts of point-and-figure, namely the law of supply and demand and the discretization of price. Onto those concepts we build layer upon layer of more detailed information. The technical chapter – which constitutes the last part of the book – should help to resolve any remaining questions.

How to make the most out of the book

Novices

If you are new to point-and-figure and would like to apply the technique to guide your investment strategy, then the introductory chapters are a must. You have to become proficient in drawing a p&f chart yourself, and therefore it is *imperative that you do the exercises*. Once you have gone through the basics, we suggest that you do p&f charts of your favourite stocks.

When you feel you are familiar with the concept, you should continue to increase your knowledge base so that you will be able to apply point-and-figure to real trading. You will probably have to buy one of the software programs we recommend or subscribe to a chart service (some products allow for free trial periods). On page 24 we have listed the services which we use personally, with contact information provided on page 46.

Experienced traders

If you are knowledgeable about investing or trading, but want to know more about point-and-figure charting, we still recommend that you go through the introduction and the basics, and try the charting exercises. Once you are able to draw the charts set out in the exercises, study the trend lines and pyramiding, because both are different – although more precise – than in bar chart analysis. Then go to the chapter which is related to your investment or trading style. You will probably not need to go through the technical chapter.

Professional traders

If you are a professional trader and already have an understanding of point-and-figure, but would like to increase your arsenal of trading concepts, then you should read quickly through the basics and trading applications, where you may well learn something new, and then study in-depth the subject you are most interested in, be it day-trading, swing trading or optimisations.

Point-and-figure experts

If you are already an expert in point-and-figure, but are looking for some additional gems, we suggest you read through the Chapter 4 on optimisation, and Chapter 6 on technical matters. You will probably also want to study Chapter 5 on profitability analysis, because it includes new research. Note, too, the section entitled *'Tips from experienced traders'* which is part of Chapter 3.

Terminology

A quick note on the format of company codes used in the text.

All company codes use the format:

   [Company symbol].[Exchange]

For example:

   VOD.L   -   Vodafone shares trading in London
   AEGN.AS -   Aegon shares trading in Amsterdam
   CARR.PA -   Carrefour shares trading in Paris
   SAPG.DE -   SAP shares trading on Xetra

This is a standard code system used by information services such as Reuters.

Supporting website

The website supporting this book can be found at:

http://www.harriman-house.com/pointandfigure

Conclusion

The objective of this book is to provide the reader with all of the basics and the most significant technical topics to point-and-figure charting. It represents a training manual explaining everything you need to know to become a successful chartist in an easy-to-understand manner through a few words, accompanied by lots of examples and figures.

When you have worked through the book, you will know how to do it! It is a p&f 'cookbook'. The recipe works, and the product is great.

We hope that you enjoy the book and that it will help you to become an even more successful market participant. Point-and-figure is easy to do, the best of all technical analysis systems, and therefore we encourage you to start implementing it for your benefit as soon as possible.

So let's get started!

Introduction

Why point-and-figure?

There are a number of charting methodologies including line, bar, candlestick, Kagi and point-and-figure, to name but a few. Each of these is illustrated below.

Chart 0.1 — Line chart of NASDAQ rise and decline

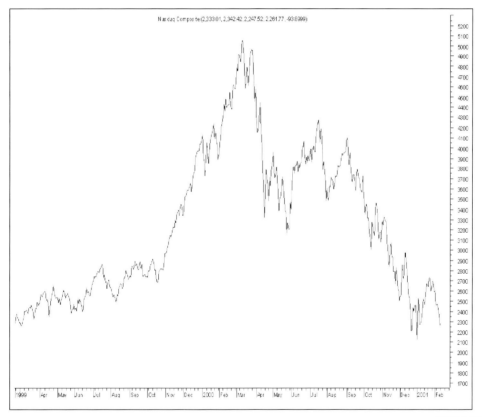

Source: MetaStock

The *line chart* is the simplest way to display the price history of a security, namely by connecting subsequent closing prices. It is the standard method used to display any kind of sequential data, e.g. temperature.

Chart 0.2 – Bar chart of NASDAQ rise and decline

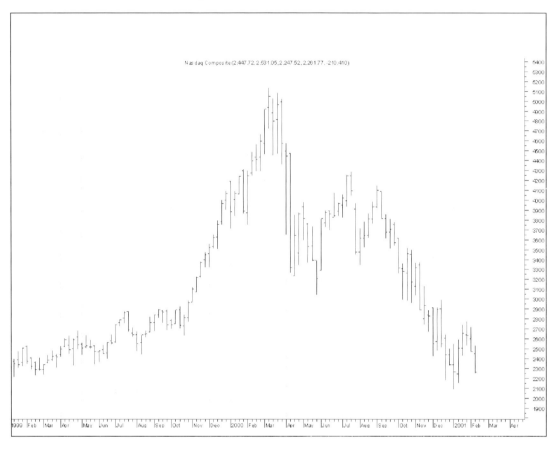

Source: MetaStock

In contrast to a line chart, the above *bar chart* – the most widely used chart type – also shows the trading range (open, high, low) in addition to the closing price. The high and low of the day define the length of the bar. The open is marked with a tick on the left and the close with a tick on the right side of the bar.

Like the line chart, the bar chart shows how the price moves over time using equal-spaced time intervals. In the chart above, you can see that calm periods like April 1999 are given the same importance as highly volatile periods like April 2000.

Chart 0.3 – Candlestick chart of NASDAQ rise and decline

Source: MetaStock

The *candlestick chart* tries to highlight patterns by colouring the rectangle formed by the high and the low either black (if close below open) or white (if close above open). This feature is used for visual analysis by identifying specific patterns, like a "big black candle" or a "morning star". Interestingly, candlesticks are a very old concept, being used to analyse rice contracts in Japan around 1600.

Chart 0.4 – Kagi chart of NASDAQ rise and decline

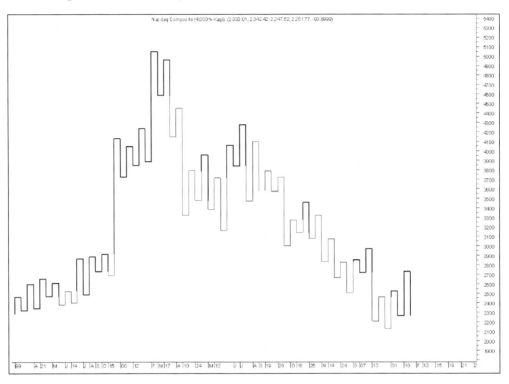

The *Kagi chart* is a sort of Japanese point-and-figure chart. It dates back to the opening of the Japanese stock market and was introduced in the West much later. Its strengths are similar to the p&f charting technique – for example, in its use of a variable time axis.

Chart 0.5 – Point-and-figure chart of NASDAQ rise and decline

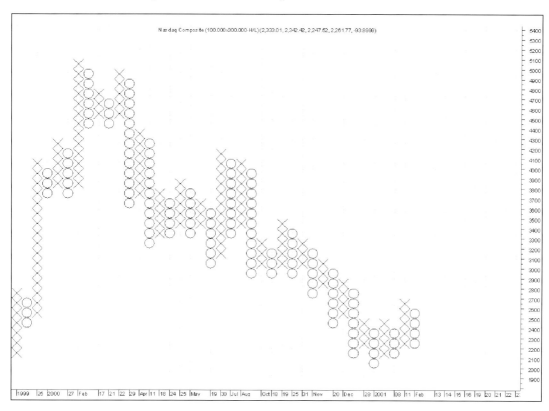

Source: MetaStock

Finally, the point-and-figure chart.

Much has been written on all the charting types mentioned above, and there are strong supporters of each technique. But there are significant advantages of point-and-figure over all other charting systems. And so major are these benefits that if you know point-and-figure charting, there is no need to use any other system.

The powerful advantages of point-and-figure

Point-and-figure is truly superior to all other charting approaches for the following reasons:

- **It is easy to understand.**
  It takes only a few minutes to become an expert p&f chartist! The techniques are simple. No maths skills, prior market knowledge or special tools are required. Just learn a few basics and you are up and running.

- **It focuses on what really matters: price movements.**
  All other technical analysis is based on a fixed time axis, whereas p&f only considers price movements and therefore prevents erroneous trading signals originating from timeline-induced distortions.

- **The methodology is a chart and trading system in one.**
  Not only does the p&f chart depict price moves, but most importantly the charts translate directly into a trading methodology, producing buy and sell signals!

- **It has been rigorously tested and it works.**
  Numerous academic studies have been conducted over a span of decades and the results are always the same: p&f charting is profitable.

- **There are exact decision rules.**
  You know exactly where to enter and exit trades. There is absolutely no guessing required.

- **It is universal.**
  Once you know the basic rules you can chart every investment media including stocks, commodities, mutual funds, stock and commodity options, indexes, and even coins, stamps and art. The same techniques apply for all investment products.

- **It always gets you in on a major move.**
  You will never miss a major move since there will always be an entry signal. You might choose not to trade the signal, but the signal is always there.

- **It works for long and short positions, and always displays stop-loss points.**
  Whether you trade only long, only short, or both, the charts display all exact entry points as well as exact stop points. No guessing is required.

- **It concentrates money in the trending positions and keeps little in the whippy ones.**
  The inherent pyramiding technique shifts money automatically into the profitable trades, exactly where you want your money to be.

- **It generates crystal-clear trend lines.**
  In contrast to the typical bar chart and other charting methods, point-and-figure is non-ambiguous about where to trace the all-important trend lines. Again, no guessing is required.

- **The charts are simple to maintain.**
  In 10 minutes a day you can manually maintain 100 charts. No computer or expensive subscription or data service is needed. All that is required is the daily newspaper, a pencil and graph paper.

Why is point-and-figure so appealing visually?

Because it is totally symmetric as defined by the two forces of supply and demand, described by the symbols O for supply and X for demand. This symmetry can be further appreciated in the instructions for drawing the charts which consist of two symmetric sets of instructions. Also, buy signals are the exact reverse of sell signals, and trend lines only exist with three angles: horizontal, diagonal up and diagonal down. Beauty through simplicity.

The investment decision

Investing involves a very limited number of decisions:

1. What stock (futures contract, equity option, index option, commodity option or other item) should I buy?

2. At which price level should I buy it?

3. Having purchased it, at which price level should I sell it?

To be a successful investor, one needs not only to select the best stocks to own, but buy them at the right time, and then employ appropriate exit strategies to stop-losses and let profits run.

The limitations of fundamental analysis

Most investment services, newsletters, advisors, and brokerage firms select stocks to purchase through the use of fundamental analysis, the reason being that wrong advice is easy to justify by pointing at a change in some exogenous variable, market environment or geopolitical situation.

Fundamental analysis involves the study of the quality of the company, its sales, earnings, management, and other factors relating to how the company has performed over recent history, how it should fare in the future and how it compares with other firms within its industry sector. There are hundreds of factors, ratios and indicators that can and are employed to track past performance, anticipate future results and measure one company against its peer group.

But as important as knowing what stock to buy, is knowing *when to buy it*. How often have the fundamentals pointed to a very positive scenario, only to have the securities price collapse? Technical analysis is employed to determine *when* to buy the fundamentally strong stock.

The ideal investment approach marries fundamentals to technical analysis in order i) to identify the best stocks and ii) to select the most efficient entry and exit points. To use only one, fundamental or technical analysis, is to admit that the quality of the company does not matter, or that it is not important when to buy and sell. Both are needed.

If we had to decide whether fundamental or technical analysis is most important, and could employ only one, we would select technical methods. It is always preferable to own a beautifully market-performing stock, with well orchestrated buy and sell points, than an extremely strong fundamental stock that is going nowhere in the market.

There are dozens upon dozens of methodologies for evaluating security price movements (i.e. technical analysis). There are technical methods that utilize bar charts, moving averages, Bollinger Bands, Gann Arcs, Fibonacci Fans, Renko, Candlesticks, Standard Deviations and Price Rate-of-Change, to name but a few. Some are old, some new, some time-tested, and many totally untested. A few are simple to employ, but most are confusing. Others require a high degree of mathematical expertise, a fast PC with lots of hard drive space, and a person who desires to delve into the mysteries of the incomprehensible.

Then there is point-and-figure, one of the oldest, easiest to understand, simplest to employ, academically tested, and most profitable of the lot.

Since when has point-and-figure been used?

Point-and-figure charts have been around since the late 19th century. There is some anecdotal evidence that early forms of the technique were used by European traders even before Wall Street was founded in 1792. They were considered as an ideal way to keep track of stocks since they show the past history in a very concise, readable form and are easy to keep up and study. An experienced chartist can manually update 100 charts in 10 to 15 minutes per day. But it was not until 1958 when A. W. Cohen first published his book, *The Three Box Reversal Method of Point and Figure Stock Market Trading* that the techniques became widely recognized as a valuable market strategy. The original publisher of the Cohen book was Chartcraft, Inc., which is today the major supplier of subscription charts in the US.

Examples of point-and-figure in action

The success of point-and-figure charting is revealed by examining a handful of trading signals yielded by the system in recent years.

Chart 0.6 – BAE Systems [BA.L]

```
400 _____   400
390 .....................|...X.X......................  390
380 X..........X.X.......|...XOX6.+...................  380
370 1OX.........XOXO.....|.X.XOXO+...................   370
360 .OXO......X.XO8OX.B...|.XOXO5O...................   360
350 _OXO__X_X_X7XO_OXOXO__2_XOXO+O_____   350
340 .OXO..45XOXOX..OXOAOX.XOXO4+.■.................   340
330 .OXO..XOXOXO...OXOXOXOXOXO+..OX..............     330
320 .OXOX.XO.O.....9XOXOXOXO3+...7XO8.............    320
310 .OXO2OX........OXOXO.O1O+....OXOXO............    310
300 _OXOXO3_____O_OX__C_+_____O_OXO_____    300
290 .OXOXO..........OX...........OXO..............    290
280 .OXOX...........O....|........OX9.............    280
270 .OXOX................|........O.O.............    270
260 .O.O.................|........O...............    260
250 _____|_____O_____    250
240 .....................|.......O................    240
230 .....................|.......O................    230
220 .....................|.......O................    220
210 .....................|.......O..X.X...........    210
200 _____O__AOXO_+_____    200
195 .....................|.......O..▓OXO+.........    195
190 .....................|.......OX.XOXOX.........    190
185 .....................|.......OXOXO+OXB........    185
180 .....................|.......OXOX+.■XOX.X.....    180
175 _____OXO+__O_OXOXO___    175
170 .....................|.......OX+.....OXOXO.....   170
165 .....................|.......O+......OXOCO.....   165
160 .....................|.......+......O.O.O......   160
155 .....................|..............O.........    155
150 _____O_____    150
145 .....................|..............O.........    145
140 .....................|..............O.........    140
135 .....................|..............O.........    135
130 .....................|..............O.........    130
125 _____OX_____    125
120 .....................|..............OX.....      120
115 .....................|..............OX.....      115
110 .....................|..............OX.....      110
105 .....................|..............OX.....      105
100 _____OX_____    100
 95 -------------------0----------------------O------  95
 90 -------------------2---------------------------    90
```

This BAE Systems [BA.L] chart covers the time span January 2001 until end of 2002. A trading range during the first 18 months between 260 and 390 is observed. Then a breakout which is defined by a simple signal and the breaking of a bullish support line. This strong sell signal, at 340 in autumn 2002, heralds the decline of the stock toward 100. Although a certain resistance to that move is experienced in the 175 to 200 region, which generates a small whipsaw: a buy signal is given at 195, and shortly afterwards another sell signal at 180. Thereafter, the downtrend continues, again introduced by the break of a support and a simple sell.

What do the different colours mean?

We use throughout the book green for a buy signal, red for a sell signal and yellow for other interesting characteristics, such as trend lines.

Chart 0.7 – BSKYB [BSY.L]

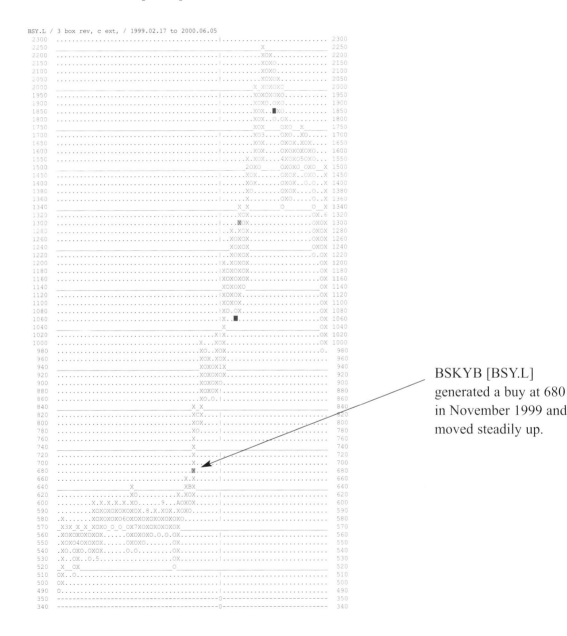

BSKYB [BSY.L] generated a buy at 680 in November 1999 and moved steadily up.

Chart 0.8 – Safeway [SFW.L]

```
420   .....|..X....|..................... 420
410   .....|..X7...|..................... 410
400   _____6_XO_____ 400
390   .....|XOXO...|..................... 390
380   .....|XOXO...|..................... 380
370   .....|XO.O...|..................... 370
360   .....|X..■B..|..................... 360
350   _____X_X__OXO_____ 350
340   ....XO5..8XO.|..................... 340
330   ....XOX..9XO.|..................... 330
320   ....XOX..OAOX|X.................... 320
310   ....XOX..O.OX4X6................... 310
300   _____XCX____OXOXO_____ 300
290   ..■.X2X....C.O5OX.................. 290
285   X.XBX3.......O.OXO7................ 285
280   XOXOX|.......|.OXOXO............... 280
275   XOXO.|.......|.OXOXOX.............. 275
270   _O_____O_OXOXO_____ 270
265   .....|.......|...O.OXO............. 265
260   .....|.......|.....OXOX............ 260
255   .....|.......|.....OXOXO........... 255
250   .....|.......|.....O.OXO....■.X..... 250
245   _____OXOX_X_XOXO_____ 245
240   .....|.......|.......O.OXOX8XOXO.... 240
235   .....|.......|........OXOXOXOXO.... 235
230   .....|.......|........OXOXO.OXO.... 230
225   .....|.......|........OXOX..O.OX... 225
220   _____O_OX_____■XO__ 220
215   .....|.......|...........O.....OXOX. 215
210   .....|.......|...............9XOXA 210
205   .....|.......|...............OXOXO 205
200   .....|.......|...............O.OXO 200
195   _____OXO 195
190   .....|.......|...................O.O 190
185   .....|.......|...................O 185
180   .....|.......|...................O 180
175   .....|.......|..................... 175
150   -----0-------0--------------------- 150
145   -----1-------2--------------------- 145
```

As the chart above shows, point-and-figure got you well into a short in the down move of Safeway [SFW.L] during 2001-2002.

And, in particular, all the telecoms, dotcoms and techs generated sell signals and had you short over the major part of the meltdown – not to forget that p&f had you on the long side during the aggressive up move.

This is thus an introduction to point-and-figure charting. It is the beginning set of do-it-yourself instructions with the later chapters devoted to more detailed aspects of the process.

But for now, let's learn the tools.

1

Drawing
point-and-figure charts

- Background

- How to draw the charts

- Computerised charting

Background

Point-and-figure charting has long been associated with images of serious-minded men hunched over notebooks in dark corners of brokerage offices and trading floors, making cryptic marks on box-ruled paper. Part-time speculators usually think of it as a valuable tool that is beyond their grasp, either because it demands too much time, or is too complicated, or requires access to time and sales data that isn't always available.

Hopefully, this book will correct these misconceptions. Anyone can keep p&f charts just as he can the more common bar graphs. All that's needed is a pencil and eraser, graph paper, daily high-low prices for each stock or contract to be plotted, and an understanding of a few simple rules. The result is a trading tool that is more useful than the standard bar chart, and that presents clearer pictures of what prices are doing, more precise indications of where to get in and out of a market, and more reliable predictions of how far price moves are likely to go.

The underlying philosophy: supply and demand

The basic premise of p&f charting and trading is that the *Laws of Supply and Demand*, and nothing else, govern the price of a security or commodity.

- When demand is stronger than supply, the stock's price rises;
- When supply exceeds demand, the price falls;
- When supply and demand are contesting for supremacy, the price moves sideways.

Point-and-figure extracts the essence of that battle for equilibrium between supply and demand by creating an interpretable graphic, the p&f chart. The chart is used to determine investment or trading strategy.

Representing the forces of supply and demand

Every p&f chart contains the following elements:

Long columns of Xs	Long columns of Os	Short alternating columns of Xs and Os
Signify greater demand than supply and therefore a rising price.	Signify greater supply than demand and therefore a falling price.	Signify a contest for supremacy between supply and demand from a relatively equal position.

The p&f chart is a pictorial record of the contest between the forces of supply and demand.

Chart 1.1 – Supply and demand in the case of Aegon [AEGN.AS]

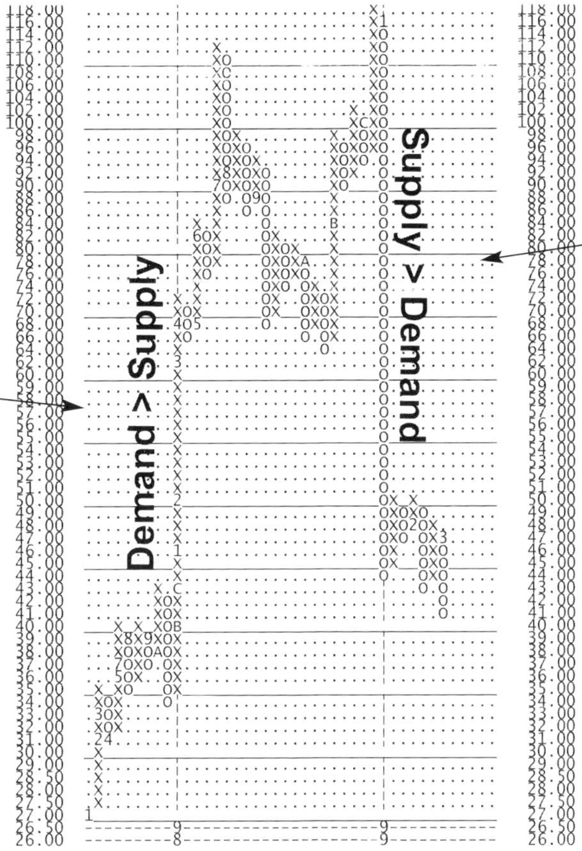
Demand > Supply
Supply > Demand
The long column of Xs – *rising prices* – means that demand at that time was greater than supply.
The long column of Os – *falling prices* – means that at that time supply was greater than demand.

General principles

Point-and-figure charts are unique in three ways:

1. Only **large significant moves** are noted, and minor fluctuations are ignored as having no relevance to the overall trend.

2. P&F charts **ignore the passage of time**. Dates may be indicated on the chart, but this is done solely as a matter of convenience, and has no relevance to decision making or to signal descriptions.

3. P&F charts **denote movements by the letters "X" and "O"** and not by lines, as in the more commonly seen line/bar charts.

How to draw the charts

The tools

Pencil and paper

As already mentioned, the only things necessary for successful p&f charting of stocks, commodity future contracts, options or any other investment are a pencil and paper, daily high and low prices for each investment being monitored, and an understanding of a few simple rules.

The pencil should be soft lead type which can be easily erased. The eraser should leave the paper smudge-free and the paper should have either the US ten squares to the inch with heavy rulings every five boxes, or the European 4mm grid. The 1mm engineering grid is, however, too tiny. Graph paper of the appropriate type is readily available at most office supply stores.

Pencil and paper in the computer age? In the modern world of computers and the internet, the reference to pencil and paper may seem rather old-fashioned. But we firmly believe that to thoroughly understand p&f charts, you have to spend some time manually drawing them. Only by doing this will you properly appreciate the subtleties of p&f. Once you have drawn charts manually, you may well decide to move on to using a computer. However, be aware that many of the most accomplished traders still prefer to maintain their p&f charts by hand.

Computer

Even if you take our advice and start by drawing charts manually, you will probably end up using a computer for p&f charting. Point-and-figure programs work on any standard PC. Below is a short description of the equipment that we use:

- **Reasonable hardware** (at the time of writing, we use as a desktop a Pentium IV, 2GHz, 512MB, 100GB Hard disk, and as a portable a Pentium IV, 2.66GHz, 256 MB Ram, 30 GB Hard disk). Because hardware gets cheaper and cheaper we recommend, the bigger the better. However, a reasonable PC should not cost a fortune.

- A reliable and fast **back-up device**; we use an IOMEGA Zip drive and a CD-Burner.

- Good p&f **software**. We recommend MetaStock, PFScan and Updata.

- **A very good screen**. Because p&f is so fascinating, you will spend a lot of time looking at the screen!

- **Fast access** to the data providers, especially for downloading prices of a large number of stocks. We use broadband internet.

Remember the most important task in computing is: back up!

Chapter 6 details the use of computers and the programming of p&f charting in more detail.

Learning by doing

The best way to learn how to draw a p&f chart is to work through an example. This is what we will do in this section.

The table below should be considered an excerpt of stock data. It is shown in the most widely used format, namely:

1. Date
2. Opening price
3. Highest price of the day
4. Lowest price of the day
5. Closing price
6. Number of stocks traded

Table 1.1 – Figures for p&f drawing example

Date	Open	High	Low	Close	Vol
1-Jan-01	37.25	38.25	35.75	37.50	1234000
2-Jan-01	39.50	40.12	39.25	40.00	1567000
3-Jan-01	37.50	38.50	37.00	37.25	1456000
4-Jan-01	37.00	37.50	36.50	37.00	1789000
5-Jan-01	37.00	40.25	37.00	39.00	2345000

Please read through the instructions overleaf, then roll your sleeves up, take a piece of paper and a pencil, and try to do the chart yourself.

Scaling the chart

As the prices are in the 29 to 60 range the box size of 1 is used (explained in the *How to scale the chart* section on page 31).

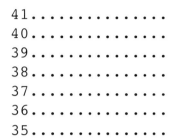

```
41...............
40...............
39...............
38...............
37...............
36...............
35...............
```

Day 1 - Starting the chart

Once the chart is scaled for the stock, the next step is to enter price movements. This is accomplished by *observing the daily highs and lows for the stock.*

If we start a new chart manually on blank paper we have to decide whether to put Xs or Os in the first column of the chart. Since there are no entries yet on the chart, the spread between the first day's high and low is important.

If the spread spans the value of three or more boxes *and* the price closes above the centre of the range, draw the appropriate number of Xs.

How does this work in practice?

In our example, Day 1, 1st January 2001, had a high of 38.25, a low of 35.75, and closed at 37.50. Because the high and low spans 3 boxes (36, 37, 38), with our pencil we would place a dot in the 36, 37 and 38 boxes, as shown in the chart below.

```
41...............
40...............
39...............
38...*...........
37...*...........
36...*...........
35...............
```

Since the closing price (37.50) is above the middle of the range (37.0), we would change the dots to Xs in the 36, 37, and 38 boxes, as shown opposite.

```
41...............
40...............
39...............
38...X...........
37...X...........
36...X...........
35...............
```

Had the close been below the centre of the range, the entries would have been Os.

Note that if the range between the high and low had failed to span three boxes, dots would be placed in the boxes that were spanned, as temporary markers. For example, had the high on Day 1 been 37.50 and the low 35.75, dots would be placed only in the 36 and 37 boxes. The dots would serve as reminders of which boxes have been crossed until more days' price data became available.

If, on Day 2, the stock had a high of 38.25 and a low of 36.75, a third, and higher box (38) would have been reached, so the two dots in the 36 and 37 boxes would be replaced with Xs and a third X drawn at 38.

If, on Day 2, the range had been 37.25 to 34.75, a *lower* box (35) would have been crossed. The dots in boxes 36 and 37 would be replaced with Os, and a third O drawn at 35.

Once the first column of Xs or Os has been entered in the chart, *closing prices are no longer used in the charting process*. From now on, only high and low prices play a role.

Rising prices

On Day 1 in our example, the price advanced from box levels 36 to 38. Accordingly, we have a column of Xs in the 36, 37, and 38 boxes. Now that the first column has been drawn, the *continuation becomes considerably easier*.

The technique is as follows:

• If the current or most recent column is composed of Xs, look at the high for the day under consideration (the 'daily high'). If it is at least one box higher than the highest X in the current column, draw in the appropriate number of additional Xs.

For instance, if the current column has Xs at 36, 37, and 38 and the daily high is 39.25, you would draw a new X at 39. If the daily high was 40.125, you would draw new Xs at 39 *and* 40. Note that a box is considered crossed if the price hits the exact price point of the box. For example, if the daily high was 40 you *would* draw an X in the 40 box, just as you would if the high was 40.875. The 41 box could not be filled with an X until the price reached at least 41.

Day 2 - A new high

In our example, because on Day 2, 2nd January 01, there was a high of 40.12, two extra Xs are marked in boxes 39 and 40. The updated chart is shown below.

```
41...............
40...X...........
39...X...........
38...X...........
37...X...........
36...X...........
35...............
```

If the daily high is high enough to require the drawing of one or more additional Xs in the current column, the *daily low is totally ignored*. This procedure of looking first at the highs and drawing more Xs continues as long as each succeeding daily high is one or more boxes higher than the last X drawn in the current column.

Price reversal

At some point, there will come a time when the daily high does *not* permit the drawing of new Xs. Only when this occurs is the daily low of interest. If the daily high is not at least one box higher than the highest X, the daily low is reviewed to determine whether the price advance has reversed. If the low is lower than the highest X by the value of three boxes, the price advance is considered temporally broken. In this case we look at the daily low to see if we have a price reversal and should thus draw three Os. If we can draw three Os, the new column is drawn with the first O being placed one column to the right of the X column and one box below the highest X.

Day 3 - A price reversal from up to down

On Day 3, since the 38.50 is not high enough to permit the entry of a new X, attention is focused on the daily low: 37. Because the low of 37 allows for three boxes (39, 38 and 37) below the highest marked box (40) to be filled, the trend is considered in the p&f chart as reversed, and Os are drawn downwards beginning one column to the right of the X column and with the highest O one box below the highest X. The chart at the top of the next page shows this price reversal.

```
41...............
40...X...........
39...XO..........
38...XO..........
37...XO..........
36...X...........
35...............
```

Had the low been 36, four Os would have been drawn (39, 38, 37, and 36). Had the low been 35, five Os would have been drawn (39, 38, 37, 36 and 35). And so on.

But if the low had been 37.50, *only two* boxes would have been penetrated, and, since the three-box reversal method of p&f does not consider a trend to have been reversed until *three* boxes are spanned, no entries would be made for the day and the price would be regarded as still on the advance.

If neither one new X nor three new Os can be drawn, no entry would be made and the procedure would begin anew on the following day.

On the following and each succeeding day and as long as the trend is still up (meaning the current column is an X column) the high is reviewed first for new entries and only if no new Xs can be drawn is the low analysed for a three-box reversal. Regardless of how low the low may be, if the high permits the drawing of at least one new X, the trend is still up and the low must be disregarded. If the trend has truly reversed, even though a new X was drawn, the directional change will be revealed the following day when a higher high is lacking and the low is three or more boxes below the highest X.

Falling prices

If the current column is a declining column or a column of Os, the daily procedures are reversed. The daily low is analysed first. If the low is one or more boxes below the lowest O in the current column, the appropriate number of additional Os are drawn and the daily high is ignored.

For instance, if the current column runs from 39 down to 37 and the day's low is 35.75, a new O is entered at 36, and the high price for the day is of no concern. If, on the other hand, the low fails to permit the entry of one or more additional Os, as in a low of 36.50, the high would be analysed to determine if a three-box reversal had occurred. If the high were 40 or above, a reversal has occurred and a new column of Xs is drawn immediately to the right of the Os with the lowest X being entered one row higher than the lowest O in the most current of O columns.

If no new Os can be added and a reversal has failed to occur, no entries are made for the day and the procedure begins again the following day.

Day 4 - No new lower low and no price reversal, wait for the next day

On Day 4, the low price is 36.50, but would have to have been 36, lower, to add another zero. As a new lower low is not recorded, and the day's high is not high enough to signal a three-box reversal, we do nothing and wait for the next day's prices.

Day 5 - Subsequent reversal, this time from down to up

On Day 5, 5th January 01, a reversal is made, as no new lower low is made, and the high of that day is above 40 – signalling a three-box reversal. The chart now looks as follows:

```
41...............
40...X_X.........
39...XOX.........
38...XOX.........
37...XO..........
36...X...........
35...............
```

The simple example above, using prices over 5 days, demonstrates nearly all the major features of a point-and-figure chart.

The basic elements of construction

From the previous example, we learnt that the major elements of p&f chart construction are:

1.   How to scale the chart
2.   How to start a new chart
3.   When the box can be filled
4.   When a reversal occurs

We'll now look at these elements in more detail.

1. How to scale the chart

The first task in drawing a p&f chart is to scale it properly. This means assigning a value-range to the boxes. We say *value-range* because each box has an upper limit and a lower limit.

Definition of a box

The following figure explains what is referred to as a *box*. Manual p&f charts are always drawn on paper with a pre-printed grid, which is either filled with Xs or Os. Nowadays with computer-generated charts the grid is not explicitly present, as you will see throughout this book.

The figure below shows an excerpt from a typical computer-drawn p&f chart with a grid put over it. The grid that is put over the chart divides it into boxes. These are the *boxes* we refer to in the context of point-and-figure.

Figure 1.1 – Scaling for the Dow at 40 - 1897 and again in 1932

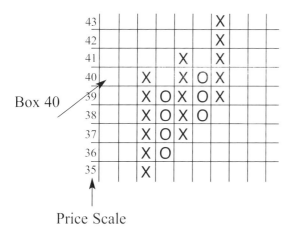

Price Scale

You can see on the figure that the numbers on the left refer to the box itself. *Box 40* is box 40, and not the continuous area between 39 and 40 or 39.5 and 40.5, just simply box 40. This follows from the 'discretizing' of price and it differs from continuous scales like the one found on a ruler, where between 39 and 40, 39.5 can be found or estimated.

In point-and-figure only 39 and 40 exist, nothing in-between.

Why is discretization of price far superior to discretization of time?

Discretization means the division into small individual elements. In technical analysis – other than point-and-figure – the information is sliced into individual elements according to the time axis. The data or information is partitioned into weeks, days or multiples of minutes, and hence the horizontal time-axis or time-line is equally spaced. That is *discretization of time*.

But does time matter for a long or short position?

No, or only to a minimal extent. In point-and-figure the data is divided according to price; that is *discretization of price*. Does price matter? You bet! Point-and-figure has an advantage over other technical analysis methods through this fundamental difference in discretization of the information.

Think of it. It really does not matter if the Dow moves to 10,000 over 1 or 4 weeks. What matters is that it does move to 10,000. Does it matter if your favourite stock moves to a new high on a Tuesday or a Thursday? In bar-charts, yes, because it alters trend lines. In p&f it does not, and hence especially avoids fuzziness of such trend lines. The new high on Tuesday is treated like the new-high on Thursday in p&f, and a year with little price move action takes little room on a chart and a year like 1987 or 2001 with a lot of movement takes considerably more room; and that is what we believe is the correct representation of a market. Like in a history book where the era of the Neanderthals should occupy fewer pages than the 20th Century. In the bar-chart world, the 20th Century would be described in the same number of pages as 100 years of our ancestors fighting the sabre-tooth tigers and catching mammoths!

A final comment

Sure, if you trade options or derivatives for benefiting from the decay in time-value things are different and time obviously matters. However, for the great majority of traders out there in the markets what matters most are price moves. Only point-and-figure treats the importance of price moves in a way that we think is adequate – hence the superiority, in our view, of point-and-figure.

What constitutes Box 40 (or any other particular box) depends on your perspective:

1. If you are coming **from above with falling prices**, i.e. you are testing whether you can fill box 40 with an O, then the low has to be equal or smaller than 40.

2. If you are coming **from below with rising prices**, i.e. you are testing whether the box can be filled with an X, then the high has to be equal or greater than 40.

It is as simple as that.

Variable box sizes

The p&f chart tracks price moves. Price moves are relative, which means that the absolute level of the price matters. That is why a 200-point down move on the Dow at a level of 10,000 is totally different from a 200-point down move at 1,200. At the lower level of 1,200 such a move is a crash whereas at the higher level of 10,000 it is only a slightly bigger-than-average move. The crash should be represented by a column of many Os, as Os mean descending prices, whereas the slightly bigger-than-average move should be depicted by only one or two boxes filled with Os. In order to achieve this sense of proportion, you have to use variable box-sizes. As a general principle: the higher the absolute price, the bigger the box.

We propose – again, generally speaking – that *a box should represent about 2% of a price move*. On that basis, the box for the Dow at a level of 1,200 would be of the size of 25 and at the level of 10,000 it would be 200. If you adopted these box sizes:

*   with the Dow at 1,200, the 200-point 'crash' move would be marked by filling 8 boxes;
*   with the Dow at 10,000, the 200-point slightly bigger-than-average move would be marked by filling only 1 box.

The chart below scales the Dow around a level of 10,000. The differences between the boxes are 200, and therefore we say that the *box size* is 200.

Figure 1.2 – Scaling for the Dow at 10,000

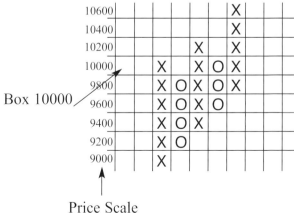

We will give some more details on scaling stock indices in a later chapter. But we would like to mention already at this point that a box size of 200 for the Dow between 6000 and 14000 would be chosen if a high level of compression were desired, e.g. for a long-term chart spanning several decades. For shorter time spans, box sizes for the Dow at that level of 100 or even 50 are more common. Intraday charts would be drawn with a box size of 20.

Standard box sizes

What you should keep in mind is that the box sizes become bigger as price increases. However, they can easily be found in the following table, where you see which box size you have to apply for which price range.

Table 1.2 – Standard box sizes

Price		Box Size
from	to	
6	14	0.2
14	29	0.5
29	60	1
60	140	2
140	290	5
290	600	10
600	1400	20

As an example, if a stock has a price history in the range of 30 to 40, from the table you can see that a box size of 1 is appropriate, because the price range lies within the 29 to 60 bracket.

Extension of the standard scale

What you also see is that the previous table consists of repeating numbers. For the price range limits the repeating numbers are 29, 60, 140 and for the box sizes 1, 2, 5. With those numbers you can – by multiplication by 10 – get to any scale-values you want. For example, the Dow in a range of 6,000 (better not!) and 14,000 (hopefully) you use simply a box size of 200, found by multiplying the last row on the table by 10.

Example 1.1 – Variable box sizes

The scale is based on areas made out of 101 boxes, namely:

- 6 to 14, box size 0.2, (40 boxes)
- 14 to 29, box size 0.5, (30 boxes)
- 29 to 60, box size 1, (31 boxes)

then in order to get the scale for bigger values you multiply the range limits and the box size by 10, 100, 1000, 10000 etc. If you want a scale for smaller values you divide range and box sizes by 10 or 100.

Let's say that you want a scale for a stock that traded between 230 and 780. You multiply the above values once by 10, and you get:

- 60 to 140, box size 2, (40 boxes)
- 140 to 290, box size 5, (30 boxes)
- 290 to 600, box size 10, (31 boxes)

then you multiply by 10 once more to get

- 600 to 1400, box size 20
- 1400 to 2900, box size 50
- 2900 to 6000, box size 100.

Now you take values that allow the inclusion of 230 to 780. The result is thus:

- 140 to 290, box size 5
- 290 to 600, box size 10
- 600 to 1400 step, box size 20

That's it!

2. How to start a new chart

Strategy 1

Wait until 3 boxes can be filled and decide based on the closing price and the range (highest high to lowest low or, if not available, highest close to lowest close) whether to use Xs or Os. If close is higher than the mid-point of the range, use X and if close is lower use O. If on the first day it is impossible to fill 3 boxes, wait more days until this can be done. The decision to use Xs or Os for the first column is then based on where the last box is drawn. If it is filled on the high side, use X, if it is filled on the low side use O.

Strategy 2 (simplification)

If high and low are available: take first available price data and decide on range (high to low) whether to use Xs or Os. If close is higher than the mid-point between high and low, use X and if close is lower use O. We use this method in our computer programs.

3. When can the box be filled ?

The expression *box* has its origin in the use of a paper with grid lines for manual charting. The *box number* refers to the number on the vertical price-scale identifying the box. Testing whether a box can be filled depends on the direction of the price move. Two cases exist, either you come from above, testing for Os (falling prices) or you come from below, testing for Xs (rising prices). The box can be filled if and only if the price range – defined by the high and low – includes the box number.

Therefore:

- X – the price used in the charting process (normally the high of the day) has to be higher than or equal to the box number in order to draw the X.

- O – the price used in the charting process (normally the low of the day) has to be lower than or equal to the box number in order to draw the O.

Example 1.2 – Testing when a box can be filled

Assume we are testing if box 40 can be filled. In the case of:

– testing for **rising prices** the X can be drawn if the high is higher or equal to 40; or

– testing for **declining prices** the O can be marked if the low is lower or equal to 40.

4. When does a reversal occur?

The reversal occurs when no new same symbol can be added to the current column; instead, a certain number – traditionally 3 – of boxes can be filled in the opposite direction, starting on a box one higher in the case of a reversal from O to X or one lower in the case of X to O.

Note that in order for the box to be filled, the price has to touch or move beyond the limit of the box. The following graphic serves as an illustration. The dots refer to the boxes that have to be checked.

Figure 1.3 – Reversal patterns

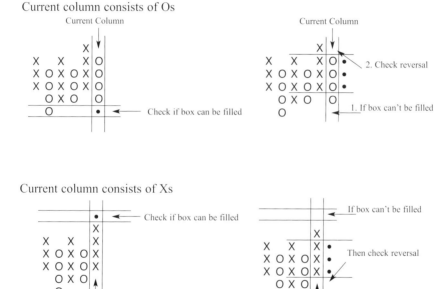

Advanced topics of chart construction

Price data used

In the following section, we answer questions related to the data input on charts. Our instructions are geared towards the most common type of charting which uses end-of-day data. However, some traders use different time horizons than an entire trading day and they use either:

- **price intervals**, typically *high*, *low,* or
- **real-time** charting, using the *last price* only.

Real-time charting is based on the continuous real-time stream of market prices. It is used when day-trading liquid markets. For the construction of the chart only these transaction-per-transaction prices are used and not the highs and lows used in end-of-day charting.

On the other side of the liquidity spectrum we find assets such as real-estate or illiquid bonds. Here, too, the last published transaction price is used instead of highs and lows, for the simple reason that the lack of liquidity means there are no daily highs and lows.

The following decision rules are based on the typical use of high, low, close for end-of-the-day charting of *liquid stocks*. However, in the other cases mentioned above you would substitute both high and low with the price given, either real-time or close/settle.

Summary of price data used for p&f charts

- **Typical end-of-day** (EOD) chart: *high, low, close*.
- **Real-time**: *last* (use as substitute for both high or low when applying rules for the typical EOD).
- **Illiquid asset**: *close* or *settle* (use as substitute for both high and low within EOD rules).

Crossing of box size levels

This is a relevant point if you use a variable box size scale like the standard scale and do the chart manually. Remember that the standard scale uses:

- box sizes of 1 for prices between 29 and 60,
- box sizes of 2 for prices between 60 to 140 and
- box sizes of 5 between 140 and 290.

Therefore, when your stock is hovering around a level like 60, 140 or 290 you would have to pay particular attention to the box sizes.

Let's look at the case where your stock – in which you hopefully have a short position – trades 150 points down from 240 to 90. For each down move of 5 points until 140 you will have to fill a box with an O. From there on, a 2 point move fills a box, as the new box size is now 2 points. So for the fall from 240 to 90 you would have to fill 45 boxes (20 from 240 to 140; 25 from 140 to 90). In comparison to a 150 point crash from 290 to 140, which would only affect 30 boxes.

The secret is to pay attention to those levels, that's all. First take a quick glance at the scale, then fill in the appropriate boxes.

Adjusting a chart for a dividend or capital issue

In the case of bonus issues, rights issues, extraordinary large dividends or any other material change in the equity-structure, the chart should be adjusted to reflect that change. As a rule of thumb: dividends, both stock and cash, of less than 10% are ignored.

Manual charting

For manual charting you would calculate a new scale, e.g. for a 1 to 2 split, the new scale would have scale values of half the old ones. You would then draw the new scale on the right hand side of the chart and use the new scale for the ex-split values. The same would be done for the dividend adjustment.

In adjusting a chart manually, it should always be borne in mind that some of the chart patterns in the old chart can disappear in the new chart. And in some cases, an adjustment will even change a chart from being bullish to being bearish or vice versa.

The problem arises when the stock data after the split gets situated exactly in a range where box size levels are crossed, most likely from above 200 to below 100. This is obviously a problem which is only temporary. If you feel that it disturbs your analysis, it can be overcome by using two charts in parallel, one with the old scale and one with the new scale. Then you have to inversely adjust the prices to be used in the chart with the old scale.

Computer charting

If you use a computer for your charts, you would simply adjust the data-series or download it after the split date – as data providers normally adjust data rapidly and correctly – and have the computer redraw the chart from scratch.

Time indication on charts

In the chart over the page all the basic features of a point-and-figure are included. On both sides of the chart the box size scale is displayed. A trend line consisting of '+' is also included.

Chart 1.2 – EuroSTOXX50 [.STOXX50E]

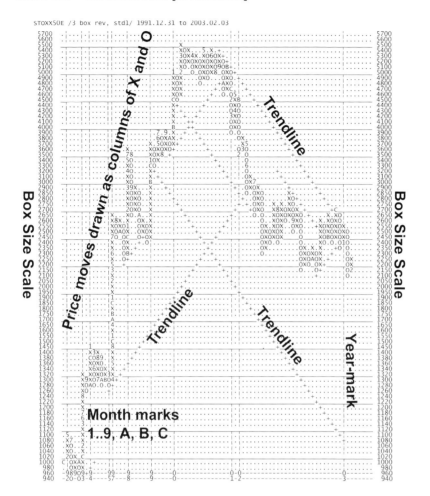

Table 1.3	
Month codes	
Jan	1
Feb	2
Mar	3
April	4
May	5
June	6
July	7
Aug	8
Sept	9
Oct	A
Nov	B
Dec	C

As mentioned, **point-and-figure ignores the passage of time**. However, for the purpose of comparability, but not for trading, letters are often used to mark the start of a new month, or a line to mark the start of a new year. Examples of both are shown above, with years indicated by vertical lines and, at the bottom, the last two year digits are printed. Months are drawn inside the chart, substituting Xs or Os with the month codes show in the table above right.

Another practical example

Just to make you an expert in charting, we have included another example: mmO2 PLC [OOM.L], The data for mm02 in this period from January to February 2002 is printed opposite. It is in the format of: date/open/high/close/volume.

Starting on page 42 we will plot this data on a p&f chart.

Table 1.4 – Example price data for mmO2

Date	Open	High	Low	Close	Volume
02-01-2002	86.00	90.25	86.00	89.00	32571772
03-01-2002	89.10	91.75	87.25	90.89	96608224
04-01-2002	92.00	92.75	88.75	91.25	83221424
07-01-2002	92.00	92.25	88.00	90.72	80453848
08-01-2002	89.61	92.50	88.50	91.56	149584448
09-01-2002	91.00	91.50	86.66	89.22	104319984
10-01-2002	87.50	87.75	85.25	86.50	134468912
11-01-2002	87.50	89.50	86.50	88.50	48392516
14-01-2002	85.25	87.50	84.81	85.03	34868488
15-01-2002	85.00	90.00	84.50	88.00	76452320
16-01-2002	86.50	90.00	80.00	88.00	73580800
17-01-2002	86.53	88.25	85.90	86.25	72097752
18-01-2002	86.75	88.25	85.00	85.53	104493032
21-01-2002	85.25	86.50	84.25	85.25	27617188
22-01-2002	85.00	86.84	82.50	84.94	48338120
23-01-2002	82.00	83.00	80.00	81.53	105278408
24-01-2002	81.03	84.25	81.00	82.47	94844912
25-01-2002	82.63	83.31	80.25	81.25	26047040
28-01-2002	81.28	84.00	79.00	79.43	69077912
29-01-2002	81.28	81.95	79.00	80.25	74353048
30-01-2002	79.53	79.53	75.50	78.00	94711624
31-01-2002	76.28	80.00	76.22	76.75	63062104
01-02-2002	77.28	80.16	75.00	79.13	85325560
04-02-2002	78.25	78.57	74.75	75.52	48750840
05-02-2002	75.00	76.00	72.25	73.81	101264192
06-02-2002	75.03	75.03	70.00	71.61	55556080
07-02-2002	70.72	74.25	68.00	71.70	83176912
08-02-2002	71.97	75.00	71.32	73.28	55047380
11-02-2002	72.22	75.00	71.25	71.50	45950152
12-02-2002	71.50	73.66	69.50	71.10	49905948
13-02-2002	71.53	72.38	66.10	68.27	153598560
14-02-2002	68.02	69.75	66.50	67.94	68061024
15-02-2002	67.98	70.50	66.50	67.25	78512064
18-02-2002	68.27	68.48	65.25	66.04	57734716
19-02-2002	65.98	66.50	62.50	64.66	70843168
20-02-2002	64.94	64.94	58.00	60.04	109770192
21-02-2002	63.00	63.75	58.98	62.00	71520240
22-02-2002	62.98	64.25	61.25	62.41	38584116
25-02-2002	61.73	63.75	60.00	61.45	84168552
26-02-2002	61.73	67.00	61.18	64.29	139078592
27-02-2002	65.23	68.00	63.50	64.00	98475920
28-02-2002	67.77	68.06	64.25	66.00	42747032

1. Constant box size

First, use the simplest scale, namely a constant box size of 1. Your grid will be made up of boxes which all have the same size 1, with the lowest box being 57 and the highest 93 (the range of the mmO2 data).

Below is the result of charting the data. We hope you get a chart that looks exactly the same.

Chart 1.3 – OOM p&f chart with a constant box size of 1

```
93    ..........................    93
92    X.X.......................    92
91    XOXO......................    91
90    1OXO__X_____    90
89    .OXOX.XO..................    89
88    .O.OXOXOX.................    88
87    ...OXOXOXO................    87
86    ...O.OXOXO................    86
85    _____O_OXO_____    85
84    .......OXOX...............    84
83    .......OXOXO..............    83
82    .......OXOXO..............    82
81    .......OXOXO..............    81
80    _____O_O_OX_____    80
79    ...........OX2............    79
78    ...........OXOX...........    78
77    ...........OXOXO..........    77
76    ..........O.OXO...........    76
75    _____O_OX_____    75
74    .............OXO..........    74
73    .............OXO..........    73
72    .............OXO..........    72
71    .............OXO..........    71
70    _____OXOX_____    70
69    .............OXOXO........    69
68    .............O.OXO..X......    68
67    ...............O.O..XO.....    67
66    ................O..XO.....    66
65    _____O___XO_____    65
64    .................OX.X......    64
63    .................OXOX......    63
62    .................OXOX......    62
61    .................OXOX......    61
60    _____OXO_____    60
59    .................OX........    59
58    .................O.........    58
57    ..........................    57
```

You might have forgotten to include the '2' on line 79 indicating the start of February (month '2') and the end of January (month '1'). The marking of months or any other time reference is not strictly necessary in p&f charting, because, as you know by now, p&f charts ignore the passage of time. Nevertheless, it is a common convention to mark new months with a number, because traders often like a maximum of information.

The numbering for months is very simple: 1-9 for January to September, and then the letters A, B and C for October, November and December respectively.

2. Standard box size

Now, and this is very important for your learning process, do the same chart with the standard scale. Remember the standard scale changes the size of the boxes. The size of the box increases – although in a staggered way – with the increase of the price.

Look up the box values in the *Standard box size* table on page 34. The information that you take from that table is that the boxes will have the size of 1 between 29 and 60, and 2 between 60 and 140. Now, using the standard scale, the chart should look like this:

Chart 1.4 – OOM with standard scale

```
94   . . . . . . . . . . .      94
92   X_____      92
90   1O. . . . . . . . . .      90
88   .OX. . . . . . . .         88
86   .OXO. . . . . . .          86
84   .OXO. . . . . . .          84
82   _OXO_____       82
80   .O.O. . . . . . .          80
78   . . .O. . . . . . .        78
76   . . .O. . . . . . .        76
74   . . .2X. . . . . . .       74
72   ___OXO_____          72
70   . . .OXO. . . . . .        70
68   . . .O.OX. . . . .         68
66   . . . . .OX. . . . .       66
64   . . . . .OX. . . . .       64
62   _____OX_____       62
60   . . . . .OX. . . . .       60
59   . . . . .OX. . . . .       59
58   . . . . .O. . . . . .      58
57   -----------                57
56   -----------                56
```

If you succeeded in drawing the two charts correctly, you have shown that you understand the basics. Congratulations! There is nothing more to learn in respect of drawing the basic chart.

What you do still need to learn is how to insert trend lines and, most of all, how to interpret a p&f chart and apply it to real trading.

You have observed with the above two charts two important aspects, namely that:

1. The standard scale is easy to do, and

2. The bigger the box size, the fewer columns, as reversals are less frequent.

Summary

We have noted the basic characteristics of point-and-figure charts:

- Xs indicate rising prices.
- Os indicate falling prices.
- A column can never include both Xs and Os.
- Columns of Xs alternate with columns of Os.

Concise instruction for creating point-and-figure charts

1. If the current column consists of Xs, check if new Xs can be added, or, if the current column consists of Os, check if new Os can be added. If they can, add them.

2. If no new same symbol can be added to the current column, check if a reversal has happened and if so, start a new column with the opposite symbol. If no reversal has happened, wait for the next day's price data.

3. Interpret the chart for new buy or sell signals.

The above can also be represented as a flow chart:

Figure 1.4 – Flow chart describing p&f chart construction

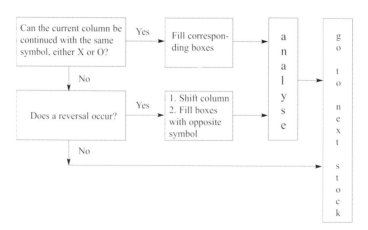

What about volume?

Point-and-figure charts do not display volume in the way that bar-charts do. In our opinion this is not problematic, because volume often switches between being a leading and a lagging indicator and so is no use at all for predicting price moves. Moreover, we have not seen any scientific study that shows that volume can be used to forecast price moves. And one more consideration: reported volume figures are flawed because they are not consolidated with trading volume generated by derivatives or OTC trading.

Computerised charting

With the proliferation of PCs it is rare to find an active trader who does not have at least two computers, a portable and a PDA at hand! Recently we counted the number of PCs in our office and at home, and the number was surprising. But one can spend money in much more silly ways, and of course we have somehow to finance the turnaround of the tech markets. *So let's buy more hardware*!

But jokes aside, a good computer with fast internet access is indispensable. Therefore in this book we cover the aspects of computer application to point-and-figure extensively.

Price data

If you are computer literate, and willing to spend the time and money, historic price data is available from a number of data vendors. Depending on the vendor, the data may go back several decades and be available for download to your computer, or it may be on CD ROM. Current day data would be downloaded daily to update the historic data accumulated on your hard drive or on the CD ROM. Some databases give access to the historic data for free, the best known being *Yahoo*.

Recommended data vendors

- ADVFN   www.advfn.com
- E-Signal   www.esignal.com   all major markets at a reasonable price
- Global Fin. Data   www.globalfindata.com   expensive though complete
- LSE   www.londonstockexchange.com
- MetaStock   www.equis.com   with Reuters Data Link
- Olsen   www.olsen.ch   for tick data
- Paritech   www.paritech.co.uk
- TickData   www.tickdata.com   for US tick data
- Updata   www.updata.co.uk   Trader II Professional's own data feed
- Yahoo   finance.yahoo.com   in combination with the utility Hquote

Software programs

You will need a software package that can create p&f charts from the daily high and low price data. There are several that do an excellent job. Often they also generate bar charts, candlestick charts, do technical analysis, and many even allow the user to view fundamental information on the selected investment.

45

A good p&f software program should include:

- Different possibilities to scale a chart (logarithmic, linear, user-defined).
- Drawing of automatic trend lines.
- Facility to access (in a user-friendly way) many different historical price series.

Robust software packages that create p&f charts include *MetaStock*, *PFScan* and *Updata Technical Analyst* and *Updata Trader*.

In each package you select the box size or scaling, and number of box reversal desired, and the system will automatically produce the chart. The charts generated from each program are accurate and very useable.

Even though each product produces excellent charts, there are significant differences in price and features of each software package. Some versions allow for intraday charts, others not. Some are configured so as to be connected directly to specific data feeds; others are independent of data vendors and feeds.

Recommended software programs

We have extensively tested the high end products of MetaStock, PFScan and Updata, and can happily endorse all three for the chartist interested in utilizing a PC to maintain point-and-figure charts.

- **MetaStock** (www.equis.com): for very basic point-and-figure.

- **PFScan** (www.pfscan.com): a software boutique's outstanding application with unique features for scanning entire markets for breakout signals.

- **Updata** (www.updata.co.uk): probably the worlds best point-and-figure charts. Moreover, Updata is an integrated trading platform, one of the best we know.

Example screen shots from each of these software programs – two in each case – appear on the next 6 pages.

MetaStock

Figure 1.5 – Banco Santander [SAN.MC] with volume displayed by MetaStock

This is the basic screen layout of the MetaStock program. Because it is a universal technical analysis package it does not offer the advanced features one finds in PFScan or Updata. MetaStock p&f price-scales are always linear. They can, however, be changed in size.

Figure 1.6 – Ibex35 [.IBEX] and Repsol [REP.MC], both with volume, by MetaStock

As shown above, it is useful to be able to have various charts in different windows for comparisons.

PFScan

Figure 1.7 – PFScan with trend lines, counts and signals

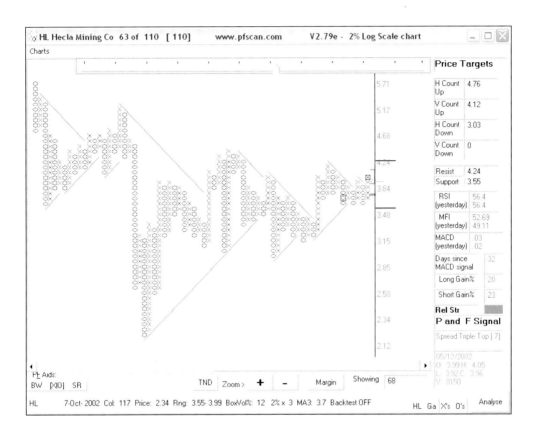

In this screenshot of PFScan, you can see automatic trend lines (bullish support and bearish resistance), plus current resistance and support levels (on the scale at the right side).

There is a list of additional indicators, price targets and signals shown in the right split-window.

At the bottom are various buttons which allow the charts to be zoomed, analysed or to be tested for signals and profitability.

Figure 1.8 – PFScan with trend lines, counts and signals

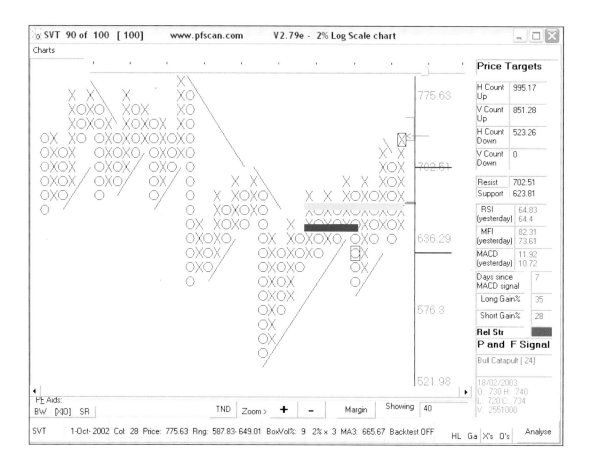

Here we have zoomed in on a chart to increase the visibility of the price targets, indicators and signals. Note also that the most recent trading signals are indicated with framed boxes and thick horizontal bars.

Updata

Figure 1.9 – Updata, point-and-figure

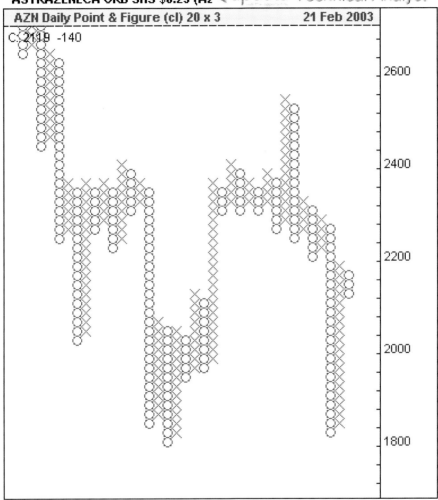

In this window showing AstraZeneca [AZN] p&f chart, you can appreciate the aesthetics of the Updata design. For this chart, a linear 20-point box size scale has been used. Updata allows a highly flexible definition of the box size scale.

Figure 1.10 – Updata, point-and-figure with horizontal and vertical counts

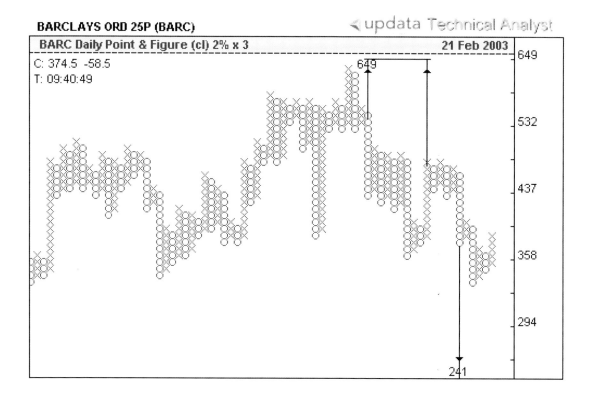

One of Updata's valuable features is the automatic performance of precise horizontal and vertical counts. The chart is based on a logarithmic box size scale.

Note: further references for software and data can be found in Appendix 3 on page 249.

Subscription charts

Besides constructing the charts yourself, there are a number of independent services that offer 'ready-made' p&f charts. We mention a couple of the better known ones below.

Chartcraft

If you are interested in US stocks you can subscribe to the excellent products of *Chartcraft* (www.chartcraft.com). They range from annual long-term chart books providing chart history going back many years, to monthly chart books with less historic data, but more current charts,. They also offer weekly and daily email-based services, with the latest comments and charts. Their subscription charts are available for most US securities as Chartcraft is the oldest, largest, and most respected of the p&f charting services. All of their charts are also easily accessible online on the web.

Stockcube

You can also subscribe to Chartcraft's sister company's service *Stockcube* (www.stockcube.co.uk), which provides online p&f charts for non-US stocks, currencies and financial futures. However, note that Stockcube creates its charts based on closing prices.

Both Chartcraft and Stockcube are known for their immaculate products and professional service.

For the professional trader we consider a subscription to such a service a *nice to have*. Most especially in order to complement your own charts, either drawn by hand or computer.

Interpreting the charts

- Buy and sell formations

- Trend lines

Buy and sell formations

The basic chart patterns

Point-and-figure chart patterns are neither shrouded in mystery nor are they merely random configurations, because they repeat themselves with statistical relevance.

The cumulative actions of buyers and sellers, whether they are long-term investors, or speculators, must necessarily be reflected in price changes. Every purchase and sale of a security is made at a certain price level; this affects the trading price, and ultimately can change the trading price. The method used to record these price changes is what causes the appearance of recurring patterns of Xs and Os in p&f charts. The ability to recognize and interpret these patterns provides the chartist with the knowledge of the correct position to take at any particular time. These patterns are referred to as *formations* and range from very simple to very complex patterns.

Simple Buy and Simple Sell

The most basic of all formations – and necessary elements in more complex formations – are the Simple Buy and Simple Sell formations; sometimes called the *Double Top* and *Double Bottom* formations.

Figure 2.1 – Simple Buy and Simple Sell formations

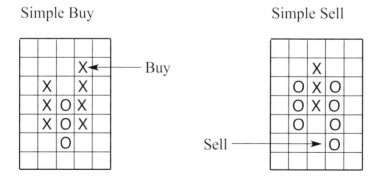

Simple Buy

The *Simple Buy* formation (or *Double Top*), as shown in the figure above, occurs when the current X column rises one box higher than the top X in the prior column of Xs. The simple buy formation is more than an entry point for a long position. It also represents the price at which any short position in the contract should be covered. Thus, the simple buy formation is both:

1. an entry signal for longs, and a
2. stop-loss point for shorts.

Simple Sell

The other basic formation is the *Simple Sell* (or *Double Bottom)*. It is composed of two columns of Os and one intervening column of Xs and occurs when the current column of Os falls one box below the lowest O of the prior column. An example of this type of formation is also highlighted in the FTSE chart (2.1) on page 59, coloured red on the third column. The Simple Sell formation signals two market strategies:

1. to liquidate long positions, providing guidance for the placing of stop-loss orders, and to
2. short the security.

Point-and-figure signals in the framework of market psychology

Technical analysis like the one based on point-and-figure charts follows the argument that the price is always right, and therefore that past price movements have to be analysed in order to forecast future price moves. Neither market sentiment, nor different market players' needs and their strategies, are considered.

The reasons, however, that point-and-figure signals work are easily discovered in the framework of market psychology and market structure. Prices of individual stocks are a function of the market view and the portfolio constraints of many professional and private speculators, traders and investors. They all know that prices fluctuate around a trend or drift. Therefore they continuously scrutinize the markets for trend changes, trading ranges or breakouts from previous trading ranges.

The Simple Buy signal works because it represents the move – whether coincidental or driven by insiders – towards new highs, a retracement and a rise above the old high. Such price action, which is typical and frequent in securities markets, is observed by many market participants, attracts their interest and therefore increases demand. Moreover, short sellers usually cover their short positions in this situation which increases demand further. All the above events trigger a chain reaction which leads the price towards higher levels and is the market behavioral reason why the Simple Buy works.

The Simple Sell is a down move that stops, rebounds and then turns down again. Market participants with long positions reason that the rebound had no staying power and therefore the stock is weak. This convinces them to liquidate all or some of their positions which results in an increase of supply. If this happens – as it normally does – the additional supply accelerates the down move of the stock because more investors liquidate and short-sellers enter the scene. The down move continues to the point where market participants feel that the stock is cheap and they start buying. A bottom formation is created and eventually a Simple Buy signal occurs.

'Bullish' and 'bearish' p&f charts

If the last signal on a chart is a buy, the chart is described as *bullish*, whereas if the last signal is a sell, it is described as *bearish*. This again is a very practical feature of point-and-figure, which allows you to automatically classify markets into bullish and bearish phases based on very clear rules. At any one moment, every chart is either bearish or bullish. No guessing required and no fuzziness.

Examples: Simple Buy and Simple Sell

On the next two pages we have reproduced p&f charts of the FTSE Index [.FTSE] and Gallagher Group [GLH.L]. One goes south, the other north.

On both you see a series of simple sells and buys. On both charts we have selected only the most instructive simple buys and simple sells. As usual we highlight the buys with green and the sells with red. Again, if you are new to point-and-figure charting, don't be confused by the month codes (numbers). They are often used in place of Xs and Os to show the beginning of a new month, but are not mandatory.

You might like to compare the Charts 2.1 and 2.2 with more familiar bar charts of the same data.

Chart 2.1 – FTSE [.FTSE]

```
FTSE / 3 box / 2000.01.04 to 2003.01.10
7050  ....|....................................|...............................|.....  7050
6900  ....|....................................|...............................|.....  6900
6750  _X_9_____  6750
6600  1X4XO...................................|...............................|.....  6600
6450  OXO6O...................................|...............................|.....  6450
6300  OXOXO...................................|...............................|.....  6300
6150  23OXO...................................|...............................|.....  6150
6000  O_OX2_____  6000
5940  ..█.O....X.X.X.X........................|...............................|.....  5940
5880  ....3....X5XOXOXO.......................|...............................|.....  5880
5820  ....O....XOXUXO6O.......................|...............................|.....  5820
5760  ....O....XO.OXO.O.......................|...............................|.....  5760
5700  _____OX_X_X__O___█X_____  5700
5640  ...OXOXOX......OXOX.....................|...............................|.....  5640
5580  ...OXOXOX......O7O8O....................|...............................|.....  5580
5520  ....O.OXOX.....O.OXO....................|...............................|.....  5520
5460  ....|.OX4X........OXO...................|...............................|.....  5460
5400  _____OXO._____OXO_____X_____  5400
5340  ....|.OX..........OXO.........X.XOX.....................................|.....  5340
5280  ....|.O...........O.9.........X.XOXO1O..X.X.............................|.....  5280
5220  ....|................O.....X.X.XOXOCOXOX.X5XO...........................|.....  5220
5160  ....|................O.....XOXOXOXO.OXOXOXOXO...........................|.....  5160
5100  _____O_____XOXOXO___OXOXO3O_O_____  5100
5040  ....|................O......XO.OB....O|2.O...█......................|.....  5040
4980  ....|................O......X..O......|.......6.........................|.....  4980
4920  ....|................OX...X.X.........|......O.........................|.....  4920
4860  ....|................OXOX.XAX.........|......O.........................|.....  4860
4800  _____OXOXOXOX_____O_____  4800
4740  ....|................OXOXOXO..........|......O.........................|.....  4740
4680  ....|................O.O.OX...........|....OX..........................|.....  4680
4620  ....|..................OX.............|....OXOX.........................|.....  4620
4560  ....|..................OX.............|....O7OXO........................|.....  4560
4500  _____OX_____._____O_OXO_____  4500
4440  ....|..................OX.............|......O.O....X...................|.....  4440
4380  ....|..................OX.............|......O...XO....................|.....  4380
4320  ....|..................OX.............|......O...XO....................|.....  4320
4260  ....|..................O..............|......OX.X.XO....................|.....  4260
4200  _____OXOX8XOX_____X_____  4200
4140  ....|................................|......OXOXOX9XOX.....X.XC|.....  4140
4080  ....|................................|......OXOXOXOXOXO....XOXO|.....  4080
4020  ....|................................|......OXOXOXOXOXO....XOBOX.....  4020
3960  ....|................................|......OXOXO.O.O.O..X.XO.OX.....  3960
3900  _____O_OX_____OX_XOX__O1_____  3900
3840  ....|................................|......OX.....OXOXOX..O|.....  3840
3780  ....|................................|......OX.....OXOAOX...|.....  3780
3720  ....|................................|......OX.....OXO.O....|.....  3720
3660  ....|................................|......O.......O.......|.....  3660
3600  ----0-------------------------------0--------------------------0-----  3600
3540  ----1-------------------------------2--------------------.--------3-----  3540
```

Note that all three of the highlighted sell signals on the FTSE chart are precursors of important down moves.

Chart 2.2 – Gallaher Group [GLH.L]

```
730   ..........|.......................................  730
720   ..........|.....................X.....X........     720
710   ..........|....................X.XO....XO.......    710
700   _____XOXO____XO_____   700
690   ..........|......X...........X.X.XOXO....XO......   690
680   ..........|......XO.........9OXOXO.O....XO.......   680
670   ..........|......XO........X.XOXOX..O..X.XO..X....  670
660   ..........|......XO........XOXOXO...O..XOXOX.XO...  660
650   _____X_XOX_____XOXOX_____O__XOXOXOXO___   650
640   ..........|....X6XOXO......XOXOX....OX.XOXOXOXO...  640
630   ..........|..X.XOXOXO....X.XOXOX....OXOXO.OBO.O...  630
620   ..........|..XOXO.OXO....X8XO.O.....OAOX..O...O..X  620
610   ..........|..XOX..O7O....XOX........O.O.......OX.X  610
600   _____5O___O_O____XO_____OXOX  600
590   ..........|..X......OX...X..................OXOX    590
580   ..........|..X......OXO..X..................OXO.    580
570   ..........|..X......OXO..X..................OX..    570
560   ..........|..4......O.OX.X..................OC..    560
550   _____X_____OXOX_____O___   550
540   ..........|..X......OXOX.......................     540
530   ..........|..X......OXO........................     530
520   ..........|..X......O..........................     520
510   ..........|2.X.................................     510
500   X_____X3X_____    500
490   XO.......X|XOX.................................     490
480   XO..B.....X1XO.................................     480
470   9OA.XOX...XOX..................................     470
460   .OXOXOX.XOX...................................      460
450   _OXOXOXOXOXOX_____     450
440   .OXOXOXOCOXO..................................      440
430   .OXOXO.O.O.|..................................      430
420   .O.O......|...................................      420
410   ..........|...................................      410
200   ----------0----------------------------------       200
195   ----------2----------------------------------       195
```

This chart includes various buy signals. The two which are marked are simple buys – the X is higher than the X on the previous X column – and again the chart shows nicely how they herald bullish moves.

To reiterate what was said on page 58:

With point-and-figure the chart is either bullish or bearish. It is never neutral.

- If the last signal was a **buy signal**, the stock is *bullish*. If you like the stock, you would buy it, thus going long. If you do not like it, you would not hold a position – and would have covered any short position.

- Conversely, if the last signal was a **sell signal**, the stock is *bearish*. No matter how much you like the security, you should liquidate any long position. If you believe the stock is weak, you would go short.

Therefore your decisions are simple:

- When a **buy signal** occurs (the security becomes bullish), you cover all shorts and go long (if you like the stock), or stay out of the security; and

- When a **sell signal** occurs (the security becomes bearish), you liquidate all long positions and go short (if you believe it is weak), or stay out totally.

Depending on your view of the security, you may decide not to be in a position. But if you choose to have a stake, *only go long of bullish stocks* (those with the most recent signal was a buy) and short bearish ones (where the last signal was a sell).

If you have a position, you always close it when an opposite signal occurs. This closing of positions is a required discipline of point-and-figure trading. It is very important and an enormous help for traders who would otherwise often fail to cut losses or take profits at the right time.

Summary

Name of signal	Indicated by	Action
Simple Buy	Higher X than highest X on nearest X column to the left.	Always cover shorts, then go long or stay out.
Simple Sell	Lower O than lowest O on nearest O column to the left.	Always sell longs, then go short or stay out.

Why the P&F chart is never neutral, and never ambiguous

A p&f chart always includes a clearly distinguishable most recent signal, either bullish or bearish. Neutral signals don't exist.

The p&f chart is bullish, if the most recent, or last, signal was a buy and is bearish if the most recent signal was a sell.

Therefore, a p&f chart is bullish or bearish, never neutral or fuzzy – which makes them completely different from brokers' recommendations: *hold, buy, strong buy, very strong buy, sell, coverage ceased*! For example, the FTSE chart on page 59 is bearish, as the last signal is sell, generated on the second last column.

Complex buy and sell formations

Although the Simple Buy and Simple Sell formations discussed above are the basic patterns upon which p&f trading is built, their brief formulation and simplicity often hides information which is evident in more complex patterns. For this reason a number of other, more complex, patterns, all using the simple patterns as a necessary element, have been developed to provide the most realistic picture of past price action and the best possible prediction of future price movement.

Filtering the many signals

There is another reason for the development and use of more complex patterns. They can serve as an effective screen or filter for trading where investment capital is limited.

Since all patterns contain a simple signal, *to trade on all simple patterns would require a considerably larger capital commitment* than if you restrict your trades to occurrences of a specific complex formation. For instance, a trader taking only signals generated by a Triple Top formation, one of the eight buy signals, would be trading only 15.3% of all buy signals (a research finding of R. E. Davis) as defined by simple formations.

There are eight buy and eight sell signals, including the basic Simple Buy and Simple Sell, that we consider useful. They are summarised in the table overleaf. Before looking at them, you may want to remind yourself of the basic signals:

Figure 2.2 – Reminder of the two basic signals, Simple Buy and Simple Sell

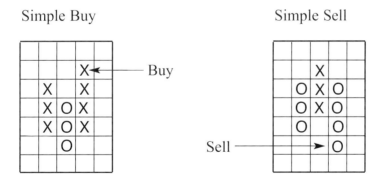

Table 2.1 – Point-and-figure buy and sell formations

	BUY SIGNALS		SELL SIGNALS
B-1	Simple Bullish Buy (or Double Top)	S-1	Simple Bearish Sell (or Double Bottom)
B-2	Simple Bullish Buy with a Rising Bottom	S-2	Simple Bearish Sell with a Declining Top
B-3	Breakout of a Triple Top	S-3	Breakout of a Triple Bottom
B-4	Ascending Triple Top	S-4	Descending Triple Bottom
B-5	Spread Triple Top	S-5	Spread Triple Bottom
B-6	Upside Breakout above a Bullish Triangle	S-6	Downside Breakout of a Bearish Triangle
B-7	Upside Breakout above a Bullish Resistance Line	S-7	Downside Breakout Below a Bullish Support Line
B-8	Upside Breakout above a Bearish Resistance Line	S-8	Downside Breakout below a Bearish Support Line

The remainder of this chapter is devoted to these sixteen formations.

The symbols used for the signals, B-1 to S-8, are taken from the Davis Study. We describe this study in detail in Chapter 5, but at this point it is worth noting its status as the first rigorous academic study of the profitability of point-and-figure. R.E. Davis, who was professor of chemistry at Purdue University, researched the frequency of occurrence of the 16 complex p&f signals listed above, based on a large sample of US stocks and over a long time period. The interesting findings are reproduced in the table opposite.

Table 2.2 – The Davis Study - frequency of buy and sell formations

Buys	Freq in %	Sells	Freq in %
B1	12.8	S1	13.5
B2	56.9	S2	56.4
B3	15.3	S3	15.5
B4	6.6	S4	8.4
B5	2.4	S5	1.6
B6	1.2	S6	2.6
B7	3.9	S7	1.4
B8	0.7		
	99.8		99.4

Non-standard complex signals

As happens in all technical analysis, several chartists have developed a myriad of different point-and-figure signals and they also combine them with various other indicators. Often they – the signals – have strange names, such as the *descending long tail trampoline* or the like, and occur once in a lifetime. We firmly believe that it is much more profitable to *stick with the basic signals* and that it is dangerous to complicate or confuse the trading process.

The buy signals

We use the same format to picture the eight basic buy signals as we use throughout the book to chart the different stocks. Please note that there are trend lines used in the three last signals. We'll come back to the subject of trend lines in a later chapter. But for the moment keep in mind that trend lines are used to signal certain patterns such as supports and resistances, are always drawn in 45 degree angles and marked with '+'.

B-1 – Simple Bullish Buy signal (or Double Top)

The most basic of all signals is the *Simple Bullish Buy* signal, sometimes called the *Double Top* formation. It is formed by a column of Xs, then a column of Os, then a column of Xs, which rises one box above the prior column of Xs. This is the Simple Buy we looked at on page 56.

Figure 2.3

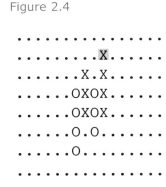

B-2 – Simple Bullish Buy with a Rising Bottom

The second formation, the *Simple Bullish Buy with a Rising Bottom*, is similar to the B-1 in that the tops are identical in both cases, meaning that the current column of Xs exceeds the top X of the prior X column by one box. But the bottoms of the B-1 and B-2 differ. In the case of the Simple Bullish Buy Signal with a Rising Bottom (B-2), the bottom O in the most recent column of Os is higher than the lowest O of the preceding O column, a condition not present in the B-1, where the lowest O of the most recent column is horizontal to the lowest O of the prior O column.

Figure 2.4

Having rising bottoms is significant, because it means that support is coming into the market at progressively higher prices with each decline. And that makes the signal stronger than the Simple Bullish Buy which doesn't have rising bottoms.

At least one of the Simple Bullish Buy signals, B-1 and B-2, is contained as an element of all of the more complicated buy signals, and when either occurs alone or as an element of a more complex formation, all shorts should be covered. Entries on the long side may be made or the trader may hold off, waiting for a specific and more complex formation to evolve, but *all short positions must be covered*, because the security is now bullish with the degree of bullishness forecast by the type of formation which ultimately evolves. Because the position is bullish, there is absolutely no justification for remaining short.

B-3 – Breakout of a Triple Top

The third formation, but the first of the complex formations, is the *Breakout of a Triple Top*. It is made up of five columns, three of Xs and two of Os. The first two columns of Xs peak at the same level, while the current X column rises one box higher than the tops of the prior two columns.

Figure 2.5

```
. . . . . . . . . . . . . . . . . .
. . . . . . . . .X. . . . . . .
. . . . .X.X.X. . . . . .
. . . . .XOXOX. . . . . .
. . . . .XOXOX. . . . . .
. . . . .XO.O. . . . . . .
. . . . .X. . . . . . . . . .
. . . . . . . . . . . . . . . . . .
```

B-4 – Ascending Triple Top

The fourth buy signal is the *Ascending Triple Top* which is nothing more than two simple bullish signals (B-1 and/or B-2) given in succession in five columns. If the bottoms are rising along with the rising tops, the formation is more bullish than if the bottoms are horizontal.

The Triple Top formation is stronger than either of the Simple Bullish Buy Signals, B-1 and B-2, because it represents a breakout of a resistance level which held more times than in the simple formations, and it is considered a complex formation because it contains a simple signal as an element as well as requiring a wider span of columns than either of the simple formations.

Figure 2.6

```
. . . . . . . . . . . . . . . . .
. . . . . . . . .X. . . . . .
. . . . . . . .X.X. . . . . .
. . . . .X.XOX. . . . . .
. . . . .XOXOX. . . . . .
. . . . .XOXO. . . . . . .
. . . . . . .O. . . . . . . . .
. . . . . . . . . . . . . . . . .
. . . . . . . . . . . . . . . . .
```

B-5 – Spread Triple Top

The *Spread Triple Top* is the fifth formation. It is similar to the Breakout of. a Triple Top (B-3) except that it is spread over seven rather than five columns because one rally failed to match or exceed the highs of the prior X columns and it thus takes an additional X column to break the horizontal resistance.

Figure 2.7

```
. . . . . . . . . . . . . . . .
. . . . . . . . . .X. . . . . .
. . .X.X. . .X. . . . . .
. . .XOX.XOX. . . . . .
. . .XOXOXOX. . . . . .
. . . .OXOX. . . . . . . .
. . . . . .O. . . . . . . . .
. . . . . . . . . . . . . . . .
. . . . . . . . . . . . . . . .
```

The next three formations deal with the combined relationship of support and resistance lines to the height of the tops of X columns and the bottoms of O columns.

B-6 – Upside Breakout above a Bullish Triangle

The sixth formation is the *Upside Breakout above a Bullish Triangle*. This formation is created by resistance (supply) coming into the market at progressively lower levels with each rally, thus keeping each succeeding column of Xs from rising as high as the prior column, while support (demand) comes in at progressively higher levels with each decline as revealed by rising bottoms.

The formation is completed and a buy signal generated when the upside breakout occurs, meaning that a column of Xs rises one box higher than the high of the preceding X column. The triangle is bullish because the last signal prior to the start of the triangle was a buy signal.

Figure 2.8

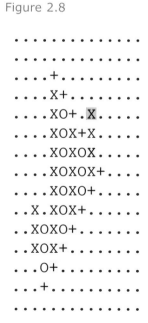

B-7 – Upside Breakout above a Bullish Resistance Line

The seventh signal is the *Upside Breakout above a Bullish Resistance Line*. The resistance line in this case is drawn as a 45 degree line up and to the right beginning from the lower right hand corner of the lowest box containing an exposed O, i.e. an O not bordered by an X on its right. The longer the resistance line holds, i.e. the more columns of Xs that approach the resistance line but fail to break through, the more bullish the ultimate breakout.

A breakout is defined as a penetration which completely clears the resistance line and not just straddles the box through which it crosses. Chart 2.3 provides an example of both a straddled position (not a breakout) and a true breakout.

Figure 2.9

```
. . . . . . . . . . . . . . . . .
. . . . . . . . . . . .X+. . .
. . . . . . . . . . . .X. . . .
. . . . . . . . . . +X. . . .
. . . . . . . . . +OX. . . .
. . . .O. . .+.OX. . . .
. . . .O. .+.XOX. . . .
. . . .O.+.OXOX. . . .
. . . .O+.XOXOX. . . .
. . . .OX.XO.O. . . . .
. . . .OXOXO. . . . . . .
. . . .OXO. . . . . . . . .
. . . .O.O. . . . . . . . .
. . . . . . . . . . . . . . . . .
```

B-8 – Upside Breakout above a Bearish Resistance Line

In B-7 signals, the security is already bullish and prices have been steadily rising prior to the signal. But in the eighth formation, an *Upside Breakout above a Bearish Resistance Line*, the security is in a steady decline, trading within a bearish channel defined by an upper resistance line and a lower support line both moving down at a 45 degree angle as they extend from left to right.

In the B-8, the support line may be well defined or almost non-existent, yet there must be a resistance line declining at a 45 degree angle from top left to lower right drawn as the best-fit 45 degree line to the declining tops of the X columns. The buy signal occurs when an X column both breaks through the resistance line and rises one box higher than the highest X of the prior column.

Figure 2.10

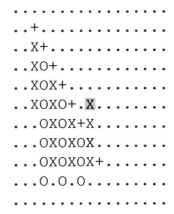

```
. . . . . . . . . . . . . . . . . .
. .+. . . . . . . . . . . . . . .
. .X+. . . . . . . . . . . . .
. .XO+. . . . . . . . . . . .
. .XOX+. . . . . . . . . . .
. .XOXO+.X. . . . . . . .
. . .OXOX+X. . . . . . . .
. . .OXOXOX. . . . . . . .
. . .OXOXOX+. . . . . . .
. . .O.O.O. . . . . . . . .
. . . . . . . . . . . . . . . . . .
```

Breaking or straddling of trend lines

In order to illustrate the difference between breaking a trend line and straddling a trend line we use a 2 year chart of British Telecom [BT.L].

Chart 2.3 – BT [BT.L]: touching, straddling and finally breaking of a bearish resistance

```
BT.L / 3 box rev, classic/ 2001.04.17 to 2003.01.10
 560   ...+..................................|.....................|.......   560
 550   ___X+_____ 550
 540   .X.XO+...........+....................|.....................|.......   540
 530   .XOXO.+..........+...................|.....................|.......    530
 520   .XO5O..+.........+....................|.....................|.......   520
 510   OXOXO...+.........+...................|.....................|.......   510
 500   OXOXO____+_____X+_____ 500
 490   OXOXOX....+......X...8O+..............|.....................|.......   490
 480   O.OXOXO....+.....XO..XO.+.............|.....................|.......   480
 470   .+O.OXOX...+..X.XOX.XOX.+.............|.....................|.......   470
 460   +...OXOXO..X.+.7OXOXOXOXOX+...........|.....................|.......   460
 450   +____O_OXOX_XOX+XOXOXOXOXOXO+_____ 450
 440   .+....O.OXOXOXOXO.O.O.O.OXO.+.........|.....................|.......   440
 430   ..+....O6OXOXOX+.......OXO..+.........|.....................|.......   430
 420   ...+....O.O.O.OX.+......O.O...+.......|.....................|.......   420
 410   ....+.........O...+.......9....+......|.....................|.......   410
 400   _____+_____+_____OX____+_____ 400
 390   .....+................+.....OXO....+....|.....................|.......  390
 380   .......+.............+....OXOX.X.X+...|...................... |.......  380
 370   ........+............+...OXOXOXOXO+..|.....................|.......     370
 360   .........+............+..OXOXOXOXOX+.|.....................|.......     360
 350   _____+_____+_OXO_OXOXOXO+_____ 350
 340   ..........+..........+O...OAOXOXO.+..................|.......          340
 330   ...........+.........+...O.OXBXO.|+..................|.......          330
 320   ...........+.........+....O.OXO.|.+.................|.......           320
 310   ...........+.........+....O.O.|..+.................|.......            310
 300   _____+_____+_____O_____+._____       300
 290   ...........+.........+.....O.|....X.................|.......           290
 280   ...........+.........+....OX|3.X.X6................|.......            280
 270   +..........+.........+...OXOX4XOXO+..............|.......              270
 260   .+.........+.........+..OCOXOXOXO.+..............|.......              260
 250   __+_____+_____+_____+_O_OXO_OXOX_+._____         250
 240   ...+.......+.........+.......+..1X..5.OXO.+..........|.......           240
 230   ....+......+.........+......+.OX....7XO..+...........|.......           230
 220   .....+.....+.........+.....+O2....OXO..X+........X.|.......            220
 210   ......+....+.........+....O....O.O..X9X.......XC1.......               210
 200   _____+____+_____+_____+_____OX_XOXO._____XOX_____         200
 195   ........+..+.........+..........|.+.....OX8XOXO+.....XOX........        195
 190   .........+.+.........+..........|..+....OXOXOXO.+..X.XOX........        190
 185   ...........+.........+..........|...+...O.O.O.O..+.XOXO|.......        185
 180   ...........+.........+..........|....+........O...+XOB.|.......        180
 175   _____+_____+_____|_____+_____OX_X_XO_____        175
 170   ...........+.........+..........+......|......+......OXOXOX+..|.......  170
 165   ...........+.........+..........+......|.....+....OXOAOX.+.|.......    165
 160   ...........+.........+..........+....|.........+....OXO.OX..+|.......  160
 155   ----------------+-----------------+---O-------------O---O+---O-------  155
 150   ----------------+-----------------+--2-----------------+----3-------   150
```

You will see that in the first two instances (June, September 2002) the bearish resistance trend line was only straddled and in the third instance (October 2002) the extrapolated trend line was truly broken.

(If you're trying to work out where these months occur on the chart, look for the month codes in the columns. June, for example, is indicated by a '6' at a height of 280.)

Chart 2.4 – Buy signals on the € / $

```
ECU / standard / 3 box rev / 2001.12.06 to 2003.06.05
1.19   .|.......|...X..... 1.19
1.18   .|.......|...X..... 1.18
1.17   _____X_____  1.17
1.16   .|.......|...X..... 1.16
1.15   .|.......|...X..... 1.15
1.14   .|.......|...X..... 1.14
1.13   .|.......|...5..... 1.13
1.12   _____X_____  1.12
1.11   .|.......X...X..... 1.11
1.10   .|.......3O..X..... 1.10
1.09   .|.......XOX.X..... 1.09
1.08   .|.......XOX4X..... 1.08
1.07   _____XOXOX_____  1.07
1.06   .|.......1OXO...... 1.06
1.05   .|.......XO........ 1.05
1.04   .|.......X......... 1.04
1.03   .|.......X......... 1.03
1.02   _____X___C_____  1.02
1.01   .|...XO..X......... 1.01
1.00   .|.X.XO9.B......... 1.00
0.99   .|.X7XOXOX........  0.99
0.98   .|.XOXOXOX.+......  0.98
0.97   ___XO_8XOX+_____  0.97
0.96   .|.X..O.O+........  0.96
0.95   .|.6....+|........  0.95
0.94   .|.X.....|........  0.94
0.93   .|.X.....|........  0.93
0.92   ___X_____  0.92
0.91   .X.5.....|........  0.91
0.90   .XO4.....|........  0.90
0.89   CXOX.....|........  0.89
0.88   O1OX.....|........  0.88
0.87   O.O3.............  0.87
0.86   ..O..............  0.86
       -O-------O---------
       -2-------3---------
```

Point-and-figure detects all major moves, as shown here on the rally of the Euro against the Dollar. The chart is said to be bullish, because the last signal was a buy.

When is a support or resistance line broken?

The line is broken if an entire box can be filled above (resistance line) or below (support line). If the filled box only coincides with the line, the X or O is said to 'straddle' the line.

Summary of buy signals

Figure 2.11 – Buy signal summary

```
630  B1...B2....B3.....B4.....B5.......B6........B7.........+B8.............  630
620  ......................................+.....................+............  620
610  .........................................+.....................X+............  610
600  .........................................X+...................XO+...........  600
590  ..X.....X......X......X........X...XO+.X...........X+..XOX+...........  590
580  X.X...X.X..X.X.X....X.X..X.X...X...XOX+X...........X...XOXO+.X.......  580
570  XOX..OXOX..XOXOX..X.XOX..XOXOX.X...XOXOX.+........+X....OXOX+X.......  570
560  XOX..OXOX..XOXOX..XOXOX..XOXOXOX...XOXOX+........+OX....OXOXOX.......  560
550  .O...OXO....O.O...XOXO....OXOXOX...XOXO+.+..O...+.OX....OXOXOX+......  550
540  .....O...........O.....O.O.O..X.XOX+.....O..+.XOX....O.O.O.........  540
530  ..................................XOXO+......O.+.OXOX.................  530
520  .................................XOX+......O+.XOXOX.................  520
510  ................................O+........OX.XO.O.................  510
500  .............................+.........OXOXO....................  500
490  ......................................OXO...................  490
480  ...................................O.O.....................  480
470  ............................................................  470
```

The sell signals

Based on point-and-figure's symmetry, all sell signals are the exact opposite of the buy signals, so if you want to, you can skip the next few paragraphs. You may, however, find the discussion and illustrations of the sell signals helps to clear up any confusion, as well as serve as an indirect review of the buy signals.

S-1 – Simple Bearish Sell

The *Simple Bearish Sell* signal occurs when the price falls, rises and falls again with the current decline or current column of Os dropping one box below the lowest O of the prior column of Os.

The occurrence of the Simple Sell formation calls for two responses. It demands that all long positions be liquidated and also suggests, but does not demand, that consideration be given to a short sale.

Figure 2.12

```
. . . . . . . . . . .
. . . . X . . . . . .
. . . OXO . . . . .
. . . OXO . . . . .
. . . O . O . . . . .
. . . . . . O . . . . .
. . . . . . . . . . .
```

The trader should never wait around for a more complex sell formation to evolve before closing out his longs, because the occurrence of the S-1 signal immediately indicates a bearish posture. But a short need not be taken if the trader prefers not to be on the short side at all or would prefer to wait for a more bearish formation before shorting.

S-2 – Simple Bearish Sell with a Declining Top

The *Simple Bearish Sell with a Declining Top* is the second of the sell formations. The S-2 is more bearish than its cousin the S-1, for it has a declining top as evidence that selling pressure is coming in at lower levels with each rally.

Figure 2.13

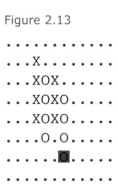

```
. . . . . . . . . . . .
. . . X . . . . . . . .
. . . XOX . . . . . .
. . . XOXO . . . . .
. . . XOXO . . . . .
. . . . O . O . . . . .
. . . . . . O . . . . .
. . . . . . . . . . . .
```

The third and remaining sell signals are not really sell signals for the closing out of longs because this is always done on an S-1 or S-2. Instead, these more complex formations only signal the opportunity for effective short selling. They are considered more complex formations in that they involve at least five columns, three of Os and two of Xs, and all contain within their pattern at least one of the two basic signals, S-1 and S-2.

S-3 – Breakout of a Triple Bottom

The third sell signal is called the *Breakout of a Triple Bottom* regardless of whether the tops are level or declining. Declining tops represent the more bearish pattern.

The Breakout of a Triple Bottom evolves from a price decline, an upside reversal, a second decline that meets downside support at the same level as the lowest O of the prior declining column, a second rally which fails to break out on the upside and a third decline which drops one box below the lowest Os of the prior two columns.

Figure 2.14

```
. . . . . . . . . . . . .
. . . . X . X . . . . . .
. . . O X O X O . . . . .
. . . O X O X O . . . . .
. . . O . O . O . . . . .
. . . . . . . ▣ . . . . .
. . . . . . . . . . . . .
```

Never anticipate the completion of the S-3 before it happens by shorting in anticipation, because the support which stopped the decline of the first and second columns of Os might hold a third time and be strong enough to send the price up to a topside breakout.

There is never any assurance that a signal will occur until it does occur, and thus signals must never be anticipated or traded prematurely.

S-4 – Descending Triple Bottom

The next formation is the *Descending Triple Bottom*. It is simply two successive S-1 and/or S-2 formations in five consecutive columns. Or, defined differently, it is composed of a column of Os, a rally of Xs, a second column of Os which declines one box below the low of the prior declining column, followed by a second price rise succeeded by a third decline signalling the sell by falling one box below the low of the prior decline.

Figure 2.15

```
. . . . . . . . . . . . .
. . . . X . . . . . . . .
. . . O X O X . . . . . .
. . . O X O X O . . . . .
. . . O X O X O . . . . .
. . . . . . O . O . . . .
. . . . . . . ▣ . . . . .
. . . . . . . . . . . . .
```

S-5 – Spread Triple Bottom

The fifth sell pattern, the *Spread Triple Bottom*, has the basic triple bottom design of the S-3, yet the formation is spread over seven rather than five columns.

Figure 2.16

```
. . . . . . . . . . . . . . . . .
. . . . X . . . X . . . . . . . .
. . . . XOXOXO . . . . . .
. . . OXOXOXO . . . . . .
. . . OXOXO . O . . . . . .
. . . O . O . . . O . . . . . .
. . . . . . . . . O . . . . . .
. . . . . . . . . . . . . . . . .
```

S-6 – Downside Breakout of a Bearish Triangle

The *Downside Breakout of a Bearish Triangle* is the sixth of eight sell signals. This formation originates from an earlier sell signal followed by a major decline.

After the decline, support develops and a rally occurs which finally gives way to a new decline that bottoms higher than the low of the prior declining column. The next rally falls short of the high of the preceding rally and the price again declines.

This pattern of rising bottoms and falling tops can continue for any number of columns and defines the sides of the triangle. The formation is finally completed and a sell signal generated when an O column declines below the lower support line.

Figure 2.17

```
. . . . . . . . . . . .
. . + . . . . . . . . .
. . X+ . . . . . . . .
. OXO+ . . . . . . .
. OXOX+ . . . . . .
. O . OXO+ . . . . .
. . . OXOX+ . . . .
. . . OXOXO+ . . .
. . . OXOXO . . . .
. . . OXO+ O . . . .
. . . OX+ . . . . . .
. . . O+ . . . . . . .
. . . + . . . . . . . .
. . . . . . . . . . . .
```

S-7 – Downside Breakout Below a Bullish Support Line

The next formation, the *Downside Breakout Below a Bullish Support Line*, occurs when there is a downward penetration of a well defined bullish support line. The bullish support line is the 45 degree best-fit line of bottoms and the penetration must completely clear the support line, not just touch or straddle the box through which it crosses from lower left to upper right, as well as decline one box below the lowest O of the prior column.

Figure 2.18

```
. . . . . . . . . . . . . . .
. . . . . . . . . . . . . . .
. . X . X . . . . . . . . . .
. . XOXOX . . . . . . . .
. . XOXOXO . + . . . . .
. . XOXOXO+ . . . . . .
. . XOXOXO . . . . . . .
. . XOXO+O . . . . . . .
. OXOX+ . ▣ . . . . . . .
. OXO+ . . . . . . . . . .
. OX+ . . . . . . . . . . .
. O+ . . . . . . . . . . . .
. + . . . . . . . . . . . . .
. . . . . . . . . . . . . . .
```

S-8 – Downside Breakout below a Bearish Support Line

The eighth and last of the sell signals is the *Downside Breakout below a Bearish Support Line*. This pattern evolves from a sudden breakout below a bearish support line running from upper left to lower right at a 45 degree angle which has repeatedly held in the past.

Figure 2.19

```
. . . . . . . . . . . . . . .
. . . . . . . . . . . . . . .
. . X . X . . . . . . . . .
. . XOXO . . . . . . . .
. . XOXOX . . . . . . .
. . XO . OXOX . . . . .
. . X+ . OXOXO . . . .
. . X . +O . OXO . . . .
. . X . . + . O . O . . . .
. . X . . . + . . O . . . .
. . X . . . . + . O . . . .
. . . . . . . . +O . . . .
. . . . . . . . . O . . . .
. . . . . . . . . ◉+ . . .
. . . . . . . . . . . . . .
```

Examples of sell signals

There are lots of great examples of sell signals that we could show you, especially in the actual market environment. The ones below are of a typical high-tech stock and the Nikkei-225 index.

Chart 2.5 – Sell-signals on ARM Holdings [ARM.L]: S3 and S8

```
ARM.L / 3 box rev,
 250 _____        250
 245 .X...........................................           245
 240 .XO..........................................           240
 235 .XOX.........................................           235
 230 .XOXO........................................           230
 225 OXOXO_____            225
 220 OXOXO........................................           220
 215 O.O.O........................................           215
 210 ....O........................................           210
 205 ....O........................................           205
 200 ____O_____           200
 195 ....O........................................           195
 190 ....O........................................           190
 185 ....OX.................X.X...................           185
 180 ....OX6X...............XOXO..................           180
 175 ____OXOXO_____XOXO_____            175
 170 ....OXOXO........X......X.O..................           170
 165 ....O.OXO........XO.......X..O...............           165
 160 ......OXO........XO.......X.X..O.............           160
 155 ......O.O........XO.....8.XOX..O.............           155
 150 ____O_X_____XOX_X____XOXOX__9_X_____            150
 145 ........OX.X7X...XOXOXOX.XOXO...OX.XO........           145
 140 ........OXOXOXO..XOXOXOXOXOX....OXOXO........           140
 138 ........OXOXOXO..XOXOXOXOXO..OXOXO..X........           138
 136 ........OXOXOXO..XOXOXOXO.OX...OXO.O..XO.....           136
 134 _____OXOXOXOX_XOXOXOX___OX____OX__O__XO____           134
 132 ......OXOXOXOXOXOX..OX....OX..OX.XO.........+           132
 130 ......O.OXOXOXOXOXOX..OX....OX..OXOXOX......+.           130
 128 ......OXO.OXOXOXO..OX....O...OXOXOXO.....+..           128
 126 ......OX..OXOXO.O.....O.......OXOXOXO....+...           126
 124 _____OX__OXO_____OXOXOXO____+_____           124
 122 ........OX..OX.................OXOXOAO..+.....           122
 120 .........O...OX................O.OXO.O.+......           120
 118 .........O...O.................OX..O+........           118
 116 ...............................OX..+.........           116
 114 _____OX_+O_____           114
 112 ...............................OX+.O.........           112
 110 ...............................O+..O.........           110
 108 .................................+...O.......           108
 106 .....................................O.......           106
 104 _____O_____           104
  62 .....................................O.......            62
  60 .....................................O.......            60
  59 .....................................O.......            59
  58 .....................................O.....X.            58
  57 _____O_____XO_           57
  56 .....................................O.....XO            56
  55 .....................................O.....XO            55
  54 .....................................O.....XO            54
  53 .....................................O.....XO            53
  52 _____O_____XO_           52
  51 .....................................O.....XO            51
  50 .....................................O.....X.            50
  49 .....................................O..X...X.            49
  48 .....................................O..XO..X.            48
  47 _____O__XOX_X_           47
  46 .....................................O..XOXOX.            46
  45 .....................................OX.XOXOX.            45
  44 .....................................OXOXOXOX.            44
  43 .....................................OXOXOXOX.            43
  42 _____OXOXOXOX_           42
  41 .....................................OXOXO.OX.            41
  40 .....................................O.OX..OX.            40
  39 ......................................O...OX.            39
  38 --------------------------------------O--                38
  37 ---------------------------------------                  37
```

In this example, we see the formation of a base at 215 which is eventually broken, generating a breakout from a triple bottom.

Later, not only a Simple Sell is formed, but also a bullish support is broken. Such a chart shouts: *Sell!*

A sell around 110 would nicely be covered at 46, based on a Simple Buy signal.

Chart 2.6 – Nikkei-225 and its first sell signal: a Simple Sell or Double Bottom breakout

```
N225 / 4 box rev / 1988.01.18 to 2003.01.15
38000  C|.........|.....|.....|.|.||| ....|...||..|.............|..............|38000
37000  X2.........|.....|.....|.|.||| ....|...||..|.............|..............|37000
36000  BO.........|.....|.....|.|.||||....||..|.............|..............|36000
35000  8O_____35000
34000  5O.........|.....|.....|.|.||| ....|...||..|.............|..............|34000
33000  4OX........|.....|.....|.|.||| ....|...||..|.............|..............|33000
32000  23X8.......|.....|.....|.|.||| ....|...||..|.............|..............|32000
31000  1O5O.......|.....|.....|.|.||| ....|...||..|.............|..............|31000
30000  COXO_____30000
29000  XOXO.......|.....|.....|.|||| ....|...||..|.............|..............|29000
28500  B4XO.......|.....|.....|.|||| ....|...||..|.............|..............|28500
28000  6OXOX......|.....|.....|.|||| ....|...||..|.............|..............|28000
27500  5O.OX......|.....|.....|.|||| ....|...||..|.............|..............|27500
27000  X  ■OXO      3_____27000
26500  4|.OXO.....|X6....|.....|.||| ....|...||..|.............|..............|26500
26000  X|.O.OX....|XO....|.....|.||| ....|...||..|.............|..............|26000
25500  3|...OX9...|XO....|.....|.||| ....|...||..|.............|..............|25500
25000  X|...OXOX.X|XO..X.|.....|.||| ....|...||..|.............|..............|25000
24500  X   OXOXBX1XO  AB_____24500
24000  2|...O.OXOXOXOX.XO|.....|.||| ....|...||..|.............|..............|24000
23500  X|.....OXOXOXOX8XOX.....|.||| ....|...||..|.............|..............|23500
23000  X|.....OXOXO27XOXOXO....|.||| ....|...||..|.............|..............|23000
22500  1|.....OXOCO.OXOXCXO....|.|6|....|...||..|.............|..............|22500
22000       OXO   O O9O1O      X8_____22000
21500  ||.....OX..|...O.O|O....|.6|4O....|...||..|.............|..............|21500
21000  ||.....OX..|.....|O...5.59XO...|...||..|.............|..............|21000
20500  ||.....AX..|.....|2...XB2O1OX..|...3..|.............|..............|20500
20000  ||.....O...|.....|3...XOXOX9X8.|....|24.|.............|..............|20000
19500           O    4OXOXCXO        1O_____19500
19000  ||.........|.....|4X.X.XOXBCOXO..|....|BO.|.............|..............|19000
18500  ||.........|.....|OX69AXO1191XO..|....|XO.|.............|..............|18500
18000  ||.........|.....|OXOXOXOXOXO05O..|....|7O.|.............|..............|18000
17500  ||.........|.....|O5OXOXOX28O.A..|....|65.|.............|..............|17500
17000           O OXOXOXOX _OX_X    XO_____17000
16500  ||.........|.....|..OXB3OC3X|.OXCX6...|40.|.............|..............|16500
16000  ||.........|.....|..OXO|O|OX|.BXOXO...|XO.|.............|..............|16000
15500  ||.........|.....|..7X.|.|OX|.OXO1O...|X7.|.............|..............|15500
15000  ||.........|.....|..8X.|.|67|.O.O|O..B|3A.|.............|..............|15000
14500           O    O      8 _X1XO       5_____14500
14000  ||.........|.....|.|||| ....|O..XOXCX|X.....XO....|.............|..............|14000
13800  ||.........|.....|.|| ....|OX.XOXOX1X2X....XO....|.............|..............|13800
13600  ||.........|.....|.||| ....|9XOXOXOXOXOX.XO....|.............|..............|13600
13400  ||.........|.....|.|||| ....|AXOXOXOXOXOXOXOXO....|.............|..............|13400
13200           OXOXO_O_O_OXOXOX6_____13200
13000  ||.........|.....|.||| ....|O.OX||..|.OXOXOXO....|.............|..............|13000
12800  ||.........|.....|.||| ....|..O.||..|.OX4.OXO....|.............|..............|12800
12600  ||.........|.....|.||| ....|.....||..|.3X..O.O....|.............|..............|12600
12400  ||.........|.....|.||| ....|.....||..|.OX....7X...|.............|..............|12400
12200                        OX    OXO_____12200
12000  ||.........|.....|.|.||| ....|....||.|.OX....OXO...|X.5..........|..............|12000
11800  ||.........|.....|.||| ....|....||.|.OX....O8O...|XOX6.........|..............|11800
11600  ||.........|.....|.||| ....|....||.|.O....O.O...|XOXO.........|..............|11600
11400  ||.........|.....|.||| ....|....||.|....O...|XOXO.........|..............|11400
11200                                O    XOXO_____11200
11000  ||.........|.....|.||| ....|....||.|.....OX.X|X4.OX.........|..............|11000
10800  ||.........|.....|.||| ....|....||.|.....OXBXC3..OXO.........|..............|10800
10600  ||.........|.....|.||| ....|....||.|.....9XOXOX..OXO.........|..............|10600
10400  ||.........|.....|.||| ....|....||.|.....OXOXOX..O7O.........|..............|10400
10200                                      OXOXOX_O_O_____10200
10000  ||.........|.....|.|.||| ....|....||.|.....OXO.1X...O.........|..............|10000
 9800  ||.........|.....|.||| ....|....||.|.....OX..2X....OX.........| 9800
 9600  ||.........|.....|.||| ....|....||.|.....OA..O.....OXA........| 9600
 9400  ||.........|.....|.||| ....|....||..|.....O...|...9XO........| 9400
 9200                                           OXOB_____ 9200
 9000  ||.........|.....|.||| ....|....||..|.....|.......O.OXC..... 9000
 8800  ||.........|.....|.||| ....|....||..|.....|.......OXO..... 8800
 8600  ||.........|.....|.||| ....|....||..|.....|.......OXO..... 8600
 8400  ||.........|.....|.||| ....|....||..|.....|.......OXO..... 8400
 8200  89---------9------9-----9-9999----9----90--0-------------0--------------- 8200
 8000  90---------1------2-----3-4567----8----90--1-------------2--------------- 8000
```

The Nikkei during the period 1990-2002 is a tremendous example of a bear market and should never be forgotten – showing that bear markets can last for a very long time. Therefore we have included this long-term Nikkei point-and-figure chart, where we see a first sell on the fourth column and thereafter many more sell signals can be detected.

Summary of sell signals

Figure 2.20 – Sell signal summary

```
470  S1...S2....S3.....S4......S5......S6...........S7............ S8........  470
460  ..............................................+.................................  460
450  ............................................X+.............................  450
440  .....X..........................X......X...X...OXO+..................XOXO......  440
430  .X...XOX....X.X...OXOX....XOXOXO..OXOX+..........X.X.........XOXOX.....  430
420  OXO..XOXO..OXOXO..OXOX0..OXOXOXO..O.OXO+........XOXOX.......XO.OXOX...  420
410  OXO..XOXO..OXOXO..OXOXO..OXOXO.0...OXOX+.......XOXOXO.+.....X+.OXOXO..  410
400  O.O...O.O..O.O.O....O.O..O.O...O....OXOXO+......XOXOXO+.....X.+O.OXO..  400
390  ..■.....■.....■.....■.......■....OXOXO.......XOXOXO......X..+.O.O..  390
380  ................................................OXO+■.......XOXO+O.......X...+..O..  380
370  ................................................OX+.........OXOX+.■.......X...+.O..  370
360  ................................................O+........OXO+..............+O..  360
350  ................................................+..........OX+.................O..  350
340  ...............................................+............O+.................■+.  340
330  ..............................................................................  330
```

Which signals really matter?

According to the original Davis study 93% of all trading signals are made up by the formations S1 to S4 and B1 to B4.

```
B1...B2....B3.....B4.......S1...S2....S3.....S4.....
..................................................
.........................................
..■....■.....■.....■........X.............X.....
X.X...X.X..X.X.X....X.X.....X...XOX....X.X...OXOX...
XOX..OXOX..XOXOX..X.XOX....OXO..XOXO..OXOXO..OXOXO..
XOX..OXOX..XOXOX..XOXOX....OXO..XOXO..OXOXO..OXOXO..
.O...OXO....O.O...XOXO.....O.O...O.O..O.O.O....O.O..
.....O...........O.........■....■.....■.....■..
..................................................
```

Note: We take a highly pragmatic approach to point-and-figure, to make it comprehensive and scientifically correct. We go out of our way to avoid unnecessary complications. So in this book we have not included the dozens and dozens of buy and sell formations which, though possible, are very rare.

What is the signal/trade gap?

A crucial concept often forgotten is the gap between the time the trading signal is generated and the trade taking place.

If you look at a chart you can spot the trading signals, but you will not be able to derive their profitability. The reason is simple: the signal is generated and then the trading action is initiated.

However, the price may have changed in the meantime. If you have high speed access to the markets and are continuously watching over the prices, the signal/trade gap is not significant. However, if you do all your charting in the evening and give orders to your broker the next day to buy or sell on the opening, the signal/trade gap becomes significant. Always make realistic assumptions on your ability to trade on a signal.

Discussion of the application of complex signals

Because of the speed and size of market movements in recent years, there is seldom enough backing and filling action to generate the five or more columns within the relatively tight price ranges necessary for the creation of the more complex formations.

The most extensive study on point-and-figure reveals the frequency of occurrence of fifteen of the sixteen formations for 1100 US stocks for the period 1954 through 1964, and two stocks between 1914 and 1964, as computed by Robert E. Davis and discussed in his book *Profit and Probability* published in 1965. Because there are thousands of stocks actively traded on the US national and regional exchanges and in the over-the-counter markets, and because the entry fee for a round lot is often considerably higher than the margin required for trading one futures contract, the stock investor must limit his universe of signals to a favourite few.

Bond and stock option traders, and especially common stock traders, have a more difficult problem. They must find the one or more formations best suited to their financial resources. If they have plenty of investment capital, they have the option of using the more commonly occurring signals. If their funds available for investment are severely limited, however, they have to use the less common signals.

Does it work?

Point-and-figure charting is a valuable trading tool. It yields specific prices at which to take longs and go short, and the location of stop-loss points. It provides order, meaning, rationality, consistency, and forces discipline in the trading world where this most important ingredient is so often lacking. But best of all, it works.

True, there are whipsaws and false signals. The system is not perfect. But, as a rule, it cuts losses short, lets profits run, and is right a high percentage of the time. It is also always *in* on the major moves. These are the components of a good trading system and p&f charting does it in an easy-to-understand format.

The system can be coupled with fundamentals to comprise a matchless trading team. The fundamental data will indicate the securities to trade and the long-term trends (i.e. bullish or bearish) and provide some guidance as to whether you should take only buy signals to enter long positions because the fundamentals are extremely strong, take only sell signals to go short, or take all signals given weak and deteriorating fundamentals, or take all signals. The chart will provide the timing of the trades.

Alternatively, point-and-figure can be used alone if you subscribe to the philosophy that all fundamentally caused movements will ultimately be reflected on the chart so why bother with fundamentals? But regardless of which method you use, the system will work.

The later chapters of this book will discuss more complex point-and figure formations using the charts to predict price movements, and the actual real-trading profit record for the system spanning seventy years of history and numerous professional and academic studies of profitability.

Summary

- There are **eight basic buy and eight basic sell** signals used in point-and-figure charting.

- The first two buy signals, referred to as the **Simple Buy** signals and comprised of three or four columns, play a dual role of determining the price level at which shorts must be covered as well as signalling the opportunity for the establishment of new long positions.

- The more **complex buy** signals, all comprised of five or more columns and all containing one or more of the simple signals within their structure, permit the establishment of long positions but are not used to close out shorts, since short positions are always covered on simple signals.

- The **Simple Sell** signals covering three or four columns always signal the need for the liquidation of long positions as well as suggest the possibility of a short sale.

- The more **complex sell** signals, more correctly termed *short-sale signals*, contain more columns of reversals and one or more of the Simple Sell formations. These complex formations are not used to close longs, since the simple signals accomplish this, but are strong indicators that the short side is the correct side of the market.

Trend lines

Stock prices do not move in totally irregular and unpredictable ways. Instead, their prices tend to rise and fall within channels or trends. Although the use of the buy, sell, and short sell formations can provide excellent returns, it is often wise to view the formations within the context of the current trend as a means of avoiding those signals running counter to the trend which have high probabilities of being false.

The four basic price channels

1. **Accumulation channel**: marked by an equilibrium position of supply and demand and a horizontal price movement normally following a major decline,

2. **Bullish channel**: marked by rising demand and thus price increasing,

3. **Distribution channel**: indicated by an equilibrium position of supply and demand and a horizontal price movement normally occurring after a major bullish move,

4. **Bearish channel**: as denoted by supply exceeding demand and thus a declining price.

Figure 2.21 – Price channels

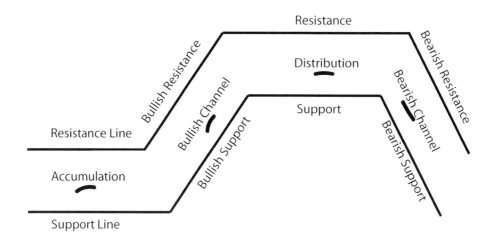

Trend lines drawn at 45 degrees

Each channel is defined by trend lines drawn on the point-and-figure chart at 45 degree rising or falling, intersecting the diagonal corners of each square. They are drawn only at 45 degree angles by convention and because the research of Robert E. Davis, as published in *Profit and Probability* showed,

> *'that the selling action points or buy points generated by these diagonal trend lines have very high probability of successful trading.'*

You will be amazed at how successful these simple diagonal 45 degree trend lines are at defining price channels. Their significance will become apparent to you in almost all charts – especially those over a longer time horizon – again and again. They will become as indispensable a tool in your trading as they are in ours.

The use of 45 degree trend lines is another unique aspect of point-and-figure charting, and one which helps eliminate ambiguity and errors of interpretation. Penetrations through p&f diagonal trend lines are absolutely clear, either true or false, and involve none of the guessing which you get with bar charts and candlesticks.

The four types of trend line

1. **Bullish support** – a line upwards and below columns
2. **Bullish resistance** – a line upwards and above columns
3. **Bearish support** – a line downwards and below columns
4. **Bearish resistance** – a line downwards and above columns

Accumulation and distribution channels

The horizontal lines defining accumulation and distribution channels are not drawn in a p&f chart because they are obvious as p&f charts are drawn in a grid structure, and such a grid makes horizontal levels evident.

Example of trend lines

The chart overleaf of the French CAC 40 [.FCHI] includes all of the four types of trend lines. They, as you can easily detect, nicely define the channels of the price moves.

Chart 2.7 – Price channels in the French market

```
FCHI / 3 box rev, log1/ 1997.01.02 to 2003.01.16
7000 _____+_____ 7000
6800 ..........|.....|.....|...9+.|........|........................ 6800
6600 ..........|.....|.....|...6O+|........|........................ 6600
6400 ..........|.....|.....|.3.XOX+......|........................ 6400
6200 ..........|.....|.....|.X4XOXB+......|........................ 6200
6000 _____1_XOXAXO_+_____ 6000
5900 ..........|.....|.....XO2OXO.O..+.....|........................ 5900
5800 ..........|.....|.....XOXO...C...+.....|........................ 5800
5700 ..........|.....|.....XOX....O..5.+...|........................ 5700
5600 ..........|.....|.....XOX....2..X6.+..|........................ 5600
5500 _____COX_____O__XO___+_____ 5500
5400 ..........|.....|.....XO.....O..XO...+|........................ 5400
5300 ..........|.....|.....X+.....3..XO....+........................ 5300
5200 ..........|.....|.....X.+...OX.XOX...|+........................ 5200
5100 ..........|.....|....+X..+..OX4XOXO..|.+....................... 5100
5000 _____+_B___+__OXOXOXO_____+_____ 5000
4900 ..........|.....|..+..X....+.O.O.78O..|...+..................... 4900
4800 ..........|.....|.+...A.....+|...O.O..|....+.................... 4800
4700 ..........|.....|+..X.9......+....+OC.X....+................... 4700
4600 ..........|.....+...7OX......|+..+.9BOXOX....+................. 4600
4500 _____+____6OX_____++__OXO1OX5____+_____ 4500
4400 ..........X...+.|...XOX......|.++..OXO|O3O.....+............... 4400
4300 ..........7O.+..X.X.XOX......|+..+.OX.|2.O......+.............. 4300
4200 ..........6O+...XOX2X8|......+....+OA.|..6.......+............. 4200
4100 ..........XOX..XOXO4.|.....+|.....OX.|..O........+............ 4100
4000 _____58XO__1OXO_____+_____OX____O_____+_____ 4000
3900 ..........4OXOX.XO....|...+..|.....OX+|..OX........+........... 3900
3800 ..........XO.OXCX.....|..+...|.....OX.+..OXO.........+......... 3800
3700 ..........X..OXOX.....|.+....|.....OX.|+.O7O..........+........ 3700
3600 ..........X..OBO|.....|+.....|.....OX.|.+O.O....X......+....... 3600
3500 _____3_9X_____+_____O_____+_OX_X_X9_____+_____ 3500
3400 ..........X..OX.|....+|......|.........|...+OXOX8XOX......+...... 3400
3300 ..........X..OX.|...+.|......|.........|....OXOXOXOXO....B.+..... 3300
3200 ..........2..OX.|..+..|......|.........|....O+OXOXOXO....XOX+..... 3200
3100 .....X.A...1..AX.|.+...|......|.........|.....OXO.O.O....XOXO+.... 3100
3000 _____78XO__X__OX__+_____OX____O____XO_O_+___ 3000
2900 .....XOXO..C..O..+.....|.....|.........|......O.+...OX.X.X.....+.. 2900
2850 .....XO9OB.X....+|.....|.....|.........|..........+..OXOXOX......+. 2850
2800 ...X.XO.OXOX...+.|.....|.....|.........|..........+.OXOAOX.......+ 2800
2750 ...XOX..OXOX..+..|.....|.....|.........|..........+OXO.OX........ 2750
2700 _3_XOX__OXOX_+_____O___OX_____ 2700
2650 .XOXOX..OXO|+....|.....|.....|.........|..........+..O.......... 2650
2600 .XOXOX..OX.+....|.....|.....|.........|.............+.......... 2600
2550 .2O5OX..OX+|.....|.....|.....|.........|..............+......... 2550
2500 .X4.6...O+.|.....|.....|.....|.........|...............+........ 2500
2450 _X_____+_____+_____ 2450
2400 .X.........|.....|.....|.....|.........|.................+...... 2400
2350 .X.........|.....|.....|.....|.........|...................+..... 2350
2300 .X.........|.....|.....|.....|.........|....................+.... 2300
2250 1..........|.....|.....|.....|.........|........................ 2250
2200 ----------9-----9-----0------0--------0------------------------- 2200
2150 ----------8-----9-----0------1--------2------------------------- 2150
```

No ambiguity

Note how well the trend lines in the above chart work. Point-and-figure only uses 45 degree trend lines and it is therefore absolutely clear where to trace them. All trend lines in this book are drawn by computer. That means no guessing and no tinkering. Just clearly defined trend lines.

Bullish support lines

Bullish support lines are drawn from the lower right corner of a low O - or exposed O - at a 45 degree angle from lower left to upper right when the chart has rising bottoms.

The 15 year FTSE 100 [.FTSE] chart shows a bullish support line which is defined by 4 columns – or 2 exposed Os with the subsequent higher Xs – and holds for 10 years.

Chart 2.8 – FTSE [.FTSE] 15 year, with bullish support line

```
FTSE / 3 box rev, log2/ 1988.01.11 to 2003.01.10
 7199  ......|.|.....|.|.....|.|.....|.|.....|.|.........|.......|......|...................... 7199
 7057  ......|.|.....|.|.....|.|.....|.|.....|.|.........|.......|......|...................... 7057
 6919  ......|.|.....|.|.....|.|.....|.|.....|.X|........|.......|......|...................... 6919
 6783  ......|.|.....|.|.....|.|.....|.|.....|...........5.....C1....X..|...................... 6783
 6650  ......|.|.....|.|.....|.|.....|.|.....|..........5___XOX__90._____ 6650
 6520  ......|.|.....|.|.....|.|.....|.|.....|.XOX...XOX4..60.......|...................... 6520
 6392  ......|.|.....|.|.....|.|.....|.|.....|.40X7X.BOXOX.XOX......|...................... 6392
 6267  ......|.|.....|.|.....|.|.....|.|.....|.XO6OX9XOXOXOXOX2.....|...................... 6267
 6144  ......|.|.....|.|.....|.|.....|.|.....X..X.XO.OXOX23O5OXOXO..|...................... 6144
 6023  _____XOXO_____1OX__8_OAO_O_O_A_O___._____ 6023
 5905  ......|.|.....|.|.....|.|.....|.3OXO.......XO2....O.|....OX....+..................... 5905
 5790  ......|.|.....|.|.....|.|.....|.X07O......X.XO.|........346...+..................... 5790
 5676  ......|.|.....|.|.....|.|.....|.X6.8...XCX.........|......OXO..+.................... 5676
 5565  ......|.|.....|.|.....|.|.....|.2..O...XOX.........|......OXO.+..................... 5565
 5456  _____X_O____BO_____OX7+___._____ 5456
 5349  ......|.|.....|.|.....|.|....A.1..OX....X.|........O.O..B.X....................... 5349
 5244  ......|.|.....|.|.....|.|....XOX..OXOX....X.|........|+9..XCX2................... 5244
 5141  ......|.|.....|.|.....|.|....9OX...OXOXA..X.|.........+.O..XO1O................. 5141
 5040  ......|.|.....|.|.....|.|....8OC..9.OXO..X.|.........+|.O..XO|O............... 5040
 4941  _____XOB____O_OX_X_____+___OX_A__6_____._____ 4941
 4844  ......|.|.....|.|.....|.|....7OX...OXOX........|...+..|.OXOX..|O............... 4844
 4749  ......|.|.....|.|.....|.|....6OX....OXOX.......|...+.....OXOX..|O............... 4749
 4656  ......|.|.....|.|.....|.|....XOX....O.O........|..+.....O.OX..|O............... 4656
 4565  ......|.|.....|.|.....|.|....XOX...............|..+........OX..|O............... 4565
 4475  _____5OX_____+_____OX__O___._____ 4475
 4388  ......|.|.....|.|.....|.|....3O|...............+.........OX.|7...X............. 4388
 4302  ......|.|.....|.|.....|.|....2.|...............+........O.|O..X.X9............ 4302
 4217  ......|.|.....|.|.....|.|....X.|...............+.......|OX.X8XOX....+B..... 4217
 4135  ......|.|.....|.|.....|.|....1.|...........+..|......|OXOXOXOXO.....XC.... 4135
 4054  _____A_____+_____OXOXOXOXOX_____XO_____ 4054
 3974  ......|.|.....|.|.....|.|....9.|...........+..|.......|OXOXO.O.OXO....XO...O 3974
 3896  ......|.|.....|.|.....|.|....8.|...........+..|.......|O.OX...OXOX.X.XO...O 3896
 3820  ......|.|.....|.|.....|.|....4.|...........+.......|...OX...O.OXOXOXO...O 3820
 3745  ......|.|.....|.|.....|.|....1.|............+.......|...OX...OXOAOX.....O 3745
 3671  _____C_____+_____O_____O_O_O_____ 3671
 3599  ......|.|.....|.|.....|.|....B.|...........+.......... 3599
 3529  ......|.|.....|.|.....|.|....2...8.|........+.......... 3529
 3460  ......|.|.....|.|.....|.|....XO...7.|........+.......... 3460
 3392  ......|.|.....|.|.....|.|....XO...6.|........+.......... 3392
 3325  _____XO___X_____+_____ 3325
 3260  ......|.|.....|.|.....|.|....COX...5.|....+.......... 3260
 3196  ......|.|.....|.|.....|.|....X3X9..4.|....+.......... 3196
 3134  ......|.|.....|.|.....|.|....AO8OX.X.|....+.......... 3134
 3072  ......|.|.....|.|.....|.|....XOXOXCX..|..+.......... 3072
 3012  _____X5XOXO3___+_____ 3012
 2953  ......|.|.....|.|.....|.|....3.XO7A.O|.|+.......... 2953
 2895  ......|.|.....|.|.....|.|....24X6....|.+.......... 2895
 2838  ......|.|.....|.|.....|.|....CO8.....|.|+.......... 2838
 2783  ......|.|.....|.|.....|.|....XO|.....+.......... 2783
 2728  _____X___B____+_____ 2728
 2674  ......|.|.....|.|....9.|.56..X.|....+.|.......... 2674
 2622  ......|.|.....|.|....8A.|XOX.X.|.....+.|.......... 2622
 2571  ......|.|.....|.|....7OX.XOXAX.|.+....|.......... 2571
 2520  ......|.|.....|.|....XO14XOXOX.|+....|.......... 2520
 2471  _____1____XBXOX7XO__+_____ 2471
 2422  ....9.XOX...3OXOXOX.|+.......... 2422
 2375  ....XOXO68...XCXO.OX.+.|.......... 2375
 2328  ....8OXOXO..XO|..89+|.|.......... 2328
 2283  ....XOCOXOX.X.|..O+.|.......... 2283
 2238  ____7AB2XOXOX___+_____ 2238
 2194  ....XOX4XOXO2.|.+...|.|.......... 2194
 2151  ....5OXO5OXOX.|+....|.|.......... 2151
 2109  ....3OXO.OXOX.+.....|.|.......... 2109
 2067  ....XO|..OXOX+|.....|.|.......... 2067
 2027  _____X____9AB+_____ 2027
 1987  ......X.|.O.+|.....|.|.......... 1987
 1948  .....X..|..+.|.....|.|.......... 1948
 1910  ......X.|..+...|.....|.|.......... 1910
 1873  ...X.1.|.+...|.....|.|.......... 1873
 1836  __X_X8X__+_____ 1836
 1800  X.X4XOX.+....|.|.....|.|.......... 1800
 1765  X2XO6O8-9-----9-9-----9-9-----9-9-----------9--------0-------0--------------------- 1765
 1730  1O3O-99-O-----1-2-----3-4-----7-8---------9---------0-------1------2--------------- 1730
```

The more times the support line has held price declines in check, the stronger the support becomes.

As long as the price remains above the bullish support line, the position is said to be *long-term bullish*.

Trading strategies for bullish support lines

In such cases there are three legitimate ways to trade the market:

1. Take all signals and thereby ignore the long-term trend.

2. Take long positions with stop-loss orders placed at sell signals, yet all short sell signals are ignored due to the long-term bullish nature of the price.

3. Ignore all sell signals occurring above the bullish support line and thereby continue to hold the longs until a sell signal occurs below the support line. In this way trading is lessened, commissions are reduced and the possibility of obtaining a long-term capital gain is increased. The disadvantage is that this third tactic is the least sensitive of the three to current market patterns.

The selection of the trading tactic to be employed is solely up to the individual and should be a function of his analysis of the fundamental prospects of the position and his personal desire for transactional action.

Chart 2.9 – Bullish support of Shire Pharmaceuticals [SHP.L]

```
SHP.L 3box rev, / 2000.01.04 to 2001.02.15
1480 ..........X.....................................................XO.........|.......... 1480
1460 ..........XO....................................................XO.........|.......... 1460
1440 ..........XO.............................X..........X.X.X.XO.......|.......... 1440
1420 ..........XO..............................XO........XOXOXOXOX.......|.......... 1420
1400        XO                                  XO          XOXOXOXOXO          1400
1380 ..........XO..............................XO.........XOXOXO.OXO.......|.......... 1380
1360 ......X.XO..............................XOX........XOXB...O.O.......|....X...... 1360
1340 ......XOXO..............................X.X.XOXO.......XOX......O....|....XO..X.X 1340
1320 ......XOXO..............................XOXOXO9O.......XOX......OX....|....XOX.XOX 1320
1300      XOXO                         X XOXOXO OX       XO      OXO      X XOXOXOX 1300
1280 ........XOXO....X........................XOXOXOXO..OXO....X.X.......+OXO.....|..XOXO2OXO. 1280
1260 ......XOXO....XO..........................XOXOXOX..XOX......+.OXO.....|..XOXO.O... 1260
1240 ......XOXO....XO..........................XOXOXOX..OXOXOX.XOX.....+..OXO.....|..XOX...... 1240
1220 ......XOXO....XO..........................XOXOXOXOXO....+..OXOX....|..XO....... 1220
1200      XO_O    XO                    XOXOX   OXOXOXOXO    +    O_OXO      X      1200
1180 ........X..O...XO......X..............X.XOXO8....O.OXOXOA....+.......OXO...|X.X........ 1180
1160 ......X..O...XO......XO...............XOXO.O.......O.O.O...+.......OXO...|XOX....... 1160
1140 ......X..O...XO......XO...............X.XOX...............+.........OXO..X|XOX....... 1140
1120 ......X..O...XO......XO...............XOXO7................+.......OXO..XOXOX....... 1120
1100      X_OX_X_XO      XO        XOXO          +        OXO  XOXOX      1100
1080 ........X..OXOXOXO.....XO...........XOX............+..........CXO..XOXOX...... 1080
1060 ......X..OXOXOXO.....XO..........X.XOX............+..........OXO..XOXOX...... 1060
1040 ......X.X..OXO4OXO.....XO....X.....XOXOX...........+.........O.O..X1XOX...... 1040
1020 ......XOX..OXO.O..O....XOX...XO....XOXO...............+.................O..XO.O........ 1020
1000      XO3_OX    O     XOXOX_XOX   XOX       +       OX_X        1000
 990 .......XO...OX....OX.X..XOXOXOXOXOX.XOX...............+................OXOX|.......... 990
 980 .......X....OX...OXOXO..XOXOXOXOXOX6XOX...............+................OXOX|.......... 980
 970 .......X....OX...OXOXO..XOXOXOXOXOXOXO...............+................OXOX|.......... 970
 960 .......X....OX...OXOXO.OXO.OXOXOX.............+................O.OX|.......... 960
 950      X    OX    OXOXO_XOX_OXOXOXOX        +            O     950
 940 .......X....OX....OXOXO..XOX..OXOXO.OX.......+................|.......... 940
 930 .......X.X...OX....OXOXO..XOX..OXO...OX.........+................|.......... 930
 920 .....XOX....O....OXOXOX.XOX..OX....O...........+................|.......... 920
 910 ...X.XOX.....OXOXOX5XOX..OX.............+................|.......... 910
 900    XOXOX       OXOXOXOXO   OX        +                900
 890 ...XOXOX.......OXOXOXOX...OX.........+................|.......... 890
 880 ...XOXOX.......OXOXOXO....OX.......+................|.......... 880
 870 ...XOXOX.......O.OXOXO...OX.......+................|.......... 870
 860 ...XOXOX.........OXOX....OX.....+................|.......... 860
 850   XOXOX        OXOX    OX     +               850
 840 ...XOXOX.......OXOX....OX......+................|.......... 840
 830 ...XO.2X.......OXOX....OX.....+................|.......... 830
 820 ...X..OX.......OXOX....OX....+................|.......... 820
 810 ...X..OX.......OXOX....O.....+................|.......... 810
 800    X_OX        OXOX       +                800
 790 ...X..OX...........OXOX......+................|.......... 790
 780 ...X..OX...........OXOX......+................|.......... 780
 770 ...X..O...........OXOX......+................|.......... 770
 760 ...X...............OXOX......+................|.......... 760
 750   X            OXOX    +                 750
 740 ...X...............OXOX....+................|.......... 740
 730 ...X...............OXOX...+................|.......... 730
 720 .X.X...............OXOX..+................|.......... 720
 710 .XOX...............OXOX..+................|.......... 710
 700  XOX            OXO_+                 700
 690 .XOX..............OX..+.................|.......... 690
 680 .XOX..............OX.+................|.......... 680
 670 .XOX..............OX+................|.......... 670
 660 .XO...............O+................|.......... 660
 650  X            +                  650
 640 .X................................|.......... 640
 630 .X................................|.......... 630
 620 .X................................|.......... 620
 610 1X................................|.......... 610
 600 OX_                               600
 590 OX................................|.......... 590
 580 O.................................|.......... 580
 390 ..................................|.......... 390
 380 ------------------------------------------------------0----------- 380
 370 ------------------------------------------------------1----------- 370
```

Here again, you can see how well the p&f 45 degree trend lines confine price movements. The low from April 2000 defines a bullish support line which holds during most of the rest of the year, and once broken gives way to an accelerated down move.

Chart 2.10 – Bullish support with Elan Corp [ELN.L]

```
ELN.L / 3 box rev, / 2000.01.04 to 2000.10.27
4700 ...................................................................... 4700
4600 ...................................................................... 4600
4500 _____ 4500
4400 ...................................................................... 4400
4300 ...................................................................... 4300
4200 ...................................................................... 4200
4100 ...................................................................... 4100
4000 _____X_____X_____ 4000
3960 ..........................................X9........XO... 3960
3920 ..........................................X.XO......XOX.. 3920
3880 ..........................................XOXO......XOXO. 3880
3840 ..........................................XOXO......XOXO. 3840
3800 ..........................................XOXOX___X___AO_O 3800
3760 ..........................................XO.OXO..XOX.X..O. 3760
3720 ..........................................X..OXOX.XOXOX..OX 3720
3680 ..........................................X..OXOXOXOXOX..OX 3680
3640 ..........................................X.X..OXOXOXO.O...OX 3640
3600 _____XOX__OXO_OX_____OX 3600
3560 ..........................................XOX..OX..O.......OX 3560
3520 ..........................................XOX..OX.........OX 3520
3480 ..........................................XO..OX.........OX 3480
3440 ..........................................8....OX.........OX 3440
3400 _____X_X_X____O_____+O 3400
3360 ..........................................XOXOX............+... 3360
3320 ..........................................XOXOX............+.... 3320
3280 ..........................................XOXOX...........+..... 3280
3240 ..........................................XOXOX..........+...... 3240
3200 _____X_XOXO_____+____ 3200
3160 ..........................................XOXO...........+........ 3160
3120 ..........................................XOX............+........ 3120
3080 ..........................................XOX..........+......... 3080
3040 ..........................................70.........+........ 3040
3000 _____X___X_X__X_____X_X_____+ 3000
2960 ...............4O..XOXO..XO....X.XOX.........+.......... 2960
2920 ...............XO..XOXOX.XO....XOXOX..........+......... 2920
2880 ...............X.XO..XOXOXOXO....XOXO.........+......... 2880
2840 ...............XOXO..XOXOXOXO...X.XOX.........+......... 2840
2800 _____XOXOX_XOXOXOXO__XOXO_____+_____ 2800
2760 ...............XOXOXOXOX5.OXO..XOX.......+........ 2760
2720 ...............XOXOXOXOX...OXO..XOX......+........ 2720
2680 ...............XOXOXO.O...OXOX.XO........+........ 2680
2640 ...............X..XOXOX....OXOX6X.......+........ 2640
2600 _____XOX_XO_OX____O_OXOX____+_____ 2600
2560 ...............XOXOX..OX.....O.OX......+.......... 2560
2520 ...............XOXOX..OX........OX.....+........ 2520
2480 ...............30.OX..OX...........OX...+........ 2480
2440 ...............X..OX..O.........O...+........ 2440
2400 _____X__O_____+____ 2400
2360 ...............X...................+.......... 2360
2320 ...............X.X.................+........ 2320
2280 ...............XOX.................+........ 2280
2240 ...............XOX.................+........ 2240
2200 _____XOX_____+___ 2200
2160 ...............XO.................+......... 2160
2120 ...............X.................+........ 2120
2080 ...............X.................+........ 2080
2040 ...............X.X...............+........ 2040
2000 _____X_XOX_____+__ 2000
1980 ...........XOXOX...........+......... 1980
1960 ...........XOXOX..........+........ 1960
1940 ...........XO.OX.........+........ 1940
1920 ...........X..O.........+........ 1920
1900 _____X_____+_____ 1900
1880 ...........X............+........ 1880
1860 ...x.X.X.....2......+......... 1860
1840 ...XOXO.....X.......+........ 1840
1820 .X.XOXO.....X.......+........ 1820
1800 _XOXOXO___X____+____ 1800
1780 .XOXO.O....X....+........ 1780
1760 .XOX..O....X....+........ 1760
1740 .XOX..O....X....+........ 1740
1720 1.OX..O....X.X...+........ 1720
1700 _O__O___XOX__+_____ 1700
1680 .....OX...XOX..+................... 1680
1660 .....OXOX.XO..+.................. 1660
1640 .....OXOXOX..+................. 1640
1620 .....OXOXOX.+................ 1620
1600 _____O_OXOX+_____ 1600
1580 .......OXO+.............. 1580
1560 ........O.+............. 1560
1540 ....................................................... 1540
1520 ....................................................... 1520
1500 ....................................................... 1500
1480 ....................................................... 1480
1460 ....................................................... 1460
  80 _____ 80
  75 ------------------------------------------------ 75
  70 ------------------------------------------------ 70
  65 ------------------------------------------------ 65
```

The Elan chart, like the Shire Pharma chart on page 87, clearly demonstrates how trend lines support forecasting of future price movements. The trend line was drawn based only on the information until January 2000, yet successfully defined price development up to November 2000.

Note: trend lines generated with bar charts are continuously changed and are therefore much less useful for forecasts and are often used for explaining the past.

Bullish resistance lines

The bottom side of a bullish channel is defined by a bullish support line while the top of the trend is bordered by a *bullish resistance* line drawn from the lower right corner of the lowest exposed O in a wall (highlighted) of two or more exposed Os at a 45 degree angle from lower left to upper right.

The bullish channel can be nicely observed on the Ericsson [ERIC.ST] chart below. You can see that the line is touched twice – in February 2000 – before it eventually breaks or gets penetrated.

Chart 2.11 – Bullish resistance by Ericsson AB [ERIC.ST]

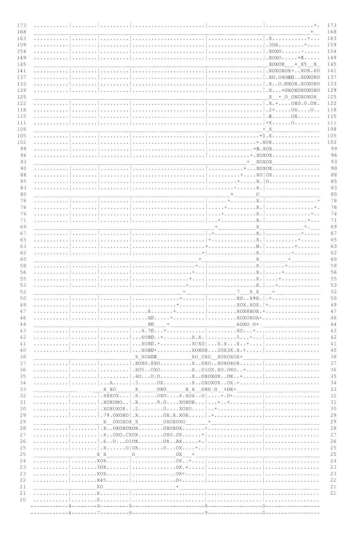

Interestingly, in the Ericsson chart the price runs through the long-term bullish resistance line, after touching it twice, then retracts and finds new levels just below the line. Some months later – as we all know – it broke strongly through the bullish support.

On the Ericsson chart we have continued the first bullish support line. It shows how this line gets reinstated after it has been broken. Just after the penetration the line straddles two columns and then towards end of 99 becomes a valid support again.

It is amazing how well these trend lines actually work!

Chart 2.12 – Bullish resistance by ABB [ABB.ST]

```
ABB.ST / 3 box rev, log1/ 1997.01.02 to 2001.08.24
290 ..............|....................|......|...+........X...........|..................  290
285 _____X_____XO_____  285
280 ..............|....................|......|.+XO.....X..XO..X.......|..................  280
275 ..............|....................|......|+.XO.....XOXOX.XO.......|..................  275
270 ..............|....................|......+..XO.....XOXOXOXO.......|..................  270
265 ..............|....................|....+|X.XOX.....XOX6XOXO.......|..................  265
260 _____+X_XOXOXO_____XOXO_O7O_____X_____  260
255 ..............|....................|...+.X1XOXOXO..X.50...0.9.......|XO...............  255
250 ..............|....................|..+..XOXOXOXO..X4X.....O......X|XO..............  250
245 ..............|....................|.+...XOXO2O.OX.XOX......OA.....X1XO.............  245
240 ..............|....................|+....XO.O...OXOX......OXO..X.XOXO...............  240
235 _____+_____X_____O3OXOX_____OXOX_XCXO_O_____  235
230 ..............|....................+|....X|.....O.OXO......OXOXOXOX|.2..............  230
225 ..............|....................+.|...9.X|.....O........O.OXOXO.|.O..............  225
220 ..............|....................+..|...XOX|....................O.OB..|.O..........  220
215 ..............|....................+...|...XOC|....................O...|.O..........  215
210 _____+_____X_XOX_____OX_____  210
205 ..............|.X............+.....|.7OXOX|......................|.OX3..............  205
200 ........X.....|.56...........+......|.XOXAB|.....................|.OXO..............  200
195 ........XO....|.XOX.........+.......|.6O8O.|.....................|.OXO...X..........  195
190 ........XO....|.XOXO......+.........|.5O...|.....................|.O.OX..5.X6........  190
185 _____XO_____4OXO_____+_____X_____OX4XOXO_____  185
180 .....X.X.XO....|.XO7O.....+.........|.X....|.....................|...OXOXOXO.........  180
175 .....6OXOX9....|.XO.O....+..........|.X....|.....................|...OXOXO.O.........  175
170 .....XO7O8O....|.X..O..+............|.4....|.....................|...O.OX..O.........  170
165 .....XO.O.A...|.3..8..+.............|.X....|.....................|...OX..OX.........  165
160 _____X_____O_____X_O_+_____X_____OX__OX7_____  160
155 ....5....O..X.|.2..O+...............|.3....|.....................|....O...OXO.......  155
150 ....X....O..XCX.X..OX...............|.X....|.....................|.....O..OX.........  150
145 .2...X....O..XOXOX..O9O.............|.X....|.....................|.......OXO.....  145
140 .XOX.X....OX.XO1OX..OXO..........X..1.X....|.....................|.......OXO.....  140
138 _XOXOX_____OXBXO_OX_OXO_____X___XCX_XOX_____O_O_____  138
136 .XOXOX....OXOX.|OX..OXO......XO..XOXOXOX....|.....................|..........O.....  136
134 .XO3OX....OXOX.|OX..OXO......XOB.XOXOXOX....|.....................|..........O.....  134
132 .XO.OX....OXO..|OX..O.O....XOXOXOXOX....|.....................|..........O.....  132
130 .X..4.....OX...|O.....O..XOXOXOXOXOX....|.....................|..........O.....  130
128 _X_____OX_____O_____XOXOXOXOXOX_____O_____  128
126 .X........OX...|......O....XOXO.OXOX....|.....................|..........O.....  126
124 .X........O....|......O...X.XOX..O.O|OX....|.....................|..........O.....  124
122 .X........O....|......O..XOXOX.....|O2....|.....................|..........OX.X..  122
120 1.............|.....OX...XOXOX.....|OX....|.....................|..........O8OXO.  120
118 _____OXOX_XOXOX_____OX_____OXOXOX_  118
116 ..............|....OXOXOXOXO.....|OX....|.....................|..........OXOXOX  116
114 ..............|....OXOXOXOX......|O.....|.....................|..........OXO.OX  114
112 ..............|....OXO.OXO.......|......|.....................|..........OX..OX  112
110 ..............|....OX..AX........|......|.....................|..........OX..O.  110
108 _____OX__OX_____O_____  108
106 ..............|....O..OX.........|......|.....................|..........O.....  106
104 ..............|........OX.........|......|.....................|..........O.....  104
102 ..............|........OX.........|......|.....................|..........O.....  102
100 ..............|........OX.........|......|.....................|..........O.....  100
 98 _____OX_____   98
 96 ..............|........O.........|......|.....................|..................   96
 94 ..............|........|.........|......|.....................|..................   94
    ------------------9--------------------9------0------------------------0-----------------
    --------------8--------------------9------0------------------------1-----------------
```

The bullish resistance line is used as a gauge of the height a column of Xs might reach on the current move. The more times it holds, the stronger it becomes.

Trading strategies for bullish resistance lines

As a trading tool, the bullish resistance line can be used:

1. As a point to **enter a short** in the expectation that upon reaching the line, the price will bounce off and down, or

2. As a place to **liquidate a long** position in a period of strength as opposed to closing it out on a regular sell signal in a period of weakness. Moreover, this is especially important when trading highly volatile commodities which may lock limit down with weakness, necessitating a liquidation on strength, not weakness.

Quite often a very bullish position will not stop at the first of the bullish resistance lines, but trade right through it as if it did not exist. This is a strong bullish indication and will generally mean that the price will rise to the next higher resistance line. For this reason all resistance lines should be drawn on the chart as done in Chart 2.13 overleaf.

Which resistance line?

Experience has led the authors to the conclusion that a strong stock or commodity will:

1. in a **neutral to bearish market** climate, generally run out of steam at the first or lowest bullish line;

2. in a **medium bullish** environment, reach the second as shown; and

3. in **exceedingly strong markets**, reach the third or fourth resistance line which is the one that finally holds.

So judge the market climate before deciding on which line to blow the long out or take a short.

Chart 2.13 – Pace Micro [PIC.L] sets the stage for the rally of the century in 1998

```
PIC.L / 3 box rev, c e/ 1997.11.12 to 1998.12.15
 114 ......................................|.........................................................................  114
 112 ......................................|.......................+.................................................  112
 110 ......................................|....................X..+..................................................  110
 108 _____XO+_____  108
 106 ......................................|....................XO.....................................................  106
 104 ......................................|....................XO.............................+.......................  104
 102 ......................................|.................+XO.............................+.......................  102
 100 ......................................|...............+.XO...........................+....................  100
  98 _____+__XO_____+_____  98
  96 ......................................|...........+..XO..............+.............................  96
  94 ......................................|...........+..XO...............+................+............  94
  92 ......................................|..........+..XO...............+................+...........  92
  90 ......................................|.........+....XOX.......+...............+...............  90
  88 _____+_____XOXOX_____+_____+_____  88
  86 ......................................|.......+.......XOXOXO..X............X..+.............  86
  84 ......................................|.......+.......XOXOXOX+XO.........X8+.......X...X..  84
  82 ......................................|......+........XOXOXOXOXO.........XO.............XOX..XOX  82
  80 ......................................|....+.........XOXO5OXOXO........XO.............XOXCXOX  80
  78 .................................+.........XOXOXO.OXO_____+XO_____XOXOXOX  78
  76 ......................................|....+............XOXOX..6XOX.X....+.XOX.........XO.OXOX  76
  74 ......................................|....+..........XOXOX..O.OXOX7..+..XOXO..........X..OXOX  74
  72 ......................................|...+............XOXOX...OXOXO..+..XOXOX......X.X..OXO.  72
  70 ......................................|...+...........XOXO....O.O.O.+...XOXOXOX.X.A.XOX..OX..  70
  68 _____+_____+XOX_____O+____XOXOXOXOXOXOXOX__OX___  68
  66 ......................................|...+.............+.XOX.........O......XO.OXOXOXOXOXOX..O...  66
  64 ......................................|...+...........+.XO..........+O......X..O.O.OXOXOXOB.....  64
  62 ......................................|..+.............+..X..........+.OX....X......OXO.OXO.......  62
  60 ......................................|..+.............+...X.........+.OXOX...X.....9X..OX.......  60
  59 _____+_____+____X_____+___OXOXO_X_____OX__OX_____  59
  58 ......................................|.+.............+...X..+....+..OXOXOX...XO..OX........  58
  57 .......................................|+..........+....X..+....O.OXOXOX....O...OX........  57
  56 ......................................O...........+....X..+........OXOXOX.........OX........  56
  55 OX.X...................+|...........+....X..+........OXOXOX.........OX......  55
  54 OXOXOX_X_____+_____+____X_+____OXO_O_____O_____  54
  53 OXOXOXOXOX........+..|...........+....X..+......OX...............  53
  52 O.O.OXOXOXOX......+..|...........+....X.+.....OX.................  52
  51 ...OXOXOXO....+....|...........+....X+....OX.................  51
  50 ....O.O.O.OCOX....+.....|.X......+........X.........O..............  50
  49 _____O_OXO_+_____XO____+_____+X_____  49
  48 ......................OXO+.....1.XO....+.............+...X...................  48
  47 ............O.OX.X.X.X.XOXO....+..............+X.X..................  47
  46 ..........OXOXOXOXOXO...+..........X..+.XOX...............  46
  45 ..........OXOXOXOXOXO.O..+..........XO.+..XOX...............  45
  44 _____O_O_O_O_OX__O_+_____XO+__XOX_____  44
  43 ...................O|..O+....X...X..XOX.X.XO4..................  43
  42 ...................|..OX...XO..XO..XOXOXOXO...................  42
  41 ...................|..OXO...XOX.XO..XOXOXOX....................  41
  40 ...................|..OXO...XOXOXOX.XOXO.O...................  40
  39 _____OXO___XOXOXOXOXO_____  39
  38 ...................|..OXO...XO.OXOXOX.........................  38
  37 ...................|..OXO...X..OXO3OX.........................  37
  36 ...................|..OXOX...X..OXO.O.........................  36
  35 ...................|..O.OXO..X..OX...........................  35
  34 _____OXO__X__O_____  34
  33 ...................|..OXOX.X..................................  33
  32 ...................|..OXOXOX...................................  32
  31 ...................|..OXOXOX...................................  31
  30 ...................|..OXO.O2...................................  30
  29 _____OX__O_____  29
  29 ...................|..OX.......................................  29
  28 ...................|..OX........................................  28
  28 ...................|..OX........................................  28
  27 ...................|..OX........................................  27
  27 _____OX_____  27
  26 ...................|..OX........................................  26
  26 ...................|..OX........................................  26
  25 ...................|..OX........................................  25
  25 ...................|..OX........................................  25
  24 _____O_____  24
  24 ...................|..........................................  24
12.80 ------------------9-------------------------------------------12.80
12.60 ------------------8-------------------------------------------12.60
```

In this chart we have extended a number of trend lines and have omitted some. We thought the chosen and extended trend lines show clearly the relevance of the bullish resistance. In standard charts you stop drawing a trend line as soon as it penetrates. However, the extended trend lines show their relevance even beyond a penetration of a column.

Chart 2.14 – Pace [PIC.L] goes for it!

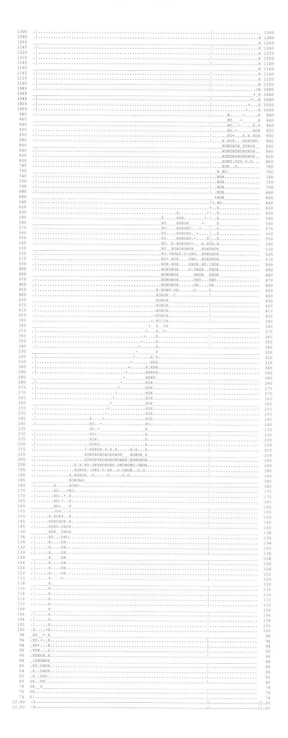

Being a super-bullish stock, Pace basically follows its long-term bullish resistance line. The bullish resistance line confines the price movements towards the upside.

Bullish stocks push against those resistance lines like prisoners against a fence. They try to break them to free the way for upside moves.

Again, we see how well p&f 45 degree trend lines can be used for price forecasts.

Chart 2.15 – Recovery of Xenova [XEN.L]

```
90 _____+_____ 90
88 .................................................+............................... 88
86 ...............................................+..............................  86
84 ..............................................+..............................  84
82 .............................................+...|............................. 82
80 _____+_____ 80
78 ...........................................+.....|............................. 78
76 .........................................+....X..|............................. 76
74 .........................................+....X1.|............................. 74
72 .........................................+......XO................................ 72
70 _____+____XO_____X_____ 70
68 ...............................+........XO...........X3.......................  68
66 ...............................+........XOX........XO..4.X....................  66
64 ...............................+........XOXO.......XO..XOX5..................  64
62 .............................+.........XOXOX.X......XOX.XOXOX.................  62
60 _____XO_____+_____+XOXOXOXOX____XOXOXOXOXO_____ 60
59 ........XO.......................................+.XO.OXOXOXO....XOXOXO.OXO....... 59
58 ........XO..............................+..........+..X|.OXOXOXO....XO.O...O.O......  58
57 ........XOX.............................+..........+...X|.O.OXO.O..X.X.......6....... 57
56 ........XOXOX...........................+..........X|.OX..2X.XOX........O........X 56
55 _____XOXOXO_____+_____+____X___O___OXOXOX_____O_____X 55
54 .....X...XOXOXOX.......................+........+...X|.......OXOXOX........O.......X 54
53 .X...XOX.XOXO.OXOX.X...................+........+...X|......OXO.OX.......OX.....X 53
52 .XO..XOXOXOX..XOXOXO..................+..........+...X|.....OX..O........OXO7.....X 52
51 .XO..XOXOXOX..O.OXOXO.................+..........+...X|.....OX..........OXOXOX...X 51
50 OXO__XO_O_O_____OXO_O__X_X_____+_____+_____X____OX____OXOXOXOX_X 50
49 OXOX.X..........6...OX.XOXO.....+..X.X.........+..........+X|......O............O.OXOXOXOX 49
48 OXOXOX.............OXO7OXO....+..XOXO.....+.........+.X|.................OXO.OXOX 48
47 O.OXO5.............OXOXOXO...+..XOXO....+...+..X|...............OX..OXOX 47
46 ..OXO..............OXOXOXO..+.....XOXO...+........+..X|..............OX..OXOX 46
45 __O_____O_OXO_O_+_____XO_O__+_____X+___X_____O___OXOX 45
44 ................OX..O+.......X..O.+.......XO...X................OXO. 44
43 ................OX..OX.X....X..9+..........+XO..X.X......................OX.. 43
42 ...............O...OXOXOX...X..OX.........+.XO..XOX..............8... 42
41 ...............OXO8OXOX.X..OXO......+..XO..XOX|................ 41
40 _____O_O_OXOXOX__OXO_____+___XOX_XO_____ 40
39 ................O.OXOX..O.O....+....XOXOX.. 39
38 ...............O.0...O....+.....XBXOX.. 38
37 ..............O..+.......XOXOX.. 37
36 ..............O..+.......XOXOX.. 36
35 _____O_+_____X_XOCO_____ 35
34 ................O+.X.....XOXO..... 34
33 ...............OX.XA....XOX..... 33
32 ...............OXOXO....XOX..... 32
31 ...............OXOXO...+XOX..... 31
30 _____OXO_O__+_XO_____ 30
29 ...............OX..O.+..X...... 29
29 ...............OX..O+...X....... 29
28 ...............O...OX...X...... 28
28 ...............OXO..X...... 28
27 _____OXO__X_____ 27
27 ...............OXOX.X....... 27
26 ...............OXOXOX....... 26
26 ...............OXOXOX....... 26
25 ...............O.O.OX...... 25
25 _____OX_____ 25
24 ...............OX...... 24
24 ------------------------------------OX--------O--------------------- 24
23 ------------------------------------O---------2--------------------- 23
```

After the fall of Xenova, the stock starts to break one bullish resistance line after another to free its way for a recovery.

Bearish support lines

Bearish support lines are drawn on bearish charts from the upper right hand corner of the highest exposed X in a wall of two or more exposed Xs (highlighted) at a 45 degree angle down from upper left to lower right. The Swiss SMI – charted with a relative big box size for an index – shows an excellent example of a bearish support line, which held for more than 3 years.

Chart 2.16 – Swiss Market Index [.SSMI], with bearish support line

```
SSMI / 3 box rev, log1/ 1997.01.03 to 2003.01.16
8600    ........|.........|..|...|.....|...............|.....  8600
8400            X             X +                              8400
8200    ........|.X8......|..|89X+.....|...............|.....  8200
8000    ........|.7O......|..|7OX2+....|...............|.....  8000
7800    ........4.XO......|..|5OCO.+...|...............|.....  7800
7600    ........XOXO......X..|4A.OX.+..|...............|.....  7600
7400            XO6O     X_1OB_X__356_+                        7400
7200    ........3O.O....XCXOX3X..OXO..+|...............|.....  7200
7000    ........X..OX...XOXOXOX..OXO...+...............|.....  7000
6800    ........X..OXO..XOX59O...O47...|+..............|.....  6800
6600    ........2..O9O..BO|8.|...O.8..X|.+.............|.....  6600
6400         1 _O_O__X+          9__B6__+                      6400
6200    ........X....O..X.+..|...|.O..AO...+..........|.....  6200
6000    X.......X....O..X.|+.|...|.O..XO7...+.........|.....  6000
5900    XOX...X.X....O..X.|.+|...|.O..XOXO...+........|.....  5900
5800    7OX8..AOC....O..X.|..+...|.OX.XOXO....+.......|.....  5800
5700    XOXOX_XOX_____AX_X____+___OXOXOXO____+_____|.....  5700
5600    XO.OXOXOB....OXOX.|..|.+.|.OXOXOXO......+.....|.....  5600
5500    X..OXOXOX....OXOX.|..|..+|.O.OXO.O..X....+....|.....  5500
5400    X..OXOXOX....OXOX.|..|...+..OX|.O..XO....+...|.....  5400
5300    6..O.O9OX....OXO..|..|...|+..OX|.OX.XO....+..|.....  5300
5200    X_____O_OX____O_____+_OX___OX8XOX_____X____  5200
5100    X......OX.........|..|...|..+OX|.OXOXOXO..B.XC|.....  5100
5000    5......O.........|..|...|.....O.|.OXOX9XO..XOXOX.....  5000
4900    X.......|.........|..|...|....+.|.OXOXO.OX.XOXOX.....  4900
4800    4.......|.........|..|...|.....+.OXOX..OXAXO.OX.....  4800
4700    X_____+OXO___OXOX__O1___  4700
4600    3.......|.........|..|...|.....|.OX....OXOX..O|.....  4600
4500    X.......|.........|..|...|.....|.OX....OXOX...|.....  4500
4400    X.......|.........|..|...|.....|.O.+...O.O....|.....  4400
4300    2.......|.........|..|...|.....|....+.........|.....  4300
4200    X_____+_____  4200
4100    X.......|.........|..|...|.....|......+.......|.....  4100
4000    X.......|.........|..|...|.....|.......+......|.....  4000
3900    1.......|.........|..|...|.....|........+.....|.....  3900
3800    --------9---------9--0---0-----0--------------0-----  3800
3700    --------8---------9--0---1-----2--------------3-----  3700
```

As usual, for explanatory reasons we have extended the support line towards the right. On a typical p&f chart the line would be drawn to the first penetration, in this case around September 2001.

Chart 2.17 – Vodafone [VOD.L] follows a bearish support line

```
VOD.L / 3 box rev, log1/ 2000.11.13 to 2002.04.04
290   ..........|.......................................................|................   290
285   ..........|.......................................................|................   285
280   .....X.X...|.......................................................|................   280
275   _____XOXO_____   275
270   .X...XOXO..|.......................................................|................   270
265   .XO..XOXO..|.......................................................|................   265
260   .XOX.XOXOX.|.......................................................|................   260
255   .XOXOXO.OXO|.X.....................................................|................   255
250   OXOXOX _OXO1_XO_____   250
245   OXOXOC.+O.OXOXO....X...............................................|................   245
240   OXOXO...+.OXOXOX.X.X2..............................................|................   240
235   O.O......+OXOXOXOXOXO..............................................|................   235
230   ..........⁻|OXOXOXOXO..............X...............................|................   230
225   _____+OXOXOXO_O_____XO_____   225
220   ..........|⁻.OXO...O...........X.XO................................|................   220
215   ..........|.+OX....O.........X.XOXO................................|................   215
210   ..........|..⁻....O....X.X.X.XOXOXO................................|................   210
205   ..........|...+....O....XOXOXOXOXO.OX.X............................|................   205
200   _____+___OX_X_XOXOXOXOX__5XOXO_____   200
195   ..........|.....+..OXOX3XOXOXOXOX..OXOXOX..................X.X..|...................   195
190   ..........|.....+.OXOXOXOXOXOXO.O4..O.O.OXO................XOXOX.X.................   190
185   ..........|......+OXOXOXO.O...O.......OXO.................XOCOXOXO.................   185
180   ..........|.......⁻.O.O.............OXO..................XO.OXOXO..............   180
175   _____+_____OXO_____X__OXO1O_____   175
170   ..........|.........+..............6.O7...............X.X.X..O.O|O..............   170
165   ..........|.........+...............OXOX...........XOXOX.....|O.............   165
160   ..........|.........+...............OXOXO8.........XOXOB.....|O.............   160
155   ..........|.........+...............OXOXOXO.........AOXO.....|O.............   155
150   _____+_____OXO_OXO__X_____XO_____O_____   150
145   ..........|..........+..............OX..OXOX.XO.....X.X..X.....|OX.......X......   145
140   ..........|...........+............O...OXOXOXO....X.XOXOX.........|2XOX...X.XOX....   140
138   ..........|...........+............OXOXOXO....XOXOXOX.........|OXOXO..XOXOXO...   138
136   ..........|...........+............OXO.O.OX.X.XOXOXOX.........|O.OXO..XOXOXO...   136
134   _____+_____O____OXOXOXO9OXOX_____OXO__XOXOXO___   134
132   ..........|...........+............OXOXOXO.OXO..........|..O.OX.X3.O.OX.X   132
130   ..........|............+............OXOXO...OX............|....OXOX....OX4X   130
128   ..........|............+............OXO...OX............|....OXOX....OXOX   128
126   ..........|............+............OX......OX............|....OXO.....O.O.   126
124   _____+_____OX_____O_____O_____   124
122   ..........|............+............OX..................|................   122
120   ..........|.............+...........OX..................|................   120
118   ..........|.............+...........OX..................|................   118
116   ..........|.............+...........OX..................|................   116
114   _____+_____OX_____   114
112   ..........|.............+...........OX..................|................   112
110   ..........|.............+..........O...................|................   110
108   ..........|..............+.............................|................   108
106   ..........|..............+.............................|................   106
104   _____+_____   104
102   ..........|..............+............................|................   102
100   ..........|...............+...........................|................   100
 98   ..........|...............+...........................|................    98
 96   ..........|...............+...........................|................    96
 94   _____    94
 47   ----------O---------------------------------------------------O----------------    47
 46   ----------1---------------------------------------------------2----------------    46
```

Vodafone follows nicely the bearish support during most of 2001.

Chart 2.18 – ARM [ARM.L]

```
ARM.L / 3 box rev,/ 2001.10.09 to 2002.10.25
450  ..................|............................................................  450
440  ........X........|............................................................  440
430  .......XO........|............................................................  430
420  .......XO....X...|............................................................  420
410  _____XOX_X_XO_____  410
400  .....X.XOXOXOCO..X...........................................................  400
390  .....XOXOXOXOXO..XO..........................................................  390
380  .....XOXOXO.OXO..XO..........................................................  380
370  .....XO.O...OXOX.1O..........................................................  370
360  ____X_B+_____OXOXOXO_____  360
350  ....XOX.+...O.OXOXO..........................................................  350
340  ...XOX..+....OXOXOX..........................................................  340
330  ..X.XOX...+..OXO|OXO...X.....................................................  330
320  X.XOXOX....+...O..|OXO....XO.................................................  320
310  XOXOXO_____+_____OXOX__XO_____  310
300  XOXO........+....|OX2XOX.XOX.X...............................................  300
290  XO...........+...|O.OXOX3XOXOXOX.............................................  290
285  X............+..|..OXOXOXOXOXOXO.............................................  285
280  X..............+.|..O.OXO.O.O.OXO............................................  280
275  X_____+_____OX____OXOX_____  275
270  X.............+...OX.....4XOXOX..............................................  270
265  X.............+...OX......OXOXO..............................................  265
260  X.............|.+-.OX.....OXOXO..............................................  260
255  .............|..+.O......OXOXOX..............................................  255
250  _____+_____O_OXOXO_____  250
245  .............|...+........OXOXO..X...........................................  245
240  .............|....+.......OXO.O..XO..........................................  240
235  .............|.....+......OX..O..XOX.........................................  235
230  .............|.....+......OX..OX.XOXO........................................  230
225  _____+_____OX___OXOXOXO_____  225
220  .............|.......+....O...OXOXOXO........................................  220
215  .............|........+.......O5O.O.O........................................  215
210  .............|........+......O.....O.........................................  210
205  .............|.........+....O.......O........................................  205
200  _____+_____O_____  200
195  .............|.........+....O................................................  195
190  .............|..........+...O................................................  190
185  .............|...........OX..................................X.X.............  185
180  .............|..........+....OX6X...................XOXO.....................  180
175  _____+_____OXOXO_____XOXO_____  175
170  .............|..........+...OXOXO.......X........XO.O........................  170
165  .............|..........+...O.OXO.......XO.........X..O......................  165
160  .............|..........+...OXO.........XO......X.X..O.......................  160
155  .............|..........+..O.O.X.......XO.....8.XOX..O.......................  155
150  _____+_____O_X_____XOX_X____XOXOX__9_X_____  150
145  .............|..........+...OX.X7X...XOXOXOX.XOXO...OX.XO....................  145
140  .............|...........+.OXOXOXO..XOXOXOXOXOX...OXOXO......................  140
138  .............|...........+.OXOXOXO..XOXOXOXOX...OXOXO..X.....................  138
136  .............|...........+OXOXOXO..XOXOXOXO.OX...OXO.O..XO...................  136
134  _____OXOXOXOX_XOXOXOX__OX____OX_O_XO_____  134
132  .............|...........OXOXOXOXOXOXOX..OX...OX..OX.XO......................  132
130  .............|...........O.OXOXOXOXOXOXOX..OX...OX..OXOXOX...................  130
128  .............|...........OXO.OXOXOXOXO...OX...O...OXOXOXO....................  128
126  .............|...........OX..OXOXO.O.....O........OXOXOXO....................  126
124  _____OX___OXO_____OXOXOXO_____  124
122  .............|...........OX..OX+.................OXOXOAO.....................  122
120  .............|...........O...OX.+................O.OXO.O.....................  120
118  .............|....................O...+...............OX..O.................  118
116  .............|....................+...............OX..O.....................  116
114  _____+_____OX___O_____  114
112  .............|........................+..........OX..O......................  112
110  .............|.........................+.........O...O......................  110
108  .............|..........................+..........O........................  108
106  .............|..........................+.........O........................  106
 38  ----------------0----------------------------------------------------------   38
 37  ----------------2----------------------------------------------------------   37
```

Like bullish charts that are chasing bullish resistance lines, bearish stocks follow bearish support lines. Again, we draw attention to the fact that the trend line in the ARM chart was drawn with the information available in October 2001 yet was giving a clear indication of the price moves for more than a year.

Chart 2.19 – Amvescap's [AVZ.L] impressive bearish support

```
AVZ.L / 2 box rev/ 2002.01.02 to 2002.10.31
1120  .X.......................................................................... 1120
1100  _XO_____ 1100
1080  .XOX........................................................................ 1080
1060  .XOXOX...................................................................... 1060
1040  .XO.OXO..................................................................... 1040
1020  .X+.O.O...............X..................................................... 1020
1000  1X_+__OX_____XOX_____ 1000
980   ....+.OXOX.X........XOXOX.................................................... 980
960   .....+0.OXO2O.......XO.O4O................................................... 960
940   ......+.O.OXO.......X..O.O................................................... 940
920   ......+..OXO.......X...O.................................................... 920
900   _____+_O_OX_X____X___OX_____ 900
880   .........+..OXOXO..X.X...OXO................................................. 880
860   .........+.OXO.OX.XO3....OXO................................................. 860
840   ..........+OX..OXOXO....O.O................................................. 840
820   ...........O...OXO...O...................................................... 820
800   _____+_O_O_____OX_____ 800
780   .............+.........OXO..X............................................... 780
760   .............+.......O.OX.XO................................................ 760
740   .............+......O5OXOX.................................................. 740
720   .............+....O.O.OXO.................................................... 720
700   _____+_____O_OX_____ 700
680   .............+........OX6................................................... 680
660   .............+........OXO................................................... 660
640   .............+.......O.O.................................................... 640
620   .............+........O..................................................... 620
600   _____+_____O_____ 600
590   .............+........OX.................................................... 590
580   .............+........OXO................................................... 580
570   .............+........OXO................................................... 570
560   .............+........OXOX.................................................. 560
550   _____+_____OXOXOX_7_____ 550
540   .............+.....O.OXOXOXO................................................ 540
530   .............+.....OXOXOXO.................................................. 530
520   .............+.....OXOXOX....X.............................................. 520
510   .............+.....OXO.OXOXOX...X...XO...................................... 510
500   _____+_____OX__OXOXOXO__XO__XO_____ 500
490   .............+.....O...OXOXO.O..XO..XO....X................................. 490
480   .............+.....O.OX..O..XOX.XO....X.XO................................. 480
470   .............+.....O...OX.XOXOXO....XOXO................................... 470
460   .............+.....OXOXOXOX8..X.XO.O........................................ 460
450   _____+_____OXOXOXOXO__XOX_O_____ 450
440   .............+.....OXOXOXO.O..XOX..O........................................ 440
430   .............+.....O.OXOX..O..XOX..O........................................ 430
420   .............+.....OXOX..O..XO...O.......................................... 420
410   .............+.....OXOX..OX.X...9X.X.X..................................X... 410
400   _____+_____O_O__OXOX____OXOXOXO_____X_X_ 400
390   .............+...........OXO....OXOXO.OX.............XOX 390
380   .............+..........OX+.....O.OX..OXO...........XO. 380
370   .............+..........OX.+......O..OXO..........X.X.. 370
360   .............+..........O..+.....O...OX.XOX.. 360
350   _____+_____+_____O_____XOXOX 350
340   .............+..........+........OX.X.....XO.OX.. 340
330   .............+..........+.......OXOXO...X+.O... 330
320   .............+..........+......O.OXOX..X.+.... 320
310   .............+..........+......OXOXO..X.+... 310
300   _____+_____+_____OXOXO__X__+ 300
290   .............+..........+......O.AXO.X...+. 290
285   .............+..........+......O.OX.X....+ 285
280   .............+..........+.......OXOX..... 280
275   .............+..........+.......OXOX..... 275
270   _____+_____+_____O_OX 270
265   .............+..........+......OX.... 265
260   .............+..........+......OX.... 260
255   .............+..........+......OX.... 255
250   .............+..........+....OX..... 250
245   _____+_____+___OX 245
240   .............+..........+..O.... 240
235   ----------------------------------------+--------------+--------- 235
230   ----------------------------------------+--------------------- 230
```

Amvescap follows its bearish support line precisely for 8 months and after that generates a new bearish support on a higher level which is followed for 2 months.

Trading strategies for bearish support lines

The bearish support line defines the lower side of a bearish channel and provides an indication of how low the position might decline before support is reached.

As a trading technique, the bearish support line can be used:

1. as an **entry point for a long** position in the hope of an immediate rally permitting a quick profit, or
2. as a place to **cover a short**.

In both cases the purchase takes place on weakness where buying competition is absent, making it easy to obtain a good fill price.

But note that this and the other trend lines discussed need not be exactly touched in order to be valid. They provide an indication of a move, not the exact level of a move and should be used only as approximate, never absolute, points. Also, bearish support lines, like bullish resistance lines, are often broken and, therefore, all possible lines should be drawn and the market climate evaluated for a best guess of which line will ultimately hold.

Which support line?

Experience again has shown that:

1. the first, or highest, line will hold for a bearish position declining in a **bullish market**,
2. the second line will normally be the one which holds a declining position in a **neutral market**, and
3. the third, or possibly the fourth, will stop the column slide in a **bearish environment**.

Such parallel supports can be seen in the DAX chart overleaf.

Chart 2.20 – German DAX [.GDAXI] with parallel supports

```
GDAXI / 3 box rev, / 1999.01.04 to 2002.06.26
 8200  .............|...............................|................|..... 8200
 8000  .............|.......X.X.........................|................|..... 8000
 7920  .............|.......XOXO.........................|................|..... 7920
 7840  .............|.......3OXO.........................|................|..... 7840
 7760  .............|.....X.XOXO.........................|................|..... 7760
 7680  .............|.....XOXOXO.........................|................|..... 7680
 7600  .............|.....XOXOXOX........................|................|..... 7600
 7520  .............|...XOXOX4XO5........................|................|..... 7520
 7440  .............|..XOXO.OXOXO..X.X.9.................|................|..... 7440
 7360  .............|....XO...OXOXOX.XOXOXO..............|................|..... 7360
 7280  .............|.X...X+...O.OXOXO6OXOXO.............|................|..... 7280
 7200  .............|.XOX.X.+...OXOXOXOXO................|................|..... 7200
 7120  .............X.XOXOX..+..OXOXOXOXOXO....B.........|................|..... 7120
 7040  ...........1OXOXOX...+..OXO.OXOX8XO....XO.........|................|..... 7040
 6960  ...........XOXOXO2...+.O...OXO7O.O...XO...........|................|..... 6960
 6880  ...........XOXO.O......+....OXO...OX...XO.........|................|..... 6880
 6800  ...........XOX+........+...O.....OXA..XOX.X.......|................|..... 6800
 6720  ...........XOX.+........+.......OXOX.XOXOXOX......|................|..... 6720
 6640  ...........XOX..+........+......OXOXOXOXOXOX2.....|................|..... 6640
 6560  ...........XOX...+........+.....OXOXOXOXOXOXO.....|................|..... 6560
 6480  ...........XOX....+........+...O.OXOXO.OCOXO......|................|..... 6480
 6400  ...........XO......+........+.....O.OX..O.OXO.....|................|..... 6400
 6320  ...........X+.......+........+.......O....OXO..5..|................|..... 6320
 6240  ...........X.+.......+........+.......O1O..XO.....|................|..... 6240
 6160  ...........X..+.......+........+......O|O..XO.....|................|..... 6160
 6080  ...........C...+.......+........+.......|O..XOX...|................|..... 6080
 6000  ...........X....+.......+........+......|3..XOXO..|................|..... 6000
 5920  ...........X.....+.......+........+.....|OX.X6XOX.|................|..... 5920
 5840  ...........X......+.......+........+....|OX4XO7OXO|................|..... 5840
 5760  ...........X.......+.......+........+...|OXOXO.OXO|................|..... 5760
 5680  ........X....X........+.......+........+.|OXOX..O8O....|................|..... 5680
 5600  ........XO....B.........+.......+........+|OXOX..O.O...|................|..... 5600
 5520  ........7O9...X..........+.......+........+|OXOX...O.........|................|..... 5520
 5440  X.....5.XOXOX.X...........+.......+........+..|O....O......|.X...5440
 5360  XO....XOXOXOXOX............+.......+........+..|O.....O......|.X4..5360
 5280  XO2...XOXOXOXOX.............+.......+........+.|.......O....X.X.XO..5280
 5200  1OXO..XOXOXOAOX..............+.......+........+|......O..X.XOX2XO..5200
 5120  .OXOX.XO6OXO.O................+.......+........+......9..XOXOXO3OX.5120
 5040  .OXOXOXO.OX...|...............+.......+........+|......O..XOXOXOXOXO5040
 4960  .OXOXOX+.8....|................+.......+........|.+.....O..XOCO1OXOXO 4960
 4880  .OXOXO4.+.....|...............+.......+........|.+.....O..XO.O|OX5XO 4880
 4800  .O.OXO+..+....|...............+.......+........|...+....OX.X...|OXO.O 4800
 4720  ...3X+....+...|...............+.......+........|...+...OXOX....|O...6 4720
 4640  ....O+......+..|...............+.......+........|....+..OXOX....|....O 4640
 4560  ...+........+.|...............+.......+........|......+.OXOB...|....O 4560
 4480  ............+|................+.......+........|......+OXO....|....O 4480
 4400  ............+|................+.......+........|.......OX+....|....O 4400
 4320  ............|+................+.......+........|......OA.+...|....O 4320
 4240  ............|.+................+.......+........|.......OX..+..|....O 4240
 4160  ............|..+................+.......+........|.......OX...+.|....O 4160
 4080  ............|...+................+.......+........|....+..OX....+|....O 4080
 4000  ............|....+................+.......+........|...+....OX....|....O 4000
 3960  ............|.....+................+.......+........|.....+...OX....|+...O 3960
 3920  ............|......+................+.......+........|.....+..OX.....|.+... 3920
 3880  ............|.......+................+.......+........|....+..OX.....|..+.. 3880
 3840  ............|........+................+.......+........|.....+OX.....|...+. 3840
 3800  ............|........+................+.......+........|......+OX.....|....+ 3800
 3760  ............|.......+................+.......+........|.+.....OX.....|..... 3760
 3720  ............|.......+................+.......+........|..+.....OX.....|..... 3720
 3680  ............|......+................+.......+........|....+.....OX.....|..... 3680
 3640  ............|......+................+.......+........|...+...OX.....|..... 3640
 3600  ............|.....+................+.......+........|.....+..OX.....|..... 3600
 3560  ............|.....+................+.......+........|......+.O.....|..... 3560
 3520  ............|....+................+.......+........|........+.....|..... 3520
 3480  ............|...+................+.......+........|..........+.....|..... 3480
 3440  ............|...+................+.......+........|...........+.....|..... 3440
       -------------0---------------------------------0---------------0-----
       -------------0---------------------------------1---------------2-----
```

In a chart like the one above of the DAX, where bearish support lines lose significance after strong up moves, new starting points for support lines – on higher levels – are identified and used to draw the new line. In the DAX chart this had to be done 3 times until a support was found (highlighted) that defined price move with precision over a significant period.

Bearish resistance lines

A *bearish resistance line* forms the top of a bearish channel and is drawn from the upper right hand corner of the highest X in a column of abnormally high Xs, down from upper left to lower right at a 45 degree angle. Royal & Sun and the Swedish market index show such resistance lines. The examples also show how such resistance lines are redrawn, in the case of HSI lower and in the case of SGE higher in January 2002.

Chart 2.21 – Royal & Sun [RSA.L], with bearish resistance line

```
RSA.L / 3 box rev,/ 2001.03.26 to 2002.10.14
560 ...................................................|.................................................... 560
550 ..............X............................................................. 550
540 ............70..............................................................|.................................................... 540
530 ...X.....XO..............................................................|.................................................... 530
520 ....XO....X.XO..............................................................|.................................................... 520
510 ...5O....XOXO..............................................................|.................................................... 510
500 X.X.XO___XOXOX__X...........................................................500
490 X4XOXOX.X.XO.OXOX.X9.........................................................|.................................................... 490
480 XOXOXOXOXOX..OXOXOXO.........................................................|.................................................... 480
470 XOXOXOXOXOX..8.OXOXO.........................................................|.................................................... 470
460 XO.O.OXO6O.....O.O.O.........................................................|.................................................... 460
450 X___O_O_____O...........................................................450
440 ..................O.........................................................|.................................................... 440
430 ..................O.........................................................+.................................................... 430
420 ..................O.......................C.X+.............................................420
410 ..................O...............X.X.XO1O+.............................................410
400 ..................O_____BOXOXOXO_+............................................400
390 ..................O..........X.XOXOXOXO...+.................................................390
380 ..................O....X.X.XOXOXO.OXO...+.................................................380
370 ..................O.....XOXOXO...O|O...+.................................................370
360 ..................O...X.XOXOXO.....|O...+.................................................360
350 ..........O_X_XOXO_O_____O____+...........................................350
340 ..................OX.XAXOX.........|O......+.................................................340
330 ..................OXOXOXO..........|OX......+.................................................330
320 ..................OXOXOX...........|2XOX....+.................................................320
310 ..................OXO.O.............|OX045.....+.................................................310
300 _____OX_____O_OXO____+.........................................300
290 ..................OX...............|.OXOX.X..X...+.................................................290
285 ..................OX...............|..OXOXOXOX6...+.................................................285
280 ..................OX...............|..OXOXOXOXO....+.................................................280
275 ..................OX...............|..OXO.O.O.O....+.................................................275
270 ..........OX_____OX____O____+...........................................270
265 ..................OX...............|..O3......O......+.................................................265
260 ..................OX...............|.O......OX...X...+.................................................260
255 ..................OX...............|.........OXOX.7O....+.................................................255
250 ..................OX...............|.........OXOXOXO....+.................................................250
245 ..........O_____O_OXOXOX_X__+........................................245
240 ................................|........OXOXOXOXO..+.................................................240
235 ................................|........O.OXOXOXO...+.................................................235
230 ................................|........OXOXO.O...+.................................................230
225 ................................|........OXOX..O...+.................................................225
220 _____O_O__O____+......................................220
215 ................................|........OX.....+.................................................215
210 ................................|........OXO.....+.................................................210
205 ................................|........OXO......+.................................................205
200 ................................|........OXO.......+.................................................200
195 _____OXO_____+......................................195
190 ................................|........O.O........+.................................................190
185 ................................|........O..........+.................................................185
180 ................................|........OX..........+.................................................180
175 ................................|........OX8..........+.................................................175
170 _____OXO_____+.................................170
165 ................................|........OXO...........+.................................................165
160 ................................|........OXO............+.................................................160
155 ................................|........OXO.............+.................................................155
150 ................................|........OXO..............+.................................................150
145 _____O_OX_____+..............................145
140 ................................|......140..OXO................+..............................140
138 ................................|........OXO................+.................................................138
136 ................................|........OXO................+.................................................136
134 ................................|........OXO...X.....X...X...+.................................................134
132 _____OXO____XO____XO__XO___+__.............................132
130 ................................|........OXO...XOX...XOX.XO....+..............................130
128 ................................|........O.O...XOXO..XOXOXO......+.............................128
126 ................................|........O....XOXO..XOXOXO......+.............................126
124 ................................|........O....XOXO..XOXOXO.......+.............................124
122 _____O__XOXOX9XOXOXO__..............................122
120 ................................|........O...XO.OXOXO.OXO........+.............................120
118 ................................|........O...X..OXOX..OXO........+.............................118
116 ................................|........OX...X..O.OX..OXO........+.............................116
114 ................................|........OXO..X...OX..OXO.........+.............................114
112 _____OXO__X____OX_OXO_____.........................112
110 ................................|........OXOX.X...OX..OXO............................110
108 ................................|........OXOXOX....O...OXOX............................108
106 ................................|........OXOXOX.......OXOXO...........................106
104 ................................|........OXOXOX.......OXOXOX...........................104
102 _____OXOX_____OXOXOXO__.......................102
100 ................................|........O.OX.......OXOXOXO....................100
98 ................................|........OX.......OXOXOX.X..................98
96 ................................|........O........OXOXOXOXOXO.................96
94 ................................|........O........O.OXOXOXOXO.................94
92 _____OXA_O_OXO___.....................92
90 ................................|................OX....OX...................90
88 -----------------------------------O------------------------O-----OX- 88
86 -----------------------------------2------------------------O-- 86
```

As long as the price trades below the bearish resistance line, the position is said to be *long-term bearish*. There may be minor rallies, but until the bearish resistance line is penetrated, the major trend is considered to be a declining one and buy signals have a high probability of being false.

Chart 2.22 – 'Polar' bearish resistance lines in Sweden [.SXAXPI]

```
SXAXPI / 3 box rev, / 1997.01.02 to 2003.01.16
430   ...|...|....|..............|..................  430
420   ...|...+....|..............|..................  420
410   ...|...X+...|..............|..................  410
400   _____XO+_____    400
390   ...|...30.+.|..............|..................  390
380   ...|...XOX.X|..............|..................  380
370   ...|...X4XOXO..............|..................  370
360   ...|...XO5O7O+.............|..................  360
350   _____20_O_O_+_____    350
340   ...|...X....8..+...........|..................  340
330   ...|...1....9...+..........|..................  330
320   ...|...X....A....+.........|..................  320
310   ...|...X....O.....+........|..................  310
300   _____X____BX____+_____    300
290   ...|...X....CX2.....+......|..................  290
285   ...|...C....OXO......+.....|..................  285
280   ...|...X....1XOX......+....|..................  280
275   ...|...X....O.OXO......+...|..................  275
270   _____X_____O3O__X____+_____    270
265   ...|...X....|.O.O..56....+.|..................  265
260   ...|...X....|...O..XO.....+|..................  260
255   ...|...B....|...O..XO......+..................  255
250   ...|...X....|...OX.XOX...X.|+.................  250
245   _____X_____OXOXOXO__COX_+_____    245
240   ...|...A....|...OXOXO7OX.XOXOX+...............  240
235   ...|...7....|...OXOXO.OX8XO1OX4+..............  235
230   ...7...X....|...O.4X..OXOXO|OXO.+.............  230
225   ...68..6....|.....O...O.OX.|O3O..+............  225
220   ___XO__X_____9B__O_O___+_____    220
215   ...4O..X....|..........OX.|..O....+..........  215
210   ...XO..4....|..........OX.|..O.....+.........  210
205   ...XO..X....|..........OX.|..O......+........  205
200   ...3OX.X....|..........OA.|..5.......+.......  200
195   ___XOXCX_____OX____6_____+_____    195
190   .8.XOXO1....|..........OX.|..O.........+.....  190
185   .XA29XO|....|..........OX.|..OX.........+....  185
180   .XOXOB.|....|..........OX.|..OXO........+...  180
175   .7OXOX.|....|..........O..|..O7O.........+..  175
170   _6OCOX_____O_O____X____+__    170
165   .5O|AX.|....|.............|....O8.X...XC....+  165
160   .3.|OX.|....|.............|....OXOX9..XO.....  160
155   .X.|OX.|....|.............|....OXOXO..BO.....  155
150   .2.|OX.|....|.............|....OXO.O..XO.....  150
145   _X__O_____O___O_X_____    145
140   .X.|...|....|.............|........OX.X......  140
138   .X.|...|....|.............|........OXOX......  138
136   1..|...|....|.............|........OXOX......  136
134   ...|...|....|.............|........OXOX......  134
132   _____O_AX__    132
130   ...|...|....|.............|..........OX......  130
128   --_9_-0----0-------------0---------OX------  128
126   ---8---0----1------------2---------O-------  126
```

Trading strategies for bearish resistance lines

When trading a *long-term bearish position*, there are three possible trading strategies. The decision as to which one of them to use is a personal one, which will depend on the importance to you of speedy capital turnover, and of close trend fits.

1. The most aggressive approach is to **ignore the bearish resistance line and take every signal** as it occurs. This strategy yields the greatest number of trades, the greatest commission cost and generally has the highest number of false signals, but it does permit the trader to profit from minor price moves within the major downtrend. It will also permit a better execution at market bottoms, but these major advantages must be weighed against the losses on false signals in trying for the bottom and the higher commission costs of increased trading activity.

2. The second strategy is to **take only the short sale and cover signals while avoiding long positions** since the trend is bearish and buy signals tend to be false.

3. The third technique requires that **short signals be taken, but once taken they are not covered on the traditional buy signal until a buy signal occurs above the bearish resistance line**. In this way the positions are held longer, the commissions costs are lowered, and potential whipsaws are reduced, but the ability to squeeze out profits on minor moves within the major trend and the opportunity of closing out the position at the best possible price is eliminated.

Redrawing bullish support and bearish resistance lines

When using either the *bearish resistance* line or a *bullish support* line, the price should give a major breakthrough, meaning that it passes completely through the line as opposed to simply straddling the line.

Chart 2.23 – Lowering of supports shown by Wolseley [WOS.L]

```
WOS.L / 2000.01.04 to 2002.08.22
780 .....................|.........................|................... 780
770 .....................|.........................|....X.............. 770
760 .....................|.........................|....XO............. 760
750 .....................|.........................|..X.XO............ 750
740 .....................|.........................|..XOXOX........... 740
730 .....................|.........................|.4OXOXO........... 730
720 .....................|.........................|..XOXOXO.......... 720
710 .....................|.........................|..XO5OXO.......... 710
700 .....................|.........................|..XO.6.O.......... 700
690 .....................|.........................|..X....OX.7....... 690
680 .....................|.........................|..X....OXOXO...... 680
670 .....................|.........................|..X....OXOXO...... 670
660 .....................|.........................|..X....OXOXO...... 660
650 .....................|.........................|..X...O.OXO....... 650
640 .....................|.........................|..X......OXO.....X 640
630 .....................|.........................|..X......O.O.....X 630
620 .....................|.........................|..X......O......X 620
610 .....................|.........................|..3..........O.....X 610
600 .....................|.........................|..X......O.....X 600
590 .....................|.........................|X.X......OX...X.X 590
580 .....................|.........................X|XOX.......OXO..80X 580
570 .....................|.........................X1XOX.......OXO..XOX 570
560 .....................|.........X.............XOXOX......+OXOX.XOX 560
550 .....................|...XO..X.............X.XOXOX.....+.OXOXOXOX 550
540 .....................|...XOX.7O.........XOXO2O......+..OXOXOXOX 540
530 .....................|...XOXOXOX.X.......XOXO.......+...OXOXOXOX 530
520 .....................|...XOXOXOXOXO........COX|......+....O.OXO.OX 520
510 .....................|...XOXOXOXO.........XO.|.....+.......O...OX 510
500 .....................|...XO6OXOXO8O.......X..|.....+...........OX 500
490 .....................|.X.XO.OXO.O.O.......X.X..|...+...........O. 490
480 .X..................|.X3X..OX...9.....X.X.XOX..|..+............. 480
470 .XO.................|.1.XOX..O....O..X.XOXOXOX..|.+.............. 470
460 .XO.................XOXO5.......O..AOXOXOXOX..|+................ 460
450 1XO.................XOXOX.......O..XOXOXOXO...+................. 450
440 OXO.................XO2OX.......O..XOXOXO....+|................. 440
430 OXO.................XO.04.......O..XO.BX....+.|................. 430
420 O.O.................X..OX.......O..X..O....+..|................. 420
410 ..O................X.X..OX.......O..X......+..|................. 410
400 ..O................XOX..OX.......+OX.X.....+....|................ 400
390 ..O.....X..........X.BOX..OX......+.OXOX....+.....|.............. 390
380 ..O....XOX.......X9XOX..O......+..OXOX...+......|............... 380
370 ..O....X.XOXOX.X.X.XOXOC.......+..OXOX..+......|............... 370
360 ..OX..XOXOXOXOX7X8XOXO|......+...O.OX.+........|............... 360
350 ..OX2..XOXOXOXOXOXOXOX.|......+.......OX+......|............... 350
340 ..OXO..XOXOXO5O6OXOXOX.|.....+........O+.......|............... 340
330 ..OXO..XOXOXO.0.OXO.OA.|....+........+........|............... 330
320 ..OXOX.XOXOX....OX..OX.|...+..................|............... 320
310 ..O.OXOXO.04....OX..OX.|..+...................|............... 310
300 ....OXOX..O.....OX..OX.|.+....................|............... 300
290 ....O3OX........OX..OX.|+.....................|............... 290
280 ....O.OX........OX..OX.+|.....................|............... 280
270 ......OX........OX..OX+|......................|............... 270
260 -------------------+-0-----------------------0--------------- 260
250 -------------------1-----------------------2--------------- 250
```

As seen in Wolseley [WOS.L], the bullish support line is no longer valid. But if the respective basic bearish or bullish nature of the market has not changed, a new and better fitting line would be drawn. So in Wolseley the bullish support is lowered.

Chart 2.24 – Lowering resistances on BTG [BGC.L]

```
BGC.L / 2000.01.04 to 2003.01.16
1970  .........|.....|........................|...... 1970
1895  ......+..|.....|........................|...... 1895
1822  X.....X+.|.....|........................|...... 1822
1752  XO...AB+|.....|........................|...... 1752
1684  XO___XO_+_____ 1684
1619  XO....XO.|+....|........................|...... 1619
1557  XO....XOX|.+...|........................|...... 1557
1497  XO....9OX1..+..|........................|...... 1497
1440  XO....XOXO...+.|........................|...... 1440
1384  XO___8OCOX___+_____ 1384
1331  XO....XOXO56...+........................|...... 1331
1280  3O....XOX2XO...|+.......................|...... 1280
1231  XO....7OXOXO...|.+......................|...... 1231
1183  XOX...XOXOXO...|..+.....................|...... 1183
1138  XOXOX_XO_3XO_____+_____ 1138
1094  X4XOXOX..OX7...|....+...................|...... 1094
1052  XOXOXOX..OXO...|.....+..................|...... 1052
1012  XOXOXOX..OXO...|......+.................|...... 1012
 973  XOXOXOX..OXO...|.......+................|......  973
 935  2OXO5OX__O4O_____+_____  935
 899  XOXO.OX..O.8...|........+...............|......  899
 865  1O...OX..|.O...|.........+..............|......  865
 831  .....O6..|.O...|..........+.............|......  831
 799  ....O...|.O..+|...........+............|......  799
 769  _____9__X+_____+_____  769
 739  .........|.OX.X1+.............'........|......  739
 711  .........|.OXOXO.+............+........|......  711
 683  .........|.OXOXO..+..........+........|......  683
 657  .........|.OAOXO...+.........+.....|......  657
 632  _____OXOXOX___+_____+_____  632
 607  .........|.OXOX2XO...+........+...|......  607
 584  .........|.OXBXO4O....+.......+..|......  584
 562  .........|.OXO.OXO.....+......+.|......  562
 540  .........|.OX..OXO......+......+|......  540
 519  _____OX__OXO_____+_____+_  519
 499  .........|.OX..3XO........+..........|+......  499
 480  .........|.OX..O.5.........+........|.+......  480
 462  .........|.O...|.O.........+........|......  462
 444  .........|.....|.O.........+.........|......  444
 427  _____O_____+_____  427
 410  .........|.....|.O.............+.......|......  410
 395  .........|.....|.OX............+......|......  395
 379  .........|.....|.OXO...........+....|......  379
 365  .........|.....|.OXO............+....|......  365
 351  _____O6O_____+_____  351
 337  .........|.....|.O.O...............+.|......  337
 324  .........|.....|...O+..............+.|......  324
 312  .........|.....|...O.+.............+|......  312
 300  .........|.....|...7...+...........+......  300
 288  _____OX_X+_____+_____  288
 277  .........|.....|...OXOXO+..............|.+.....  277
 267  .........|.....|...OXOXO.+.............|......  267
 256  .........|.....|...OXOXO..+...........|......  256
 246  .........|.....|...OXOXO...+..........|......  246
 237  _____OXOXO___+_____  237
 228  .........|.....|...OXO.8.....+........|......  228
 219  .........|.....|...OX..O.....+.......|......  219
 211  .........|.....|...OX..O.......+......|......  211
 203  .........|.....|...O...O.......+......|......  203
 195  _____9_____+_____  195
 187  .........|.....|.....O.........+....|......  187
 180  .........|.....|.....O.........+...|......  180
 173  .........|.....|.....O.+........+..|......  173
 167  .........|.....|.....O..+........+.|......  167
 160  _____O__+_____+_____  160
 154  .........|.....|.....O...+..........+......  154
 148  .........|.....|.....O...X+........+.....  148
 142  .........|.....|.....O...XO+.......|.+.....  142
 137  .........|.....|.....A....XO.+......|......  137
 132  _____O___XO__+_____  132
 127  .........|.....|.....O...XOX.X+X....|......  127
 122  .........|.....|.....OX...XOXOXOXO...|......  122
 117  .........|.....|.....OXOX.XOXOXOXOX.X|X.....  117
 112  .........|.....|.....OXOXOXOXOXOXOX1XO.....  112
 108  _____OXOXOXOXO_OXOXOXOXO_____  108
 104  .........|.....|.........O.OXOBO..OCOXOXOXO.....  104
 100  .........|.....|.........O.O.....O.OXO.O.O.....  100
  96  ---------O-----O----------------------O-------   96
  92  ---------1-----2----------------------3-------   92
```

A better-fit line might also be drawn in those cases where the movement has proved so dramatic that the old, slow moving line seemed irrelevant, as in the case of the original bearish resistance line in the tech stock BTG [BGC.L] and therefore, new and better fitting lines were subsequently introduced.

Conclusion

A chartist can be very successful in his trading by using nothing more than the simple and complex signal formations discussed earlier for the placing of orders. But there is a better way.

It involves *combining signals with trend lines*. Through the use of trend lines it is possible to predict areas where support and resistance are likely to occur. This knowledge coupled with the ability to graphically view the long-term nature of the price action aids the chartist in eliminating many potentially unreliable or false signals while permitting better executions through the technique of buying on weakness and selling into strength, an order execution philosophy unaffected by periods of limit trading.

Trading applications

- Judging the distance of a move

- The use of stop orders

- Risk and position size

- Pyramiding made simple and profitable

- Swing trading

- Day-trading, speed trading, scalping and market making

- Extending p&f to other markets

- About shorting, brokers and commissions

- Tips from experienced traders

Judging the distance of a move

Calculating price objectives with horizontal and vertical counts

There are two vital pieces of information sought by a trader:

1. the **direction** of the price trend, and
2. the probable **distance** of a move.

The direction of a trend is indicated by signals and trend lines as discussed in the first chapters, while this chapter is devoted to the prediction of the distance of a move.

Two methods of calculating price objectives

There are two methods for determining the probable distance of a move, often referred to as the *price objective*:

1. One is by the use of **trend lines** coupled with data on general market strength. In this method, as reviewed in the prior chapter, an upside price move will usually be contained by the first bullish resistance line if the general market climate is bearish, the second line is a neutral market and the third line is a bullish market. And the opposite holds true for a bearish price formation which is constrained by the first, second or third support line.

2. The other method of calculating price objectives is by the use of **horizontal and vertical counts**.

The use of counts has the advantage of yielding a precise objective, while the trend line method establishes an objective which changes with each price reversal. This occurs because each reversal moves the chart one row to the right and the resistance lines, drawn at 45 degree rising angles, two boxes higher and the support lines, drawn at 45 degree declining angles, two boxes lower.

But the two methods complement each other by displaying price objectives in different manners and the sum total of both presents the best picture, for it contains the greatest amount of data.

Calculating price objectives from a horizontal count

The size of a *base* or a *top* has a direct relationship to the price objective. The more extensive the base or top formation, meaning the more columns of Xs and Os in the formation, the greater the price objective will be above the low point of the base or below the high point of the top.

The first step in the calculation of an upside price objective involves the determining of a base.

Definition of a base

A *base* is defined as a price pattern which shows a tremendous reluctance to break into new low price ranges. The base is then measured for width, meaning the number of columns composing it.

Example 3.1 – Horizontal price objective

Chart 3.1 – Abbey National [ANL.L] horizontal price objective

```
ANL.L / 3 box rev,/ 2000.07.18 to 2001.03.27
 1360 ....................................................|.................. 1360
 1280 ....................................................|.................. 1280
 1260 ...............................................X.................. 1260
 1240 ...........................................lOX.X.....X........ 1240
 1220 ...........................................XOXOXOX.X.XO....... 1220
 1200 _____X_XOXOXOXOXO3OX_____ 1200
 1180 .......................................X.XOXOXO2OXOXOXOXO..... 1180
 1160 .....................................X.X.XOXOXOXO.O.O.OXOXO..... 1160
 1140 .........................Hu.......XOXOXOXO|O.......OXOXO....X 1140
 1120 ................................X.XOXOXOX.|........OXO.OX...X 1120
 1100 _____X_XOXOXO_O_____OX__OXO__X 1100
 1080 ...............................X.XOXOCOX.....|........O...OXOX.X 1080
 1060 ...........................XOXOXO.O......|...........OXOXOX 1060
 1040 ............................XOXO.........|...........O.OXOX 1040
 1020 ............................XO...........|...........O.OX 1020
 1000 _____X_____OX 1000
  990 ..........................X.............|..............OX  990
  980 ..........................X.............|..............OX  980
  970 ..........................X.............|..............OX  970
  960 ..........................B.............|..............O.  960
  950 _____X_____  950
  940 ..........................X.............|..............  940
  930 ..................X.......X.............|..............  930
  920 ..............XOX.........X.............|..............  920
  910 ..............X.AOXO......X.............|..............  910
  900 _____XOXOXO____X_X_X_____  900
  890 ....................XOXO.OX.X.XOXOX..........|..............  890
  880 .............X...X...X.XOX..OXOXOXOXOX...........|..............  880
  870 ...........XO..XOX.XOXOX..OXOXOXOXOX...........|..............  870
  860 ........X...XOX.XOXOXOXOX..OXO.O.O.O...........|..............  860
  850 _____XOX_XOXOXOXOXO_O___OX_____  850
  840 ......X.XOXOXOXOXO.OX......OX.................|..............  840
  830 ......XOXOXOXOXO...O......OX.................|..............  830
  820 ......XOXOXOXO...........OX.................|..............  820
  810 ......XOXO.9X.............OX.................|..............  810
  800 _____XOX__OX_____O_____  800
  790 .....X.XO...OX..........................|..............  790
  780 .X...XOX....O..........................|..............  780
  770 OXO..XOX..............................|..............  770
  760 OXO..XOX..............................|..............  760
  750 O_O__XO_____  750
  740 ..OX.X..............................|..............  740
  730 ..OX8X..............................|..............  730
  720 ..OXOX..............................|..............  720
  710 ..OXO...............................|..............  710
  700 __O_____  700
  690 ..................................|..............  690
  520 ..................................|..............  520
  510 ..................................|..............  510
  500 ----------------------------------0---------------  500
  490 ----------------------------------1---------------  490
```

ANL in the chart above has a nine-column wide base (highlighted). The width of the base is then multiplied by the value of a reversal in order to determine the distance of the move.

The value of a reversal is defined as the minimum number of boxes required for a reversal (three boxes) multiplied by the value of a box (10 points). Thus the *reversal value* for the ANL chart is 30 points (three boxes multiplied by 10 points) and the distance of the move is the nine-column width of the base multiplied by the 30-point reversal value for a total of 270 points. This figure is then added to the lowest point of the base, 860 points, which yields the horizontal price objective of 1130 as marked on the chart by the letters Hu. The calculation of the horizontal price objective can be summarized as:

Upside Horizontal Count Price Objective	=	Lowest Value in the Base in Points	+	Base's Width in Columns x Minimum Reversal Value in Boxes x Box Value in Points

or

Hu = Vlow + (W x Rm x Vbox)

ANL: 1130 = 860 + (9 x 3 x 10)

Price objectives on the downside

The calculation of the horizontal price objective on the downside is basically the reverse of the upside calculation, as we shall see in the example of ICI. The top's width is multiplied by the reversal value and this figure is subtracted from the highest point in the top.

Example 3.2 – Horizontal price objective on the downside

Chart 3.2 – ICI [ICI.L] price objective

```
ICI.L / 3 box rev / 1998.01.02 to 1999.12.09
1240 ..............X...............................|.............................. 1240
1220 ..............XO..............................|.............................. 1220
1200 ......X.....XO...............................                                   1200
1180 ......XO..X...XO.............................|.............................. 1180
1160 ...X...XO..XOX.XO............................|.............................. 1160
1140 ..XOX.XO..XOXOXO............................                                   1140
1120 ..XOXOXO..XOXOX6............................|.............................. 1120
1100 _X_XOXOXOX_XOXO5O_____                                   1100
1080 .XOXO3O.OXOXOXO.O............................                                   1080
1060 .XOXO...OXOXO...O............................                                   1060
1040 .XOX....O.O4....O............................                                   1040
1020 .XO.......O....OX............................|.............................. 1020
1000 _X_____OXO._____                                 1000
 980 .X..............OXO.........................|.............................. 980
 960 .2..............OXO.........................                                   960
 940 1X..............7.O.........................                                   940
 920 OX..............O...........................                                   920
 900 OX_____O_____                                  900
 880 O...............O...........................|.............................. 880
 860 ................O...........................                                   860
 840 ................OX..........................                                   840
 820 ................OX8.........................................X.............. 820
 800 _____OXO_____XO_____ 800
 780 ................OXO...............................|..........XO......... 780
 760 ................OXO...........................|.............XO......... 760
 740 ................OXO..........................X.X.XO......... 740
 720 ................OXO...........................|.............XOXOXO......... 720
 700 _____O_O_____X_XOXO89_____ 700
 680 ...............O...........................................XOXOXO.OA......X.. 680
 660 ...............O..........................................X.XO56X..OXO....XO. 660
 640 ...............OX.........................................XOXO.OX..OXO..X.XO. 640
 620 ...............9XO...............X...........|.............XOX..O7..OXOX.XOXO. 620
 600 _____OXO_____.____XOX__X___.X._____X__XO__O._OXOXOXOBCX_____ 600
 590 .................O.O......X.....XOXO..XO....XO.|.............XO..X......O.OXOXO.OX 590
 580 .................O.....XO...XOXOX.XO..X.XO........................XO4.X.......OXOX..OX 580
 570 .................O.....XO...XOXOXOXO..XOXO.|......X.....XOXOX.........O.O...OX 570
 560 .................O.....XO...XOXOXOXOX.XOXO.......XO.....XOXOX..............O. 560
 550 _____O._____XO____BO_OXOXOXO_O._____.X_XOX_X___XOXO_____ 550
 540 ................OX.....XO...X..O.O.OXOX..OX|....XOXOX3XOX.XOX.................. 540
 530 ...............OXO.....XO...X......OXOX..OX1...XO2OXOXOXOXOX................. 530
 520 ...............OXO.....XOX.X.X......OXOX..OXO...XO.OXO.OXOXO................. 520
 510 ...............OXO.....XOXOXOX.....OXO..OXOX..X..OX..O.O................... 510
 500 _____O_OX____XOXOXOX_____OX.._OXOXOX_X_.O_____ 500
 490 ...............OXO...XOXOXOX....OC...OXOXOXOX............................... 490
 480 ...............OXOX.X.XOXO.O......O....O.OXOXOX............................. 480
 470 ...............OXOXAXOXOX.........O.O.OX................................... 470
 460 ...............O.OXOXOXOX.................|...O........................... 460
 450 _____OXO_OXOX_____ 450
 440 ...............OX..O.O...................................................... 440
 430 ...............OX.........................|.............................. 430
 420 ...............O.........................|.............................. 420
 410 ........................................|.............................. 410
 400 _____Hd_____ 400
 390 ........................................|.............................. 390
 380 ........................................|.............................. 380
 370 ........................................|.............................. 370
 360 _____ 360
 350 _____ 350
 340 ........................................|.............................. 340
 330 ........................................|.............................. 330
```

Downside Horizontal Count Price Objective	=	Highest Value of Top in Points	–	Top's Width in Columns x Minimum Reversal Value in Boxes x Box Value in Points

or

Hd = Vtop - (W x Rm x Vbox). In the ICI example: 400 = 1240 – (14 x 3 x 20)

Summary: calculation of the horizontal count

1. Establish the width of the base. No clear rules exist, which leaves room for interpretation.

2. Multiply: width in columns x reversal in boxes x box size.

3. For up move: add calculated horizontal count number (2, above) to low of the base; for down move: substract result from high.

Calculating price objectives from a vertical count

The calculation of price objectives from vertical counts is a simpler procedure than calculating them from horizontal counts. The vertical method does not require the finding and measuring of bases and tops, often a subjective act since few tops and bases are clear and concise, and there is substantial room for disagreement among chartists as to exactly what constitutes a base or top when a specific chart is viewed.

In using the vertical count method the first step is to find the peak of a run or the bottom of a decline, and since we are working after the fact this is an exact and indisputable chart point.

Example 3.3 – Vertical count price objective

In the Johnson Matthey example on the right, the bottom is 260.

To calculate the price objective on the upside, first add up the number of boxes comprising the first up move after the bottom, or after the *final* bottom if there are two or more bottoms at the same level – 14 in our JMAT example.

This vertical box count is then multiplied by the reversal value, which (chosen purposefully) is 30, calculated as 3 x 7.5. The reversal value, as already discussed, is defined as the minimum number of boxes required for a reversal multiplied by the value of each box. The box size is put at 7.5 because the columns cross an area of change in scaling at the level of 290, namely from 10 point boxes to 5 point boxes. The net result of the multiplication of the vertical count and the reversal value is 315, calculated as 14 x 3 x 7.5. This figure is then added to the value of the lowest O at the bottom (260) and the answer (575) represents the upside price objective. Thus:

Upside Vertical Count Price Objective	=	Value in Points of the Low of the Decline	+	Number of Boxes in the First Upside Reversal after the Bottom or the Upside Reversal after the Last Level Bottom x Minimum Reversal Value in Boxes x Box Value in Points

or

Vu = Vlow + (Ru x Rm x Vbox)

JMAT: 1120 = 850 + (9 x 3 x 10)

Chart 3.3 – Vertical count with Johnson Matthey [JMAT.L]

```
760     ......................|.....................     760
740     ......................|.....................     740
720     ......................|.....................     720
700     _____     700
680     ......................|.....................     680
660     .........+..........|.............+......     660
640     .......5.X+.........|..........7.X+.....     640
620     ......X.X6XO+........|.........XOX9+.....     620
600     ____X_X4XOXO_+_____X_XOXO_+____     600
590     ....XOXOXO.O..+.......|........50XO8O..+...     590
580     ...XOXO...O..+... VU|........XOXO.OX..+..     580
570     ....XOX....OX...+.....|......X.XOX..OXO..X.     570
560     ..X.XOX....O7O...+....|......+XOXOX..AXOX.X     560
550     X_XOXOX____OXO____+_____+_XOXO6__OXOXOXO     550
540     1OXO3O.....OXO.....+..|....+..XO.O...OXOXOXO     540
530     .O2O.......OXO.......+.|..+...X.....O.O.OXO     530
520     .OX+.......OXO.......+|..+....X.....+...O.O     520
510     .OX.+......O.O........+.+...X.X....+......O     510
500     _OX__+_____O_____+___XOX___+_____+     500
490     .OX...+......O........+.+...XOX..+........+.     490
480     .OX....+.....O.......+|.X+..XOX.+........+..     480
470     .O......+....O.....+.|.XOX.XOX+........+...     470
460     ........+...O....+..|.XOX3X4+........+....     460
450     _____+_O____+_____XOXOX+_____+_____     450
440     ..........+.O...+....|.XO.O+........+......     440
430     .............+O..+...C.|.2..+........+......     430
420     .............O.+....XO|.X..........+......     420
410     ............8+.....XOX.X.......+........     410
400     _____OX____XOXOX_____+_____     400
390     ............OX9....XO1OX.......+..........     390
380     ............OXO....XO|OX......+.........     380
370     ............O.O..X.X.|OX.....+.........     370
360     ............OX.XOX.|OX....+...........     360
350     _____OXOXOX__O____+_____     350
340     ............OXOXOX.|....+.............     340
330     ............OXOBO..|...+.............     330
320     ............OAO....|..+.............     320
310     ............OX.....|.+.............     310
300     _____OX_____+_____     300
290     ............OX.....+.............     290
285     ............OX....+|.............     285
280     ............OX...+.|.............     280
275     ............OX..+..|.............     275
270     _____OX_+_____     270
265     ------------OX+----9---------------------     265
260     ------------O+-----9---------------------     260
```

To determine the *downside vertical count price objective*, the number of boxes comprising the first downside reversal after the top is multiplied by the reversal value and the net result is then subtracted from the highest x value.

Example 3.4 − Downside vertical count price objective

Chart 3.4 − Vertical count with Kingfisher [KGF.L]

```
KGF.L / 1999.01.04 to 2000.03.13
940 .....................X..........................|.............. 940
930 ................X.X.XX.........................|.............. 930
920 ...............XOXOXO..........................|.............. 920
910 ...............XOXOXO..........................|.............. 910
900 _____XOXOXO_____  900
890 ...............XOXOXO.........................|.............. 890
880 ...............XOXO.O.........................|.............. 880
870 ...............XOX..O.........................|.............. 870
860 ...............XOX..OX...X....................|.............. 860
850 _____XOX___OXO__XO_____  850
840 ...............XOX..OXO..XO....................|.............. 840
830 ...............XOX..OXOX.XO....................|.............. 830
820 ...........X.XOX..O.OXOXO......................|.............. 820
810 ............XOXOX....OXOXO60...................|.............. 810
800 _____3___XOXOX___OXO60_____  800
790 ..........XOX.XO4OX....O.O.O...................|.............. 790
780 ..........XOXOXOXOX.......O........X...........|.............. 780
770 ..........XOXOXOXOX.......O.......XO...........X.....|........ 770
760 ..........XOXOXOXOX.....OX.X...9O..........XO....|.......... 760
750 _____XOXO_OXOX_____OXOX7X___XO_____XO_____  750
740 ..........XO...OXO........OXOXOXOX.XO.........XO....|.X....... 740
730 ..........X....O.........OXOXOXOXO...........XO....|.XO...... 730
720 ..........X..............OXO.OXOXOXO.........XO....|.XO...... 720
710 ..........X..............OX..OXOXOXO.........XO....1.XO...... 710
700 _X_____X_____OX__O_OXOXO_____XO___OXOXO_____  700
690 .XO.....................OX...O80XO...........XO....OXOXO..... 690
680 .XO....X.X.X.............O....O.OXO..X.X.X...XO....OXOXO..... 680
670 .XO....XOXOX.................OXO..XAXOXOX.XO..X.XOXO......... 670
660 .XO..X.XOXOX.................O.OX.XOXOXOXOXOX.XOXOXO......... 660
650 _XOX_XOXOXOX_____OXOXOXOXOXOXOXOXO_____  650
640 .XOXOXOXOXOX................OXOXOXOBOXOXOXOXOXO.O........... 640
630 1.OXOXOXOXO................OXOXOXO.OXOXOXOX..O........... 630
620 ..OXOXOXOX................OXO.OX..O.OXO.OXOX..O........... 620
610 ..OXOX2.OX................O...OX....O...OXO...O........... 610
600 __O_OX__O_____OX_____OXOX__O_____  600
590 ....OX..................O.........OXOX..O........X.. 590
580 ....O..........VD................OXOX..OX.......XO. 580
570 .................................OXOX..OXO.....XO. 570
560 .................................OCOX..OXO.....XOX 560
550 _____O_OX__OXO_____XOX_____  550
540 .................................OX..O.O......XOX 540
530 .............................O|....O......XOX 530
520 .............................|......O......XOX 520
510 .............................|....O....X.XOX 510
500 _____O____XOXOX_____  500
490 .............................|....O..X.XOXO. 490
480 .............................|....O..XOXO3.. 480
470 .............................|....O..XOXO... 470
460 .............................|...2..XOX.... 460
450 _____OX_XOX_____  450
440 .............................|...OXOXO..... 440
430 .............................|...OXOX...... 430
420 .............................|...OXOX...... 420
410 .............................|...O.O....... 410
400 _____  400
    --------------------------------------------------0--------------
    --------------------------------------------------0--------------
```

The formula in words as well as symbols is:

Downside Vertical Count Price Objective	=	Value in Points of the High of the Rise	−	Number of Boxes in the First Downside Reversal after the Peak or the Downside Reversal after the Last Level Top x Minimum Reversal Value in Boxes x Box Value in Points

or

Vd = Vtop - (Rd x Rm x Vbox)

KGF: $580 = 940 - (12 \times 3 \times 10)$

Summary: calculation of the vertical count

*   For the **vertical upside** count: take a relevant low, determine the number of boxes (Xs) in the following column, multiply that number with the box size times minimum reversal, then add that number to the relevant low.

*   For the **vertical downside**: take a relevant high, determine the number of boxes (Os) in the following column, multiply that number with the box size times minimum reversal, then subtract that number from the relevant high.

Change of scale areas

Explaining the scaling in a previous chapter we have shown that at some values the box sizes change. Performing a vertical or horizontal count over such areas of change of scaling could cause confusion.

Horizontal counts

The horizontal count method of calculating a price objective counts the number of columns comprising a base or a top and multiplies this figure by the reversal value which is defined as the value of a box times the number of boxes comprising a minimum reversal. This result is then added to the low of the base to get an upside price objective, or subtracted from the peak of a top to establish the downside price objective.

But if the base develops in the 16 to 22 range of the US-scale where boxes change from half points to whole points, what is the box size to be used for determining the reversal value? In such cases *the reversal value is the average value of the two-box values crossed*, or 0.75.

Vertical counts

In the vertical count method of calculating the price objective, the number of boxes filled on the first reversal after the final bottom or final top is multiplied by the reversal value (box value times the minimum reversal size in boxes), and this figure is added to the bottom value, or subtracted from the top to get the appropriate price objective. If *the boxes cross a change of scale area, the boxes above and below the change level are simply treated separately*.

For example, if the first reversal has filled eight boxes over the change of scale area at 20, meaning the boxes 18.5, 19, 19.5, 20, 21, 22, 23 and 24, it can be said to have filled three half-point boxes (18.5, 19, 19.5) and five whole-point boxes (20, 21, 22, 23 and 24). These counts are each multiplied by the appropriate reversal values of 1.5 for the three half-point boxes (0.5-point boxes times three-box reversal) and three (one-point boxes times three-box reversal) for the five whole-point boxes. These results are then added (4.5 + 15) for a total of 19.5 points.

Application of price objectives

Price objectives work because their users act as if they will work and by their actions in the market tend to validate the objectives. Therefore, horizontal counts should be used to determine price objectives only where the base on top is so well defined that all chartists will agree on the formation and thereby act in unison. For only with general agreement among users will their influence be sufficiently strong to affect prices.

But conversely, since all chartists can agree after the fact as to peaks, bottoms and first reversals after such high and low prices, vertical counts are applicable to all situations.

Price objectives derived by:

- *horizontal counts*: work best in the less volatile investment media of common stocks and bonds, where the magnitude of moves are less severe than in futures;

- *vertical counts*: work equally well for stocks, commodities and most other chartable media.

Only rough guides

Furthermore, price objectives are rarely hit exactly. Often they are not reached and often they are exceeded. This does not discredit their usefulness, but only reinforces the fact that they are rough guides which indicate the probable distance of a move without regard to the time necessary to reach the calculated price level. As such they are but one additional tool to help the sophisticated chartist better analyse his market. All price objectives should be drawn on the chart and the sum total of these points coupled with trend lines present the best picture of the market as it evolves.

Why do we prefer vertical counts?

Vertical counts have less subjectivity inherent, as tops and bottoms are easy to detect and need no judging. As calculating of price objective lacks precision, we like to avoid the problems of estimating base widths.

Summary

Price objectives calculated from horizontal and vertical counts are tools which present a picture of the probable distance of a trending move. They are not exact, must be used with care and complement the variable price objectives presented by trend lines, for each one reveals a uniquely determined objective and when used in concert yields the best presentation.

The use of stop orders

Introduction

As the famous market technician and trader Jesse Livermore observed, trading success is based,

- firstly, on **acting decisively** on trading signals;
- secondly, on the use of precise **stop-loss orders**; and
- thirdly, on intelligent **money management**.

We have already explained the point-and-figure trading signals. Money management issues will be covered later in the book. Right now, we would like to explain the subject of stop orders.

Re-cap of stop orders

Stop orders are market orders that need to reach specific price levels to be triggered.

To put it simply, stop orders become market orders when the specified levels are touched. In a liquid market you can be fairly confident that you will get your trade at the level specified. For example, if you place a sell order with a stop at 80, you would expect in most cases to have the trade filled at 80. But there's usually no guarantee of this. Problems can arise, especially with illiquid markets or accelerated moves, e.g. crashes.

Stops in practice

When using a technical system like point-and-figure to trade, you can use stops to get in and out of positions.

If you are day-trading, and thus constantly observing the markets, you set such mental limits for yourself and when the price reaches the set level you proceed with the transaction. If you are not behind a screen you can give stop instructions to your broker. While liquidating positions yourself is a straight-forward process, giving stop and other orders to your broker needs investigation on your side, because the availability of different orders depends on the markets.

The best idea is to talk directly to somebody competent at your brokerage firm. The principles of stops are always the same – 'get me out or in at a certain level' – but different markets or investment instruments may have different stop procedures. You should therefore check the position carefully with your broker.

Reactive and proactive trading styles

Point-and-figure can be used with two different trading styles or a combination of both.

Reactive

You might update your chart, analyse it and if you observe a trading signal you do the required trade. If you are day-trading, you do this continuously and the trade order is entered into the market immediately after the occurrence of the signal.

If you update the charts after the market closes then you have no other alternative than to trade the next day. You can give an order to buy or sell at opening or give limit/stop orders. We call this way of trading *reactive*. This means, you do the chart, analyse and trade.

Proactive

More often chartists trade the *proactive* way. Because you know where the signals will occur, you place stops at those levels. That means, that when the signal happens you are *automatically* in the market. If you are trading proactively you have to be very meticulous about keeping control of all your open orders. We prefer to use orders that are only valid during the trading day; we have all orders cancelled when the market closes and the next day, before the markets open, we decide which stops have to be placed and introduce them one after the other.

Day-trading is usually done the reactive way. Stocks which cannot be followed real-time are usually traded in the proactive way. But you can also trade reactively, taking positions the day following the day when the signal was generated.

Which trading style is better?

We have run long-term computer simulations and can state that there is no huge advantage of one trading style over the other. Trading the proactive way generates slightly better results, but really the difference is not such that one should discard the reactive trading style.

Where to place stops

The beauty of point-and-figure is that it indicates very clearly where stops have to be placed. You place the stop at the level where the reversal or the double top/bottom would actually occur.

The proactive trader places the stop where the next signal would take place. In chart 3.5 overleaf, we have indicated where we went short, where long and where you would place the stop.

Example 3.5 – Placing a sell-stop order

Chart 3.5 – A *sell*-stop order example

```
360    ..........|.....C................    360
350    ..........|.....X................    350
340    ..X.......|.....X................    340
330    X.XO......|.....B................    330
320    XOXO......|.....X................    320
310    1OXO......|.....X................    310
300    .O.O......|.....X................    300
290    ...O......X.X...X................    290
280    ...O4.6...4OXO..X................    280
270    ...OXOXO..XO56X.A................    270
260    ...2XOXO..3O.OX9X................    260
250    ...OXOXO..X..OXOX................    250
240    ...O3OXO..2..O8OX................    240
230    ...O.5X7..X..7.OX................    230
220    .....O.O..X....O.................    220
210    .......8..1.....|................    210
200    .......A..X.....|................    200
195    .......O..X.....|................    195
190    .......OB.X.....|................    190
185    .......OXOX.....|................    185
180    .......OXOX.....|................    180
175    .......O.O......|................    175
170    ..........|.....|................    170
165    ..........|.....|................    165
160    ..........|.....|................    160
```

In the chart above we go short at 290 (red), go long at 195 (green) and at the same time place a stop at 170. 170 is the level where a sell-signal would be generated, namely a triple-bottom breakout.

If our position had the size of 1,000 shares, then we would have to give sell-stop for 2000 shares. The first 1,000 sold would liquidate the position, and the second 1000 would initiate a new short position.

In the continuation of our trading we sell and go short at 250. And we simultaneously introduce a buy stop at 280, which is the level a double-top breakout would happen (and eventually does happen).

Example 3.6 – Placing a buy-stop order

Chart 3.6 – A *buy*-stop-order example

```
360   ..........|.....C................   360
350   ..........|.....X................   350
340   ..X.......|.....X................   340
330   X.XO......|.....B................   330
320   XOXO......|.....X................   320
310   1OXO......|.....X................   310
300   .O.O......|.....X<-1.............   300
290   ...O......X.X...X................   290
280   ...O4.6...4OXO..X<-2.............   280
270   ...OXOXO..XO56X.A................   270
260   ...2XOXO..3O.OX9X................   260
250   ...OXOXO..X..■XOX................   250
240   ...O3OXO..2..O8OX................   240
230   ...O.5X7..X..7.OX................   230
220   ....O.O..X....O................   220
210   ......8..1.....|................   210
200   ......A..X.....|................   200
195   ......O..X.....|................   195
190   ......OB.X.....|................   190
185   ......OXOX.....|................   185
180   ......OXOX.....|................   180
175   ......O.O......|................   175
170   ..........|.....|................   170
165   ..........|.....|................   165
160   ........|.....|................   160
```

When we go short at 250 we know that a buy signal would be generated at 300 (triple top breakout) and put therefore a buy-stop at that level. Later, after that the following X-column reverses at 270, we can lower the stop to 280, as this is now the level where a buy would be generated, and eventually is.

Taking profits early by using stops

The most frustrating formation for the p&f chartist is the *pole*. The pole is the symbol of lost opportunity, as it represents a nice price move without an exit point at which you are prompted to realize your open profit. The *open profit or loss* is the amount of money you would make or lose if the position were liquidated immediately. It is unnerving because your portfolio can be making good open profits but, if no exit signal is generated, you may fail to take them.

Chart 3.7 – Unnerving poles on Friends Provident [FP.L]

```
FP.L / 3 box rev, 2001.07.09 to 2003.01.10
215   .|..............................................................|..   215
210   OX..............................................................|..   210
205   OX2.............................................................|..   205
200   O1O.............................................................|..   200
195   O_O__X_____       195
190   .|OX.X4.........................................................|..   190
185   .|OXOXO.........................................................|..   185
180   .|OXO3O.........................................................|..   180
175   .|O.O.5.........................................................|..   175
170   _____6_____       170
165   .|....O.........................................................|..   165
160   .|....O...................X.....................................|..   160
155   .|....O.........X.........XO........X...........................|..   155
150   .|....O..7.....XO8.......XO........XO.................C.....|..       150
145   _____O__XO__XOXO_____XO_____XO_____X_XO_____        145
140   .|....OX.XOX.X.XOXO..X...X9X.......XO..........X...X.....XOXOX...|..   140
138   .|....OXOXOXOXOXOXO..XO..XOXOX.....XO........X...XOX.XO..X.XOXOXO.|..  138
136   .|....OXOXOXOXOXOXOX.XOX.XOXOXO....XO........XO..XOXBXO..XOXOXOXO..|.. 136
134   .|....OXOXOXOXOXOXOXOXOXOXO....XO.......XOX.XOXOXO..XOXO.OXO..|..      134
132   _____OXOXOXOXOXOXOXOXOXOXOX_X_XO_____XOXOXOXOX_XOX__OXO_____        132
130   .|....OXOXO.OXOXO.OXOXOXOXOXOXOXO......X.XOXOXOXOXOXOXOX..OXO..|..     130
128   .|....OXO.OX..O.OX..OXOXO.OXOXOXOXO.....XOXOXOXO.OXOXOXO...O.O..|..    128
126   .|....O...O....OX..OXOX..O.OXOXOXOXO.....XOXOXOX..OXOXOX......OX.1..   126
124   .|.............OX..OXO....OXO.OXOXO......XO.OXO...O.OXOXO......OXOXO.  124
122   _____OX__O_____OX_O_OXO_____X_O_____OXOX_____OXOXO_   122
120   .|.............OX..........OX....OXO......X..........OXO.......O.OXO.  120
118   .|.............OX..........OX....OXOX....X...........OX........OXO.   118
116   .|.............OX..........OX....OXOXO....X..........OX........O|O.   116
114   .|.............O...........O.....OXOXOX.X.X..........OX.........|OX   114
112   _____OXOXOXOXOX_____O_____OX     112
110   .|................................OXOXOXOXOX..................|OX    110
108   .|................................OXOXOXOXOX..................|OX    108
106   .|................................OXOXOXOXOX..................|O.    106
104   .|................................OXOXOXOXOX..................|..    104
102   -0--------------------------------O-OXOAO-OX-----------------------0--  102
100   -2--------------------------------0-O---OX-----------------------3--  100
```

In the above chart two poles are highlighted, the first 114 to 150 (32% from low to high) and the second from 100 to 155 (55% from low to high). Both are tremendous moves which are not exploited by the traditional point-and-figure method. The preceding and following signals of each of the two poles are indicated as usual and fully explain how such poles frustrate the chartist.

You have various options to realize such open profits, which in the case of poles would vaporize if you simply wait for a new signal. You can use either *trailing stops or profit targets*, and in the following pages we show you how.

Trailing stops

One strategy is to use trailing stops, which means that you always maintain a profit-taking order at the price level where a reversal would occur. That strategy is best described by the following charts.

Chart 3.8 – Pole 1, initial situation

```
360    ....X...    360
350    ....X...    350
340    ..X.X...    340
330    X.XOX...    330
320    XOXOX...    320
310    XOXOX...    310
300    .O.OX...    300
290    ...OX...    290
280    ...OX...    280
270    ...OX...    270
260    ...OX...    260
250    ...OX...    250
240    ...OX...    240
230    ...OX...    230
220    ...OX...    220
210    ...OX...    210
200    ...OX...    200
190    ...OX...    190
180    ...OX...    180
170    ...OX...    170
160    ...OX...    160
150    ...OX...    150
140    ...OX...    140
130    ...O....    130
```

First we show the chart formation over the entire period. You can see a good open profit during the decline towards 130 in the short position taken at 290, which, however, is never realised. Even worse, the position would be closed with a small loss when the double-top break-out occurs around 350.

In the chart over the page we show you the same pole but this time from a couple of weeks earlier when we decided to protect our open profit with the use of a trailing stop.

Chart 3.9 – Pole 2, protecting the open profit with a trailing stop

```
360    . . . . . . . .    360
350    . . . . . . . .    350
340    . . X . . . . .    340
330    X . X O . . . .    330
320    X O X O . . . .    320
310    X O X O . . . .    310
300    . O . O . . . .    300
290    . . . 🔲 . . . .    290
280    . . . O . . . .    280
270    . . . O . . . .    270
260    . . . O . . . .    260
250    . . . O . . . .    250
240    . . . O . . . .    240
230    . . . O . . . .    230
220    . . . O . . . .    220
210    . . . . . . . .    210
200    . . . . . . . .    200
190    . . . . . . . .    190
180    . . . . . . . .    180
170    . . . . . . . .    170
160    . . . . . . . .    160
150    . . . . . . . .    150
140    . . . . . . . .    140
130    . . . . . . . .    130
```

Assume the stock made a new low and is trading around 220. Obviously we could liquidate the position and take the profits immediately, but as we believe that there is more downside potential, we put a buy-stop at the hypothetical reversal value of 250, with the intention to lower it when new Os are added to the column. Should the stock move to 250, a reversal would happen, and therefore we call it a *hypothetical reversal level*.

Chart 3.10 – Pole 3, lowering the trailing stop

```
360    . . . . . . . .    360
350    . . . . . . . .    350
340    . . X . . . . .    340
330    X . X O . . . .    330
320    X O X O . . . .    320
310    X O X O . . . .    310
300    . O . O . . . .    300
290    . . . O . . . .    290
280    . . . O . . . .    280
270    . . . O . . . .    270
260    . . . O . . . .    260
250    . . . O . . . .    250
240    . . . O . . . .    240
230    . . . O . . . .    230
220    . . . O . . . .    220
210    . . . O . . . .    210
200    . . . O . . . .    200
190    . . . O . . . .    190
180    . . . O . . . .    180
170    . . . O . . . .    170
160    . . . . . . . .    160
150    . . . . . . . .    150
140    . . . . . . . .    140
130    . . . . . . . .    130
```

On the next day the stock has a new low at 170. We lower the stop to 200 where the reversal would occur for that situation.

Chart 3.11 – Pole 4, realizing the open profit

```
360    . . . . . . . .    360
350    . . . . . . . .    350
340    . . X . . . . .    340
330    X . X O . . . .    330
320    X O X O . . . .    320
310    X O X O . . . .    310
300    . O . O . . . .    300
290    . . . O . . . .    290
280    . . . O . . . .    280
270    . . . O . . . .    270
260    . . . O . . . .    260
250    . . . O . . . .    250
240    . . . O . . . .    240
230    . . . O . . . .    230
220    . . . O . . . .    220
210    . . . O . . . .    210
200    . . . O . . . .    200
190    . . . O . . . .    190
180    . . . O . . . .    180
170    . . . O X . . .    170
160    . . . O X . . .    160
150    . . . O X . . .    150
140    . . . O X . . .    140
130    . . . O . . . .    130
```

During the next week the stock goes as far down as 130 and reverses. With a low at 130 we had lowered the trailing stop to 170, where it is eventually executed. With this strategy we have successfully protected an open profit. We have bought back the short position at 170, we have no position at all now, but just wait for the next signal, which, as we know from the first chart, is a buy at 360.

Non-trailing profit targets

Employing some statistical or simply visual studies on your favoured stocks will help you to define a price target after which you can take profits early. For example, for swing trading we have found that taking profits after 8 to 12 boxes increases profitability.

In our optimised trading strategies we also use variable non-trailing price targets similar to a moving average of price moves. We base the price targets on a series of preceding columns. A value which works well is taking 1.5 times the average size in boxes of the last 3 columns as a price target for liquidatation of a position. This is explained in the chart below.

The preceding 3 columns prior to the buy signal (280) are highlighted. They have the sizes (in boxes) of 6, 4 and 3 respectively and average 4.33. Taking 1.5 times the average of their sizes equals 6.5, which we round to 7 and determine the profit target 7 boxes higher, namely at 350. Hence, we will cover our long position, taken at 280, in full or in part at 350.

Chart 3.12 – Variable price target (moving average type)

```
360   ..........|.....C.................   360
350   ..........|.....X.................   350
340   ..X.......|.....X.................   340
330   X.XO......|.....B.................   330
320   XOXO......|.....X.................   320
310   1OXO......|.....X.................   310
300   .O.O......|.....X.................   300
290   ...O......X.X...X.................   290
280   ...O4.6...4OXO..X.................   280
270   ...OXOXO..XO56X.A.................   270
260   ...2XOXO..3O.OX9X.................   260
250   ...OXOXO..X..OXOX.................   250
240   ...O3OXO..2..O8OX.................   240
230   ...O.5X7..X..7.OX.................   230
220   .....O.O..X....O..................   220
210   .......8..1.....|................   210
200   .......A..X.....|................   200
195   .......O..X.....|................   195
190   .......OB.X.....|................   190
185   .......OXOX.....|................   185
180   .......OXOX.....|................   180
175   .......O.O......|................   175
170   ..........|.....|................   170
165   ..........|.....|................   165
160   ..........|.....|................   160
```

As the name indicates, the non-trailing profit-taking level is set at the entry of the position and is not changed until it is either touched or an opposed signal has occurred.

Conclusion

Stop orders are a crucial instrument for the point-and-figure trader. They can be used to:

- open positions
- protect positions
- take profits early

Running a big book of stop orders has to be done in a very orderly way to prevent a situation in which you confuse your broker or mess up your own order book and thus create losses due to simple errors.

Risk and position size

Your available capital and your risk appetite should define the size of your trading positions. In this chapter we talk about simple methods to estimate risk.

Keep it simple

Risk estimates can be calculated at any level of detail, involving analysis of a myriad of scenarios and with various methodologies. However, we have extensive knowledge of risk management and know that a simple comprehensible risk measure technique is what one needs.

We propose that you either simulate or estimate a maximum capital drawdown for each instrument you want to trade. Then you sum the values and deduct the diversification benefit. That's all. We assure you if Long Term Capital Management had used that approach, they would still be around today!

Estimating the maximum equity drawdown is straightforward. You estimate the trading risks by looking at the point-and-figure chart that depicts a long time span of the stock you want to trade, then you make an estimate of a worst-case regarding the potential losses.

Where does risk come from?

The risks of losing money by trading stocks with point-and-figure are twofold:

1. the **series of losing trades**, so called 'whipsawing', which is shown in the chart overleaf

   and

2. getting **locked into a wrong position** during a market discontinuity; for instance, being long over a random event like the 9/11 terrorist attack.

The problem of whipsawing

Chart 3.13 – The Achilles' heel, whipsawing!

```
96     ......................|.X.X........    96
94     ......................|.XOXOX......    94
92     ......................|.XOXOXO.....    92
90     ......................|.XO.OXO.....    90
88     ......................|.X..O.O.....    88
86     ......................|.X....O.....    86
84     ......................|.X.........    84
82     ......................|.X.......*..    82
80     ......................|.X.......*..    80
78     ......................|.X.......*..    78
76     ..............X.......|.X.......*..    76
74     _____XO_____X_____*__    74
72     ....X.........COX.....|.X.......*..    72
70     ....XO........XOXO....|.X.......*..    70
68     ....XO......X.XOXO....|.X.......*..    68
66     ....XO......XOXOXO....|.X.......*..    66
64     ____XO_____XOXO_O_____X_____*__    64
62     ....XO..X.X.XO...O....|.X.......*..    62
60     X.X.XO..XOXOXX....OX...|.X.......*..    60
59     XOXOXO..XOXOX....OXO..|.X.......*..    59
58     XOXOXOX.XOXOX....OXO..|.X.......*..    58
57     XOXOXOXOXO_OX____OXO____X_____*__    57
56     XOXOXOXOX..OX....OXOX.|.X..........    56
55     XOXOBOXOX..O.....OXOXO|.X..........    55
54     XO.O.OXOX........OXOXOX.X..........    54
53     X....OXOX........OXOXOXOX..........    53
52     X____OXO_____O_OXOXOX_____    52
51     .....OX...........O.OXOX..........    51
50     .....OX...........OXOX..........    50
49     .....O...........O1OX..........    49
48     .................O|O..........    48
47     _____    47
46     ..................|...........    46
45     ..................|...........    45
44     ..................|...........    44
```

As you can see, the first trade is long at 62, then short with a loss, then long with a loss, short with a loss, and this for a series of five trades. We would have lost about 22 points, plus transaction costs estimated at 3. That corresponds to a crash from 82 to 57, indicated on the right side with '*', which takes quite a big toll on the overall profit. But this sort of whipsawing happens quite often until a trending position is finally entered.

You can make a fair estimate of that whipsawing-risk by looking at the long-term chart and doing some paper trading, or doing a computerised analysis.

As we mentioned before, you also run the risk of discontinuities, gaps or jumps. Such risk is, however, less important with large companies than small caps. If you trade stocks that are in the FTSE, DAX or other blue-chip index, you do not have to consider that risk, because it will always be smaller than the risk associated with whipsawing.

The most significant risk of p&f trading is whipsawing. This is unlike passive investment strategies, which suffer from volatility or market crashes – where point-and-figure works especially well. Point-and-figure trading, however, is problematic in sideways markets. In such markets positions are often changed and each time a small loss is taken and those small losses add up to a big loss. Therefore, the parameter to consider in assessing risks for p&f trading is the largest *historical draw-down* and not the size of the moves of the stocks as such.

How to calculate historic draw-downs

The trading strategy is simulated with historic data. The equity – the P&L of the simulated trading account – is calculated each day during the simulation. After each new high of the equity, the following low is searched for. The difference between the two is a draw-down. Once all draw-downs are found, the biggest is determined and used in order to estimate the risks involved in the trading strategy.

Size of positions

To be prudent is a virtue. On the other hand, with tiny positions, you can't make big money. On a winning position, you always think bigger positions should have been taken, and on the losing trades you always have too big a position! Therefore a simple way of calculating levels of risks and sizes of positions is required. We'll give you a simple way of calculating your own levels of risk and capital requirements.

First you have to quantify your risk appetite. A good starting point is to establish the maximum amount of capital you are willing to lose in adverse circumstances and the number of instruments you want to trade. The amount of capital that you have at your disposition is a number we can unfortunately not change, and it does not need to be estimated. It is what it is!

For each instrument you estimate a possible worst case scenario. The easiest way is to base such estimations on historical data, i.e. long-term charts. If a certain strategy applied to a given stock had a maximum draw-down of 40%, it is reasonable to use that value for an estimate. Obviously it is conceivable that the stock will take a bigger hit than the historic maximum, though the probability is low. Such a risk should be compensated for by diversification, i.e. trading more than one security.

Then if you trade two or more low-correlated instruments, you have to calculate the diversification benefits which lowers the risk-value below the aggregate of the estimated draw-downs; or put the other way round, you can trade bigger positions. If you trade:

- 2 instruments (stocks, bonds, futures), decreases total risk by 33%
- 5 instruments, decreases total risk by 50%
- 10 instruments, decreases total risk by 80%

with the value of risk referring to the aggregate of simulated draw-downs.

Example 3.7 – Calculating maximum drawdown

You decide to trade Siemens [SIEGn.DE] and Repsol [REP.MC] with a simple p&f strategy, 1,000 shares each. You estimated the maximum drawdown at €15,000 for Siemens and €9,000 for Repsol. Therefore, you would sum the two draw-down figures – equals €24,000 – and subtract the diversification benefit of 33% – equals €8,000 – resulting in the capital-at-risk number of €16,000. To be safe and responsible in running your strategy, you have to put aside €16,000. If this number is greater than the margin requirements set by your broker, it is imperative to put it aside anyway.

Looked at from a different point of view, you want to put €20,000 in trading Repsol and Siemens with equal amounts of shares. You have estimated the maximum drawdown for Siemens to be €15 per share and €9 for Repsol. So a portfolio with 1 Repsol and 1 Siemens would incur a risk of €24 minus the diversification benefit of 33%, resulting in a risk number of €16. Therefore, you could trade €20,000 divided by €16 equals 1,250 shares, and so it would be advisable to trade not more than 1,250 shares of each company.

Pyramiding made simple and profitable

Introduction

Much has been written concerning the pros and cons of pyramiding and the right and wrong ways to do it. But unfortunately while the concept of adding to positions which are trending seems so logical and correct, its implementation usually becomes cumbersome, complicated, inexact, and more of an art than a science. And thus generally not worth the trouble.

Naturally, all traders would like the greatest concentration of positions in those stocks showing the largest positive moves, but the employment of a pyramiding strategy usually degenerates into a finger-crossing, seat-of-the-pants exercise of guesses.

But now all that can change. Pyramiding *can* become a simple, exact and easily-implemented market tool capable of substantially increasing overall portfolio returns.

What is point-and-figure pyramiding?

Point-and-figure pyramiding refers to the trading of consecutive chart signals of the same category (i.e. buys or sells), whereby on each additional signal of the same category the position is increased. The purpose of pyramiding is to concentrate the invested capital in the trending, and therefore profitable positions.

The system

The pyramiding system requires just a slight modification of the point-and-figure technique.

A quick review of non-pyramiding point-and-figure

In the non-pyramiding p&f method, only the first signal is considered. Thus, after a string of sell signals, the first buy signal would trigger a long. Once taken, the long would be held throughout the entire series of additional buy signals, with no additional positions added, and finally liquidated on the very first sell signal.

Simultaneous with the closing out of the long, a short sale would be executed which would remain on the books without additional short positions added on new sell formations, until the first buy signal where the short would be covered and a new long taken.

Pyramiding means all signals are taken

With pyramiding, the technique is changed so that positions are taken on *every* signal, not just on the first signal after a reversal. Thus on the first buy formation after a sell signal, a long is taken. On each subsequent buy signal an additional position is taken until a sell signal occurs, at which time all longs are immediately liquidated and a short taken. On each subsequent sell formation an additional short position is added until a buy signal occurs, at which time all shorts are covered and a long taken. **The result is a large accumulation of positions in stocks or contracts which are showing substantial trends, with small commitments in non-trending or whippy situations.**

Chart 3.14 – Pyramiding, ARM [ARM.L]

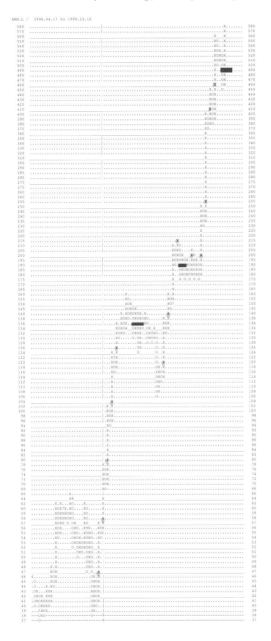

However, you only start a new position when the nature of the chart changes. If you are neutral, you do not go short on the second or a later sell signal. If you have missed the first sell, you patiently wait until a buy is generated and start your pyramiding from there.

In the chart of ARM Holdings on the left, pyramiding is demonstrated during the forceful up move in 1999. As you can see, there are up to 5 consecutive buy signals without a sell signal occurring. In the pyramiding approach to trading you would increase at each buy or long position. At the first sell formation you liquidate the entire position and go one short.

We have indicated the liquidation of the longs with a red bar of the length equal to the accumulated position.

The chart on the right shows the opposite situation, namely the pyramiding of positions is triggered during a down move.

Specifically, in the case of Cable and Wireless, one unit was sold short at 210, the market continued down and another unit sold short at 185, then the market rallied a bit (but no buy signal was given), however the rally died and the stock started falling again given another sell signal at 190 – where another unit was sold – and a final unit of shares was sold at 155. After that, there was a short rally and a buy signal at 180 indicated to close out the 4 short units, and open a long position.

Chart 3.15 – Pyramiding, Cable and Wireless [CW.L]

```
CW.L / 3 box rev, log1/ 2002.03.12 to 2003.01.10
 250 _____  250
 245 +.............................................................................. 245
 240 O+............................................................................. 240
 235 O.+............................................................................ 235
 230 OX.+........................................................................... 230
 225 OX4_+.......................................................................... 225
 220 OXO..+.+....................................................................... 220
 215 O.OX.X+X+...................................................................... 215
 210 ..■XOXOX6+..................................................................... 210
 205 ..OXOXOXO.+.................................................................... 205
 200 __OXOXOXO__+................................................................... 200
 195 ..OXOXO.O...+................................................................. 195
 190 ..O.OX..■....+................................................................ 190
 185 ....■X..OX....++.............................................................. 185
 180 ....OX..OXO..X.++............................................................. 180
 175 ___OX_O7OX_XOX++.............................................................. 175
 170 +...5...OXOXOXOX8X+............................................................ 170
 165 .+.....OXOXOXOXOX9+........................................................... 165
 160 ..+.....OXO.OXOXOXO.+......................................................... 160
 155 ...+....O...■.O.OXO..+.....B.................................................. 155
 150 ___+_____■XO___+____XO_____ 150
 145 .....+..........O.O...+...XO.................................................. 145
 140 ......+.........■....X+..XO................................................... 140
 138 ......+.........O...XOX.XO.................................................... 138
 136 .......+........O...XOXOXO.................................................... 136
 134 _____+_____O___XOXOXO+_____ 134
 132 ..........+.....O..X.XOXOX+................................................... 132
 130 .........+....OX.XOXO.O.OXO+.................................................. 130
 128 .........+....OXOXOX...■XO.+.................................................. 128
 126 ...........+...OXOXOX...OXO..+................................................ 126
 124 _____+___OXOXOX___O_O__+_____ 124
 122 ............+..OXOAOX...+..■...+.............................................. 122
 120 ............+.OXOXOX..+...O....+.............................................. 120
 118 +...........+OXOXO..+....O....+............................................... 118
 116 .+..............O.OX..+....O....+............................................. 116
 114 __+_____■X_+____O_____+_____ 114
 112 ..+...........OX+......O......+............................................... 112
 110 ....+.........O+.......O......+.............................................. 110
 108 .....+........+.......O......+.............................................. 108
 106 .....+........+.......O......+.............................................. 106
 104 _____+_____+_____O_____+_____ 104
 102 ......+.......+.......O......+............................................... 102
 100 +.....+.......+.......O......+............................................... 100
  98 .+......+.....+.......O......+............................................... 98
  96 ..+.....+.....+.......O......+............................................... 96
  94 __+_____+_____+_____O_____ 94
  92 ...+....+.....+.......O......+............................................... 92
  90 ....+...+.....+.......O...X+.................................................. 90
  88 ....+...+.....+.......XO+.................................................... 88
  86 ......+.......+.......O..X..CO.+.............................................. 86
  84 ____+_____+_____OX_XOXO__+_____ 84
  82 .....+........+.......OXOXOXO...+.............................................. 82
  80 .......+......+.......OXOXOXO...+............................................. 80
  78 .......+......+.......OXO.OXO...+............................................. 78
  76 .......+......+.......OX..■.O...+............................................. 76
  74 _____+_____+_____OX___+■____+_____ 74
  72 .......+......+.......OX..+.O....+............................................ 72
  70 .......+......+.......OX.+..O.................................................. 70
  68 .......+......+.......OX+...O.................................................. 68
  66 .......+......+.......O+....O.................................................. 66
  64 _____+_____+_+___O_____ 64
  62 ......+.......+.......+.......O................................................ 62
  60 .......+......+.......+.......O............................................... 60
  59 .......+......+.......+.......O............................................... 59
  58 .......+......+.......+.......O............................................... 58
  57 _____+_____+__O____X_____ 57
  56 .......+......+.......+..O....X............................................... 56
  55 .......+......+.......+.O....X................................................ 55
  54 .......+......+.......+O....X................................................. 54
  53 .......+......+.......O....X.................................................. 53
  52 _____+_____O____X_____ 52
  51 .......+......+.......O...X..X................................................ 51
  50 .......+......+.......O...XO..X............................................... 50
  49 .......+......+.......O..X.XO..X.............................................. 49
  48 .......+......+.......+...XOXO..X............................................. 48
  47 _____+_O__XOXOX_X_____ 47
  46 .......+......+.O..XOXOXO1................................................... 46
  45 .......+......+OX.XOXOXOX.................................................... 45
  44 .....................OXOXO.O.OX............................................... 44
  43 ...................OXOX...+■X................................................. 43
  42 _____OXOX__+_O_____ 42
  41 ...................OXOX.+....|................................................ 41
  40 ...................OXO.+....|................................................. 40
  39 ...................OX.+.....|................................................. 39
  38 -------------------OX+------O--------------------------------------------------- 38
  37 -------------------O+-------3--------------------------------------------------- 37
```

How many contracts or shares should be added on each signal?

The question usually asked in relation to pyramiding is-

'How many contracts or shares should be added on each signal?'

Most pyramiding systems get bogged down at this point in a complicated model for building a large base and adding progressively smaller units with each new signal (which is nebulous at best). In other words, a normal (non point-and-figure) pyramiding strategy would have the trader attempt to estimate the distance of the move and the number of signals which will occur in the move, both of which are difficult if not impossible to judge accurately.

In the p&f pyramiding method, no predictions are made as to the distance the price will move during the trend, nor is there any guess as to the number of consecutive signals that will occur in a string. And lastly, no attention is given to progressively smaller additions being added on each new signal. All that is required is to decide whether you want to start with one, two or more contracts, which is a function of available capital, and then add an equal number of positions on each new signal. Thus, if you start with one contract lot or one round lot (100 shares) of stock, one additional contract lot or round lot will be added on the second buy signal, one on the third and so forth, until all are liquidated on the first sell and one short is taken. If the initial position is two lots, two are added on each successive signal.

How very simple, and, as the early examples show, how effective!

Chartists contemplating the prospects of pyramiding often question the legitimacy of adding new positions rather than originally starting with a longer position and not pyramiding. They also express some concern about the total margin or capital committed in such a trading strategy, for high margin / capital commitments can sometimes lower the return on invested capital in a pyramided position.

Why?

Because if a trader knows that a certain stock is going to have a major move, he would naturally take the maximum possible commitment on the original signal, for the first signal is the one which will always prove most profitable in a run. But since few of us can accurately predict which stocks or contracts will be the big movers or estimate the timing of the start of the move, it makes more sense to let the price action lead us into the heaviest commitment on the long side in those situations which prove the strongest and the largest short positions in the ones that the market designates the weakest. This is all that the p&f pyramiding system is attempting to do – to allocate dollars to the long side of the strongest securities or commodities and to the short side of the weakest ones, while keeping a very nominal investment in the trendless issues. And best of all, the allocation process is completely automatic. Guesses are now obsolete!

Pyramiding increments

These are valid areas of concern that we would like to address in the following way.

The pyramiding program is without doubt a function of the available capital per instrument.

Say you wish to invest a certain amount of capital in a p&f trading strategy and decide to diversify equally over 5 different stocks or bonds. In this situation, we would suggest that initially you commit $\frac{1}{15}^{th}$ of the capital to each position. Then increment the positions during the process of pyramiding in steps of $\frac{1}{15}^{th}$ of the capital. The denominator 15 is the result of 3 times the number of different instruments. 3 is used as an estimate of an average number in consecutive signals triggering position increments through pyramiding.

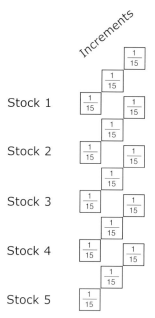

Summary

Put away your stocks dart board and the crystal ball – there is a better way! Let the market decide where your money should be concentrated.

The largest positions in your portfolio should be on the long side of the strongest stocks and the short side of the weakest ones, with only token positions in the trendless ones.

This is exactly what the p&f pyramiding system does – automatically and with exactness. All that the trader has to do is add an equal number of additional contracts to the position with each p&f signal, and automatically the big movers end up with the largest holdings.

Swing trading

Introduction

The famous chartist and trader W.D. Gann pointed out correctly that stocks oscillate, or in his words *vibrate*, and that the most profitable way to trade any security is to benefit from as many such up and down swings as possible.

Because there has been so much talk lately about swing trading, we want to explain it and show you that for the implementation of swing trading nothing more is needed than point-and-figure.

The problem with Gann's type of trading is the large number of transactions, which makes careful implementation a necessity in order to find a balance between trading those minor oscillations and keeping transaction costs under control. It is true, though, that with direct access trading through discount brokers a lot of commission costs can be spared.

What is swing trading?

As with every fashionable subject, there are many different interpretations of the term *swing trading*. Swing trading became popular again in the post-nineties, with the onset of enduring bear markets. Since swing trading does not depend on long-term up-trends, it is successful in such bear market situations. It is an alternative to the long-term buy and hold investment style.

Shorter position life-spans

In general swing trading has the same aim as point-and-figure trading, namely trading both the bearish and the bullish moves. Swing trading methodologies are based on technical analysis, and because, as mentioned many times before, point-and-figure is the best of all technical analysis, you do not need anything new in order to swing trade. However, in the consensus of the technical analysts, swing trading has slightly shorter position-life spans than standard 3 box reversal p&f trading.

In the following pages, we show you how to adapt p&f to gear it towards trading somewhat shorter cycles, in the range of one week to a couple of weeks.

We are all aware that market prices oscillate. The scholars of the markets have come up with many divisions of such fluctuations into major, minor, macro and micro trends. Remember the Dow Theory or Prechter's Elliot waves? Interestingly – and contrary to our philosophy – all the authors mentioned, Dow, Gann and Elliott, belong to the mystical crowd of traders, using biblical figures or harmonic proportions in their systems.

Swing trading is trying to profit from swings or oscillations with a duration of weeks.

Swing trading profits from fluctuations in markets that do not trend strongly upwards. The expectation that has to be set by the trader is whether he believes the markets are sideways or trending. When going into markets, you have to make a bet about the future 'trendiness'. If you believe that the markets will continue for a while without a trend, then swing trading is a good alternative.

To be a successful swing trader you just have to make minor adaptations to the traditional point-and-figure system, both in terms of box sizes and in the approach to taking profits, in order to shorten the typical life of a position.

Data to be used

End-of-day data

Swing trading is based on end-of-day data. Use the same data as for your normal point-and-figure charts. You should concentrate your swing trading on just a couple of stocks so it is easy for you to control the quality of the data. Make sure that your data is precise, because, as many signals are generated, you want to avoid glitches due to erroneous data.

Intraday data

Of course, if you want to enhance the entry points further, you could use the same methodologies as in day-trading and therefore base your graphs on intraday data. Our experience, however, has not shown a great enough improvement in order to justify the increase in complexity generated by the use of daily tick data. Moreover the use of intraday data only makes sense for screen traders, and those probably prefer day-trading anyhow or a combination of both, where positions can be taken or closed several times during the day.

How to gear p&f towards swing trading

To profit from the short-term trends of a security we use a standard scale with a box size as indicated in the table, but with a minimum reversal number of 2 instead of 3. With the smaller minimum reversal number and the smaller box size we enter and exit the swing earlier and follow the short- to mid-term oscillations of the stock more closely. Moreover we take profits on positions after 10 boxes. This is indicated on the charts with a yellow mark. After the profit is taken, the next signal (either buy or sell) is awaited and traded upon.

Table 3.1 – Scale proposed for swing trading

From	To	BoxSize
1	1.4	0.01
1.4	2.9	0.02
2.9	6	0.05
6	14	0.1
14	29	0.2
29	60	0.5
60	140	1
140	290	2
290	600	5
600	1400	10
1400	2900	20
2900	6000	50
6000	14000	100

Which markets should you swing trade?

The point with swing trading is this: if markets oscillate within trading ranges or channels, swing trading works well, but if markets trend strongly there are better ways to trade.

In order to decide whether you should switch to swing mode, you should base your decision on the study of long-term point-and-figure charts and judge whether the stock is confined by a channel or range. If that is the case, then, *yes*, go to swing trade mode.

Swing trading in practice

From the brief paragraphs in the last few pages you know enough about swing trading, at least in our opinion. Now we would like to show you how it works in practice.

Let's assume that you believe that the markets will stay confined to trading channels for a while, and so you therefore go to swing mode. You choose a strategy like:

Reversal number: 2 boxes
Scale: scale for volatile securities (cf. table 3.1)
Strategy: enter and exit on Simple Buy and Simple Sell signals, take profits early (8-12 boxes)

And you start!

On the following pages, we have included a few charts so that you can get a flavour of this trading style. Underneath each of the charts we have included a brief analysis generated by our program. The brief analysis includes the specifics of the strategy, namely the minimum reversal size, the scale type and the strategy regarding the entry and exist of positions. Then it includes the time period of the chart and the simulated trading results in points.

Testing methodology

The only strategy used is *S2iSSoSST12* which translates into:

- **Standard scale 2** box reversal
- **in on Simple signals**
- **out on Simple Signals** or **if a Target of 12 boxes** is reached

We include a summary of the different strategies in the part covering optimisations.

The profit in points can be measured against the absolute values of the prices. For example, in the case of Next, where the first trading signal is generated at a level of 950, the profit of 472 minus the deduction of an estimated 130 points of commission results in a profitability of 38% p.a., while excluding all possible leverage. Applying leverage used by professional traders and their lower commissions, the mentioned profitability gets multiplied by at least 5.

The stocks we have chosen in this section are stocks we have actually traded or followed over the shown period.

Chart 3.16 – Swing trading, Next [NXT.L]

```
NXT.L / 2 box rev, std2/ 2002.01.02 to 2002.12.06
 1120 ..............................................................................................  1120
 1110 _____X_____  1110
 1100 .............................XO...........................................................  1100
 1090 ...................X.X.X.X.X.X....XO......................................................  1090
 1080 ..................▓XOX4XOXOXOXO.....XO.....................................................  1080
 1070 ...................X.XO.OXOXOXOXO.....XO...................................................  1070
 1060 _____XOX_■_OXO_OXO__X_X_XO_____  1060
 1050 ............XO.....OX..OXOX.X5XOXOX........................................................  1050
 1040 ..............X.....O..O.OXOXOXOXOXO.......................................................  1040
 1030 ..............X.........O.O.O.O.OXOX.......................................................  1030
 1020 ..............X...........▓OXOXO...........................................................  1020
 1010 _____X_____O_OXO__X_____  1010
 1000 ..............X.............O.OX.XO........................................................  1000
  990 ..........X..X..............OX6XO..........................................................   990
  980 ..........XOX.X.............OXO.O...........................................................   980
  970 ....X.X........3OXOX............O..■.........................................................   970
  960 X___XOXO2_____XOXO_____OX____X_____X_____   960
  950 .XO..▓O.OXOX.....XO...............OXO..7.XO..................XO.............................   950
  940 .XOX.X..■XOXOX.X.X................OXO..XOXO.................XO...X.X........................   940
  930 .XOXOX..O.OXOXOXOX................OXO..XOXO.............X.X....XO...XOXO.......X............   930
  920 1.OXOX....OXO.O.O.................XOXO.XO.O.........XOXO....XO....XOAO....X.XOX.X...........   920
  910 _OXOX____O_____O_O__X_■X_____XOXOX____XOX__XO_O___X_XOXOXBXO_____   910
  900 ..OXO...............................OX.X..OXO.........XO.OXO...XOXO...X..■....XOXOXOXOXOX.X.X......   900
  890 ..O.................................OXOX..OXO..X......X..■.O...XOXO..X..O....XO.OXOXOXOXOXOXO......   890
  880 ....................................OXOX..OXO...XOX.....▓....X....XOXOX.X...O.O.OXO.OXOXO........   880
  870 ....................................O.OX..OXO..▓OXO..X.X.X...O..XOXOXOXO..O...X....■X..O.O.OX.....   870
  860 _____OX__OXOX_XOXO__▓OXOX_____O___▓O_O_O___O_X_X_____O____OXO_____   860
  850 ....................................OX..OXOXOXOXOX.XO.OX...OX.X.X........O..OX..............O.O....   850
  840 ....................................O...OXOXOXOX08OXOX..O....OX9XOX.......O..▓OX...............OX.X..   840
  830 ....................................OXOXO.OXOX.......O.O.OX.....OX.XO..................OXOXC.   830
  820 ....................................OXOXO...▓XO............O......OXOX.................OXOXO.   820
  810 _____OXOX____OX_____OXOX_____OXO_O____   810
  800 ....................................O.OX...O........................OXO............O...OX     800
  790 ....................................O........................OX...................O...OX     790
  780 .............................................................OX...................O.     780
  770 _____O_____   770
  760 _____   760
  750 _____   750
  740 ..............................................................................................   740
  730 ..............................................................................................   730
  720 ..............................................................................................   720
  710 ------------------------------------------------------------------------------------------   710
  700 ------------------------------------------------------------------------------------------   700
```

Analysis of trading NXT.L	
Minimum Reversal	2
Scale Type	Standard
Start Date	2002-01-01
End Date	2003-02-01
Strategy	S2iSSoSST12
Gross P&L	472
Trades	26
Stops hit	4

In this brief analysis you see the parameters used: the date-interval, P&L, the number of trades and the number of times profits were taken early, which shows up under 'Stops hit'. P&L is indicated in 'Gross P&L'.

Commissions

Commissions vary from broker to broker, but the tendency is clear, it gets cheaper. A moderately active trader should not pay more than 0.1%. Please compare what you would pay for trading 26 times Next, but it should be closer to 50 than to 100 points. Due to the individual cost of trading we prefer to display the gross figure.

Chart 3.17 – Swing trading Exel [EXL.L]

```
EXL.L / 2 box rev, std2/ 2002.01.02 to 2003.01.17
 950 ...........................X............................................................|........ 950
 940 ...........................XO...........................................................|........ 940
 930 ...........................XO...........................................................|........ 930
 920 ...........................XO...........................................................|........ 920
 910             XOX       X                                                                          910
 900 ...................XOXOX.X...XOX......................................................... 900
 890 .......X.......X...XO.OXOXOX.XOX6X...X..................................................... 890
 880 ....XOX.....X.XOX.X..XOXOXOXOXOXOX.XO..7................................................... 880
 870 ...X.XOXOX.X.XOXOXO...O.OXOXOXO.O.OXOXO..XO............................................... 870
 860     XOXOXOXOX4XOXOXO    5XOXOX    XOXO XO................................................ 860
 850 .XOXO.O.OXO.OXO......O.O.O.....O.OXOXO.XO................................................. 850
 840 .......XOX....X...X       .O.OXOXOXO..................................................... 840
 830 X......XO.....OX.............OXOXOXO..................................................... 830
 820 XO...X........O.........OXO.O.OX......................................................... 820
 810 XO     X                    O     XO    X................................................ 810
 800 XO..X...X...............................O.O...X8..........................X...X..|........ 800
 790 XO..XO..3...............................O....XO.........................XO..|........ 790
 780 1OX.2O..X...............................O....X.X.......................XO..|........ 780
 770 .OXOXOX.X...............................O....XO....XOXO................XO..|........ 770
 760 _O_OXOXOX................................OX   XO    XO_OX              XOX 760
 750 ...O.O.O...............................OXO..XO....X.X..OX9.............XOXO....|........ 750
 740 .......................................OXO..XO..XOX..OXO...............X.XOXO...|........ 740
 730 .......................................OXOX.XOX....XO.O.O..X...........XOXCXO..X.|........ 730
 720 .......................................OXOXOXOX.X.X.....X..XO............XOXOXO..XO|........ 720
 710                                        OXOXOXOXOXOXOX   OX XOX          XOXOXOX XOX 710
 700 .......................................OXOXOXOXOXOX.....OXOXOXO.................XOXO.OXOXO1OX.X... 700
 690 .....................................O.OXOXOXOXOXOX...OXOXOXO.............X....X......XO...XOXOXOXOXOX. 690
 680 ....................................O.OXO.O.OXO.......OXO.OXO.......XOX...XOX.X.X.X....O.O.OXOXOXOXO 680
 670 ......................................OX...X.......OX..XOX.......X.XOXO..XOXOXOXOX.......OXO.OXOXO 670
 660 ....................................O         OX   OXO     XOXO OX XOXO OXOX      O   OXO O 660
 650 ...................................O.....OXOX.X.X..XOX..XOBOX..XO..........|..O...O 650
 640 .......................................OXOXOXOXOX.XO...O.O.O................|........ 640
 630 ...................................O.OXOXOXOXOX..........................|........ 630
 620 ...................................OXO.OAO.OX..............................|........ 620
 610                                      O   O   OX 610
 600 .........................................OX.............................|........ 600
 595 .........................................OX.............................|........ 595
 590 .........................................OX.............................|........ 590
 585 .........................................OX.............................|........ 585
 580                                          OX 580
 575 .........................................OX.............................|........ 575
 570 -----------------------------------------O-------------------------O------- 570
 565                                          3------- 565
```

Analysis of trading EXL.L	
Minimum Reversal	2
Scale Type	Standard
Start Date	2002-01-01
End Date	2003-02-01
Strategy	S2iSSoSST12
Gross P&L	380
Trades	25
Stops hit	5

Chart 3.18 – Swing trading, Reckitt Benckiser [RB.L]

```
RB.L / 2 box rev, std2/ 2002.01.02 to 2002.12.09
1310 ─────────────────────────────────────────────────────────────────────────────────────── 1310
1300 ......................................................X................................... 1300
1290 .....................................................XO................................... 1290
1280 .....................................................XO................................... 1280
1270 .....................................................XOX.................................. 1270
1260 .....................................................XOXO........................X.X....... 1260
1250 .....................................................XOXO.............X.XOXO.............. 1250
1240 .............................X.....X.XOXO.............X.XOXOXOX..............X............ 1240
1230 .............................XO....XO50XOX...........XOXOXOXOXOX.X.........XO............. 1230
1220 ....................X.XOX.X.XOXOXOXO...X.X.........X............XOXOXOXOXOXOXOX......XO............. 1220
1210 ........XOXOXOXOXOXOXO_O_OX_XOXO.........XO...........9_XO_O_OXO_OXOXOXO......XO............. 1210
1200 ...............X....XO.OXOXOXOX...OX6XOXOX.........XO................XOX...O...OAOXOXOX.....XO............. 1200
1190 ...............XO..X..O.OXO.OX...OXOXO.OXO....X..XO..........X.X..XOX........O.OXOXOXO...XO..X............. 1190
1180 ...............XO..X...O...O.....OXO...OXOX.X.X7..XO..........XOXO..XOX............O.OXOXOX...XOX.XO......... 1180
1170 ...............X.XO..X..........OX...OXOXOXOXOX.XO..........XOXO..XOX...........OXOXOX.XOXOXO.......... 1170
1160 .......X.......XOXOX_X.........O.....OXOXOXOXOXOXO..........XOXO__XOX............OXOXOXOXOBOXOXO_......... 1160
1150 ............XO....XOXOXOX..................OXOXOXOXOXO.O.........XOXOX.XO...........OXOXO.OXO.OXOXOX.......X. 1150
1140 ............XOX....XOX4XOX...............OXOXOXOXO...O.......X.XO.OXOX..............OXOX..OX..O.OXOXO...X.X.XO 1140
1130 ............XOXO...XO.OXO................OXO.OXOX...O.....X.XOX..OXOX.............OXOX..O....O.O.OX.XOXOXO 1130
1120 ............XO3OX.X.X..O.................O...OXOX....O....OXOX..OXOX.............O.O...........OXOXOXOX. 1120
1110 ........X_X_XO_OXOXOX..................OXOX___OX____XOXOX__OXO........................O_OXOCOX_ 1110
1100 .......XOXOX..O.OXOX....................O.OX...OX..X.XOXO...O...........................OXO.O.. 1100
1090 ......X.....XOXOX....O.O...................O.....OXO..XOXOX.............................OX..... 1090
1080 ......XO...XOXOX..........................OXO..XOXOX..............................O...... 1080
1070 ....X.XO..X.XO.O..........................OXO..XOXO.................................... 1070
1060 ───XOXOX_XOX──────────────────────────────OXO__X8X───────────────────────────────────── 1060
1050 ...XOXOXOXO..............................OXO..XOX.................................... 1050
1040 ....XO.OXO...............................OXOX.XO.................................... 1040
1030 X.X.X..O2................................OXOXOX..................................... 1030
1020 XOXOX..O.................................O.OXOX.................................... 1020
1010 XOXO──────────────────────────────────────OXOX──────────────────────────────────────── 1010
1000 10.......................................OXOX..................................... 1000
 990 .........................................OXOX..................................... 990
 980 .........................................OXOX..................................... 980
 970 .........................................OXO..................................... 970
 960 ─────────────────────────────────────────OX───────────────────────────────────────── 960
 950 ─────────────────────────────────────────O──────────────────────────────────────── 950
```

Analysis of trading RB.L	
Minimum Reversal	2
Scale Type	Standard
Start Date	2002-01-01
End Date	2003-02-01
Strategy	S2iSSoSST12
Gross P&L	346
Trades	28
Stops hit	7

Chart 3.19 – Swing trading, Man [EMG.L]

```
EMG.L / 2 box rev, std2/ 2002.01.02 to 2002.10.02
1425 ─────────────────────────────────────────────────────────────────────────────────────────────── 1425
1400 ................................................................................................. 1400
1390 ........X........................................................................................ 1390
1380 ........XOX...................................................................................... 1380
1370 ........XOXO..................................................................................... 1370
1360 ──────XOXO─────────────────────────────────────────────────────────────────────────────────── 1360
1350 ........XOXO..................................................................................... 1350
1340 ........XOXO..................................................................................... 1340
1330 ........XOXO..................................................................................... 1330
1320 ........XOXO..................................................................................... 1320
1310 ──────XOXO─────────────────────────────────────────────────────────────────────────────────── 1310
1300 ......XOXOX.X.................................................................................... 1300
1290 ....X.XOXOXOX2................................................................................... 1290
1280 ......XOXO.OXOXO................................................................................. 1280
1270 ....XOX..OXOXO.................................................................................. 1270
1260 ──────XOX__OXOXO─────────────────────────────────────────────────────────────────────────────── 1260
1250 ...X...XOX..OXOXO............................................................................... 1250
1240 ...XO..XOX..OXOXO.............................................................................. 1240
1230 .X.XOX.XOX..OXOXO....X......................................................................... 1230
1220 .XOXOXOXO..OXO.O....XO......................................................................... 1220
1210 ─XOXO_OX___O__O___XO_____X_____ 1210
1200 .XO...OX.......O....XO..............X4X.X....................................................... 1200
1190 .X....OX.......O....XO...........XOXOXOX....................................................... 1190
1180 .X...O.........O....XO...........XOXOXOXO...................................................... 1180
1170 1..............O....XO...........XOXOXOXO...................................................... 1170
1160 ──────────O__X_XO──────────────XO_OXOXO──────────────────────────────────────────────────────── 1160
1150 .................O..XOXO.........X.X..O.OXO.................................................... 1150
1140 ................O...XOX....XOX...OXO.......................................................... 1140
1130 ..............OXOXO.O......XOX....O.O........................X................................. 1130
1120 ..............O....XOX.....O......................................XO.........................X. 1120
1110 ──────────O_OX_O─────────XOX____OX──────────────────────XO_X──────────────────────XO────────── 1110
1100 ..............OX..OX.......XOX.....OXOX..............X.XOX.XO.................X...XO........... 1100
1090 ..............OX..OXO......XOX.....OXOXO.............XOXOXOXO......X.......XOX.X.XO............ 1090
1080 ..............OX..X....XO.........OXO....XOXOXO...X.X.XO....XOX9XOXO......... 1080
1070 ..............OX..OXOX.XO....X.X.......O.OXO.......XOXO.OXOX.XOXOX....X.X.XOXOXOXOX......... 1070
1060 ──────────OX__OXOXO__X_XOX_____OXOX──────────XOX__OXOXOXOXOX_X_XOXOXOXOXOXOXO___X__ 1060
1050 ..............OX..OXOXOXO..XOXOX.......OXOXO..............X...XO...OXOXOXOXOXOXOXOXO.OXOXOXOXOX.XO. 1050
1040 ..............O....OXO3OX.XOXOX.......OXOXOX..............XOX.X...OXOXO.OXOX..OXO.O.OXOXOXO. 1040
1030 ..............OX..OXO.OXOXOXO.........OXOXOXO..X..........XO7OX...OXOXO.OXOX..OXOXO...O....OXOXOXO. 1030
1020 ..............OX..OXOXO............OXOXOX..XOX........XO.OX...OXOX..O8OX..O.O...........O.OXOXO. 1020
1010 ──────────OX_OXO─────────────O_OXOX_XOXO___X__XOXO──────X_O____OXOX_O_OX──────────────OXOXOX 1010
1000 ..............OX..OX.......................OXOXOXOXOX.X.XO..XOXOX....X.........O.O...OX...........OXOXOX 1000
990 ..............OX..OX....................OXOXOXOXOXOXOXO..XOXOXO...X............OX....OXOXAX 990
980 ..............OX..OX....................OXOXOXOXOXOXOXOX...X................O...OXOXAX 980
970 ..............OX..OX.................O.OXO.O.OXOXOXOXOX.X...............O.....O_OXO 970
960 ──────────O__O─────────────OX___OXO_OXO_OXOXOXOXOX─────────────────────────O_OXO── 960
950 .................................O5....OX..OX..OXOXOXOXOX.......................OX.. 950
940 .................................O....OX..OX..O.OXOXOXOX.......................O... 940
930 ..............................O....OX..OX...O.OXOXOX.......................O.. 930
920 .................................O....OX......OXO.OX........................ 920
910 ──────────────────────────OX────────O__O_OX───────────────────────────── 910
900 ..............................O......O...................................... 900
890 ................................................................................. 890
880 ................................................................................. 880
870 ................................................................................. 870
860 ................................................................................. 860
850 ................................................................................. 850
840 ................................................................................. 840
830 ................................................................................. 830
820 ─────────────────────────────────────────────────────────────────────────────── 820
810 ─────────────────────────────────────────────────────────────────────────────── 810
```

Analysis of trading EMG.L	
Minimum Reversal	2
Scale Type	Standard
Start Date	2002-01-01
End Date	2003-02-01
Strategy	S2iSSoSST12
Gross P&L	345
Trades	41
Stops hit	8

Chart 3.20 – Swing trading, Boots [BOOT.L]

```
BOOT.L / 2 box rev, std2/ 2002.01.02 to 2003.01.21
740 ...............................................................................................|....... 740
730 .....................................X.X...........................................................|....... 730
720 .....................................XOXO..........................................................|....... 720
710 _____XOXO_____ 710
700 .....................................XOXOX.........................................................|....... 700
690 .....................................X.X5.OXOX.....................................................|....... 690
680 .....................................X.XOX..OXO6O..................................................|....... 680
670 .....................................XO4OX..O.O.O..................................................|....... 670
660 _____XO_O_____O_____X_____ 660
650 ........X.X.X.X.X.X...X.........O......X.XO........................................................|....... 650
640 ........XOXOX2XOXOX3..X.........OX.X.X.X7XO.......................................................|....... 640
630 ........XO.O.OXOXO.OX.X.........OXOXOXOXOXO........................................................|....... 630
620 ........X....O.OX..OXOX.........O.OXOXOXO.O........................................................|....... 620
610 _____X_X_____O___O_O_____O_O_O___OX_____X_____X_____ 610
600 .X.X.X.XOX....................................OXO...........XOX.............X...BOX.X........X......|....... 600
595 .XOXOXOXO...................................................OXO............XOX....X.XOX.XOXOXO.......XO....X.X..... 595
590 1.O.OXO....................................OXO...........XOXO...........XOXOXOXOXOXOXO.......XO....X.1OXO..... 590
585 ...OX.....................................OXO...X.....X.XOXO....................OXOXO.OXOXOXOX...X.X.XO...XOXOXO..... 585
580 ___OX_____OXOX_XOX_____XOXOXO_____XOX__O_OXOXOXOX_XOXOXO____XOXOXOX 580
575 ...O.....................................OXOXOXOX8...XOXOXOXO...............XO....OXOXOXOXOXOCOXOX.X.XOXOXOXO... 575
570 .........................................OXOXOXOXOX.X.XOXOXOXO...X.........X.....OXOXOXOXOXO.OXOXOXOXOXOXOXO... 570
565 .........................................OXOXOXOXOXOXOXOXOXOXO..X.XOX.........X...O.O.O.O.O...OXOXOXOXOXOXOXOX.. 565
560 .........................................O.OXOXOXOXOXO.O.O.OXO..XOXOXO........X.........OXOXOXOXOXO.OXOX 560
555 _____O_OXOXOXOX_____OXOX_XOXOXO____X____X_____O_O_OXOXO_O___OXOX 555
550 .........................................OXOXOXOX......OXOXOXO.OXO...XA..X.X....................OXOX.|....O.OX 550
545 .........................................OXOXOXOX......OXOXOX...O.O...XOX.XOX........................O.O..|.....OX 545
540 .........................................OXOXOXOX......OXOXOX...O...XOXOXOX..........................|....OX 540
535 .........................................OXO.O.O......OXOXOX...O..XOXOXOX...........................|....OX 535
530 _____O_____O_OXO____O___XOXOXOX_____O 530
525 .................................................OX...OX.O...XO.O.O.................................|....... 525
520 .................................................O9.....O..X.X.....................................|....... 520
515 .................................................O.....O..XOX......................................|....... 515
510 .................................................OX.XOX............................................|....... 510
505 _____OXOXOX_____ 505
500 .................................................OXOXOX............................................|....... 500
495 .................................................OXOXO.............................................|....... 495
490 .................................................OXOX..............................................|....... 490
485 .................................................OXO...............................................|....... 485
480 _____OX_____ 480
475 .................................................OX...............................................|....... 475
470 .................................................OX...............................................|....... 470
465 .................................................OX...............................................|....... 465
460 .................................................OX...............................................|....... 460
455 _____O_____ 455
450 --------------------------------------------------------------------------------------O-------  450
445 --------------------------------------------------------------------------------------3-------  445
```

Analysis of trading BOOT.L	
Minimum Reversal	2
Scale Type	Standard
Start Date	2002-01-01
End Date	2003-02-01
Strategy	S2iSSoSST12
Gross P&L	335
Trades	21
Stops hit	5

Chart 3.21 – Swing trading Imperial Tobacco [IMT.L]

```
IMT.L / 2 box rev, std2/ 2002.01.02 to 2003.01.31
1180 ..................................................................X.....................................................?.............. 1180
1170 ..................................................................XO......................................................|............. 1170
1160 ...................................X_X........................XO_____|............. 1160
1150 ...................................X6XO.......................XO......................................................|............. 1150
1140 ...................................XO.O.......................XO......................................................|............. 1140
1130 ...................................X..O...X...................XO......................................................|............. 1130
1120 ...................................X..O...XOX.................X...XO..................................................|............. 1120
1110 ...................................X_O____XOXO_____XOX_X_XO_____|............. 1110
1100 .....................................X.X..OX...XO.O...........X.....XOXOXO............................................|............. 1100
1090 .....................................XOX..OXO..X..O...........XOX.X.XOXOXOXO..........................................|............. 1090
1080 .....................................XOX..OXO..7..O...........XOXOX9XOXOXOXO..........................................X............. 1080
1070 .....................................XO...O.O..X..O...........X.XOXOXOXO.OXOXO........................................10........... 1070
1060 ...........................X_____X_____O_X_O_____XOXOXOXO___OXOXOX_____XO_____ 1060
1050 .............................XO...X......OX.X..O.............XOXOXO....O.OXOXO......................X.......X.XOX......... 1050
1040 .............................XO...X......OXOX..O....X.X.X.XO.OX......OXOXO.....................XO....X.XOXOXO.......... 1040
1030 .............................XOX.X.X......O.OX..O....XOXOXOX..OX......OXO.O...................XO...XOXOXOXO..X........ 1030
1020 .............................XOXOXOX.......OX..O...XOX.X..O...OX.X.X...X.X...X....XO.....XO.O|OXOX.XO...... 1020
1010 _____X____XO_O_O_____O__O_____XOXOXO___O_____OXAXOXO_XOXO_BO_X_XO_____X____OXOXOXO_____ 1010
1000 .................XO...X.:............O...X.XOXOX.................OXOXOXOX.XOXO..XOX.XOXO......X...|O.O.O.O.... 1000
 990 .................XO...X..............O...X8XOXO...............O.OXOXOXOXO.OX.XOXOXOXO..X.X.X..|.....O........ 990
 980 .................XOX...5.............O....XOXO...............OXOXOXOX..OXOXOXOXO.O..XOXOX...|......O........ 980
 970 ...............X..XOXOX.X............O...XO.................O.OXOXOX..OXOXO.O..OX.XO.O...|.....O......... 970
 960 .........X4X_XOXOXOX_____OX__X_____OXOXOX_O_O____OXOX_____O_____ 960
 950 ...........X.XOXOXOXOXOX..........OXO..X..............:.:..OXOXO........OXOX......|.....O........ 950
 940 ...........XOXOXO.O.OXO..........OXO..X.............O.OX...........OXOX......|....OX....... 940
 930 ...........XO.OX..O..............OXO..X.............O......O......O.OX.......|....OX....... 930
 920 ...........X..OX................OXO..X....................................OC.......|....OX....... 920
 910 _____X___O_____OXOX_X_____O_____OX_____ 910
 900 .:...........X...................O.OXOX.........................................|.....O........ 900
 890 .............X...................OXOX.............................................|.....O........ 890
 880 .............X...................O.OX.............................................|.....O........ 880
 870 .............X.X.................OX...............................................|.....O........ 870
 860 .......XOX....................OX.................................................. 860
 850 .........XOX......................,..............OX.............................|......O........ 850
 840 .........XO......................O...............................................|......O........ 840
 830 ...........X....                ..............................................|......O........ 830
 820 .............X................................................................|................. 820
 810 _____X_____ 810
 800 .......X..X..................................................................|................. 800
 790 ...X.X.XO3.X................................................................|................. 790
 780 ..X.XOXOXOX..............................................................|................. 780
 770 X.XOXO.OXOXOX..............................................................|................. 770
 760 XOXO___O2O_OX_____ 760
 750 10...O..O...............................................................?........ 750
 740 -----------------------------------------------------------------------0------------ 740
 730 -----------------------------------------------------------------------3------------ 730
```

Analysis of trading IMT.L	
Minimum Reversal	2
Scale Type	Standard
Start Date	2002-01-01
End Date	2003-02-01
Strategy	S2iSSoSST12
Gross P&L	312
Trades	26
Stops hit	6

Chart 3.22 – Swing trade Glaxo Holdings [GSK.L]

```
GSK.L / 2 box rev, std2/ 2002.01.02 to 2003.01.31
1850  .....X.....X...................................................................................|............. 1850
1825  .....XO.....XO.................................................................................|............. 1825
1800  __ X XO__  XOX.................................................................................             1800
1775  ...XOXO....XOXO..X.X...........................................................................             1775
1750  .X.XOXOX.X.XO.OX.XOXO..........................................................................|............. 1750
1725  .XOXOXOXOXOX..OX3XOXO..........................................................................|............. 1725
1700  1.O.OXOXOXOX..OXOXOXOX...X.X...................................................................             1700
1675  ___OXO_OXOX__OXO_O_OXOX_XOXOX_X _____             1675
1650  ....O...O2OX..O.....OXO4OXOXOXOXO..............................................................             1650
1625  .......O.O.........OXO.OXO.OXOXO...............................................................             1625
1600  ...................O..O..O5O.O.................................................................             1600
1575  .....................O...O.....................................................................|............. 1575
1550  ....................O.........................................................................  1550
1525  ...................O..........................................................................  1525
1500  .................OX...........................................................................  1500
1475  ................OXO...........................................................................  1475
1450  .............................................................................................  1450
1425  ................O.........X...................................................................  1425
1400  ................OX..X.X...X7...............................X..................................  1400
1390  ...............OXOX.XOXO..XO.........X...................X...XO................................  1390
1380  ...............OXOXOXOXOX.XO............XO..X...........XO..XOX................................  1380
1370  ...............OXOXOXOXOXO.......XO...XOX.....XO..XOX....XO..XOX...............................  1370
1360  ...............6XOXOXOXOXOXUX_X_____XO_XOXO_____XO__XOXO_____  1360
1350  ...............OXOXOXO.OXOXOXOXO......XOX.XOXO.......X..XO..XOXO..X............................  1350
1340  ...............OXOXOX..OXOXOXOXO......XOXOXOXO.......XO..XO.XOXO.XO............................  1340
1330  ...............OXOXOX..OXOXOXOXO......XOXOXOXO.......XO..XO..XO.OX.XO..........................  1330
1320  ...............OXOXO...O.O.OXO..O.....XOXOXOXO.......XOXO..X..OXOXO............................  1320
1310  ...............OXO_____OX_O_____XOXOXO_O_____XO_XO__X__OXOXO_____  1310
1300  ......................O.....O........XOXOX..O.......XO..XOX.X..................................  1300
1290  ......................O.....X.X.X.XO.OX..O...X..XO..XOXOX..OXO.................................  1290
1280  .....................OXO..X8XOX..OX..O...XOX.XOX.XOXOX..OXOX...X...............................  1280
1270  .....................O..XOXOX..OX..O...XOXOXOXOXOXOXOX..OXOXO....XO.........X...................  1270
1260  _____OXO__XOXOX__O__O____XOXOXOXOXO_OX_OXOXOX_X_XOX_____XO_____  1260
1250  .....................OXO..XOXOX.....XO.OXOXOXOX..OX..OXOXOXOXOXO...........|.XO........:........  1250
1240  .....................OXO..XOXOX....OX9..XOXOXOXO..OX..OXOXOXOXOXO..........|.XOX...............  1240
1230  .....................OXO..XOXOX....OXO..XOXOXOXO..O...OXOXOXO.OXO.O........|..XOXO.............  1230
1220  .....................OXO..XOXOX....OXO..XOXOXOXO..O...OXOXOX..OX..OX.......X.XO.O..............  1220
1210  .....................OXOX_XOXOX_____O_OXOXOXOXOXOA_____O_OXO___O__OCOX_____XOX_O_____  1210
1200  .....................OXOXOXOXO.........OXOXOXOXOXO.........OX....O.OXO....10X..O...............  1200
1190  .....................O.OXOXO..........OXOXOXOXOX.........B.........OXOX...XOX..O...............  1190
1180  .....................OXOX............OXO.O.OXOX..............OXOXO...XO...O.....................  1180
1170  .....................OXOX..X..OXOX....................OXOXO....X...O......O....................  1170
1160  .....................OXOX........OX...OXOX...........OXOXOX X X...OX X..........................  1160
1150  .....................OXOX.........O....OXOX.............O.OXOXOXOX...OXOX......................  1150
1140  .....................OXOX............OXOX...............O.OXOXOX...OXOX........................  1140
1130  .....................OXOX............OXOX...............OXOXOX...O.OX.........................  1130
1120  .....................OXOX............OXOX...............OXOXO|.....OX.........................  1120
1110  .....................OXOX........OXO..O_O.......OX.........................  1110
1100  .....................OXOX............O...............................|...OX.....................  1100
1090  .....................OXOX...........................................|...OX.....................  1090
1080  .....................OXOX...........................................|...OX.....................  1080
1070  .....................OXOX...........................................|...OX.....................  1070
1060  .....................OXOX...................................OX....OX.....................  1060
1050  .....................O.OX...........................................|...OX.....................  1050
1040  .....................OX.............................................|...OX.....................  1040
1030  .....................OX..........................................O....................  1030
1020  .....................OX.............................................|...O......................  1020
1010  .....................OX.........................................................             1010
1000  ....................O.........................................................7..............  1000
990   ---------------------------------------------------------------------0-------------  990
980   ---------------------------------------------------------------------]-----------  980
```

Analysis of trading GSK.L	
Minimum Reversal	2
Scale Type	Standard
Start Date	2002-01-01
End Date	2003-02-01
Strategy	S2iSSoSST12
Gross P&L	311
Trades	30
Stops hit	9

The tests or simulations described on the preceding pages were carried out on our proprietary software. For input data, we used the time series from the records: date, open, high, low, close and volume. We tell the computer which strategy to use and the computer starts charting. As soon as it finds a signal, a paper trade is carried out and the simulated P&L is updated. The position taking follows the 'ex-post rule', which states that a trade can only be done at a documented price level reached imperatively *after* the occurrence of the signal and not during the formation of the signal.

If you don't have proprietary software similar to our own, you can still use standard software to produce the chart and then run the 'paper trading' simulation yourself. Obviously, it makes no sense to fool yourself, so it is imperative to use real commissions and real estimates of trading prices in order to calculate realistic hypothetical returns.

Day-trading, speed trading, scalping & market making

Introduction

This chapter is about trading styles which generate a lot of transactions. The same principles apply to scalping, high-speed day-trading, and making markets. Market-making certainly raises additional considerations, like trading against one's inventory, but essentially it is trading, whereby every change in the market price matters. What we especially cover in this section is the application of point-and-figure to a trading style where the smallest oscillations of market price are considered.

This chapter is for the professional trader. We all know about the benefits of trading during the day, such as avoiding uncontrollable overnight risks. Or we know from many studies (see www.olsen.ch) that intraday data is less chaotic or trends better than end-of-day data.

In this chapter we confine ourselves to technical aspects, because we assume that the reader interested in this section knows about trading and has a professional set-up to conduct his trading business.

The most important thing to keep in mind is that we have price data which we display on a variable time-axis, exactly like in end-of-day trading. Therefore, all that is said about signals and trend lines is as valid for intraday as for end-of-day. Probably the only difference is in the way one can pyramid, because, as mentioned above, intraday trends better, and therefore *a more aggressive approach can be taken*.

An interesting observation

The only p&f chart format that is 100% complete is the one based on tick data (or time&sales). The reason is that all other formats actually condense information and occasionally omit intraday reversals. The typical open-high-low-close data ignores a great deal of price-action information; you get to know these for points, open-high-low-close, but not the way they were reached. Have there been many ups and downs during the day or was it a regular move? For this reason we would like to encourage everyone to experiment with intraday data. In most cases, however, the handling of the sheer amount of information is the primary obstacle and if you do not day trade actively, you will probably not gain much, except for the insights and experiences of having worked for a while with the purest form of a chart.

P&F and high-frequency data

In general, charting is said to be done either *end-of-day* or *intraday*. End-of-day charting involves one price set per asset each day. Intraday charting requires market data during the trading session. If we talk about *high-frequency data*, we refer to transaction per transaction data

– time&sales or such time&sales data arranged in time-high-low-close records (or data sets) covering very small time intervals, like 1 to 5 minutes.

We recommend that you start each day-trading session with a thorough study of the traditional end-of-day p&f charts in order to assess the stocks you want to trade before the opening. Resistance and support levels should be carefully studied and a strategy devised for the trading day to come.

Normally traders who use high-frequency data are professional traders. They have a real-time data feed from the exchanges or use a data provider like e-Signal that offers real-time feeds. In such a professional trading operation, which involves high speed trading based on real-time data, there are three challenges to point-and-figure charting:

1. **Integration** of the data feed with your charting software
2. **Storage** of the real-time data
3. **Access** to historical high-frequency data

We will examine each of these points later.

Does P&F combined with high-frequency data makes sense?

The answer is a strong *Yes*. We know from many theoretical studies that intraday data is the least random, therefore the best suited to technical analysis.

As with all financial tools, one has to get used to them. That is the reason we include some charts regarding intraday point-and-figure in this chapter. We have used point-and-figure over various time spans for activities like futures-scalping, stock dealing and options market-making. And the results and experiences have always been positive.

Again p&f tells you the story of the price moves and the crossings of support levels and resistance levels with a clarity that is far superior to any other system known to us. What you want to do with the story told by p&f chart depends on your trading style, which is defined by your risk tolerance, financial strength and overall strategy, like scalping, risk arbitrage, momentum trading, and so forth. But what is certain is that the p&f chart, with its low dimensionality (in other words, just a price, not a time, dimension), does give the clearest of all signals – which is crucial for an activity as fast as day-trading. You just do not have time to do interpretations. Clarity is the major advantage of point-and-figure when applied to fast trading styles.

Scaling of the intraday chart

Scaling of the intraday chart should be done with multiples of tick-sizes. The chart should be scaled so that it does not get affected by the minimum bid-ask oscillations. Therefore, we strongly suggest never to use a box size smaller than 2 ticks.

Examples of intraday charts

In the following charts, a new day is indicated with a number on a yellow background. Otherwise, they are exactly the same as the end-of-day charts shown up to this point: 3-box reversal, using the same signals. Newcomers to intraday p&f charts should note that they may suggest continuity where there is none, and that they don't give information regarding the opening or close. Looking at the Barclays chart below, it is impossible to say where it closed on Day 1 (anywhere between 347 and 360, which are the highs and lows of the column before the column which is marked with the yellow two) or where it opened on Day 2 (it could be anywhere between 348 and 355.)

Chart 3.23 – Intraday 24.01.03 - 30.01.03, Barclays [BARC.L]

```
363    . . . . . . . . . . . . . . . . . . . . . . . . . . .    363
362    . . . . . . . . . . . . . . . . . . . . . . . . . . .    362
361    _X_X_____                     361
360    .XOXO. . . . . . . . . . . . . . . . . . . . .           360
359    .XOXO. . . . . . . . . . . . . . . . . . . . .           359
358    .XOXO. . . . . . . . . . . . . . . . . . . . .           358
357    .XOXO. . . . . . . . . . . . . . . . . . . . .           357
356    _XOXO_____             356
355    .10.OX. . . . . . . . . . . . . . . . . . . .            355
354    . . . .OXO. . . . . . . . . . . . . . . . . .            354
353    . . . .OXO. . . . . . . . . . . . . . . . . .            353
352    . . . .OXO. . . . . . . . . . . . . . . . . .            352
351    _____OXO_____            351
350    . . . .OXO. . . . . . . . . . . .X. . . . . .            350
349    . . . .OXO. . . .X. . . . . . . .XO. . . . .             349
348    . . . .O2O. .X.XO. . . . . . . .XO. . . . .              348
347    . . . .O.O. .X3XO. . . . . . . .XO. . . . .              347
346    _____O__XOXO_____XO_____          346
345    . . . . . .O. .XOXO. . . . . .X.XO. . . . .              345
344    . . . . . .O. .XOXOX. . . . .XOX. . . . . .              344
343    . . . . . .O. .XOXOXO. . . .XOX. . . . . .               343
342    . . . . . .O. .XOXOXO. . . .XO. . . . . . .              342
341    _____OX_XO_OXO_____X_____                    341
340    . . . . . .OXOX. . .OXO. . . .X. . . . . . .             340
339    . . . . . .OXOX. .O.O. . . .X. . . . . . . .             339
338    . . . . . .OXOX. . . .O. . . .X. . . . . . .             338
337    . . . . . .OXOX. . . .O. .X.X. . . . . . . .             337
336    _____OXOX____O__XOX_____                   336
335    . . . . . .OXO. . . . .O. .XOX. . . . . . . .            335
334    . . . . . .OX. . . . . .O. .XOX. . . . . . . .           334
333    . . . . . .OX. . . . . .O. .XOX. . . . . . . .           333
332    . . . . . .OX. . . . . .O. .XOX. . . . . . . .           332
331    _____O_____O__XOX_____                   331
330    . . . . . . . . . . . . . .O. .XOX. . . . . . . .        330
329    . . . . . . . . . . . . . .4. .XOX. . . . . . .          329
328    . . . . . . . . . . . . . .O. .XO5. . . . . . .          328
327    . . . . . . . . . . . . . .O. .XO. . . . . . . .         327
326    _____OX_X_____                   326
325    . . . . . . . . . . . . .OXOX. . . . . . . . .           325
324    . . . . . . . . . . . . .OXOX. . . . . . . . .           324
323    . . . . . . . . . . . . .OXOX. . . . . . . . .           323
322    . . . . . . . . . . . . .OXO. . . . . . . . . .          322
321    _____O_____            321
320    . . . . . . . . . . . . . . . . . . . . . . . . .        320
319    . . . . . . . . . . . . . . . . . . . . . . . . .        319
```

Chart 3.24 – Intraday, 06.01.03-10.01.03, Vodafone [VOD.L]

```
124.25    ..........................124.25
124.00    ___X_____124.00
123.75    ...XO.....................123.75
123.50    ...XOX....................123.50
123.25    ...XOXO...................123.25
123.00    ...XOXOX.X.........X......123.00
122.75    ___XOXOXOXO_____XO_____122.75
122.50    ...XO.O.OXO........XO.....122.50
122.25    ...2....OXO........XO.....122.25
122.00    ...X....OXO.......XOX.....122.00
121.75    ...X....OXO.......XOX.....121.75
121.50    ___X____O_O_____XOX_____121.50
121.25    ...X......O.......XOX.....121.25
121.00    ...X......O.......XOX.....121.00
120.75    ...X......O.......XOX.....120.75
120.50    ...X......O.......XOX.....120.50
120.25    ___X_____O_____XOX_____120.25
120.00    ...X......O....X...XOX.....120.00
119.75    ...X......3....X4..XOX.....119.75
119.50    .X.X......OX...XO..XOX.....119.50
119.25    .XOX......OXO..XO..XOX.....119.25
119.00    _XOX_____OXO_XO__XOX_____119.00
118.75    .XOX......OXO..XO..XOX.....118.75
118.50    .XOX......O.OX.XO..XOX.....118.50
118.25    .XOX........OXOXO..XOX.....118.25
118.00    .XO.........O.OXO..XO......118.00
117.75    _X_____OXO__5_____117.75
117.50    .1............O.O..X......117.50
117.25    ...............O..X......117.25
117.00    ...............O..X......117.00
116.75    ...............O..X......116.75
116.50    _____OX_X_____116.50
116.25    ...............OXOX......116.25
116.00    ...............OXOX......116.00
115.75    ...............OXOX......115.75
115.50    ---------------O-O-------115.50
115.25    -------------------------115.25
```

In the Vodafone chart above, you can see how good the simple signals are at capturing the accelerated moves, like the up move during Day 1 and the down move during Day 2. On Day 3, where the stock showed very little intraday volatility, you can see that the signals become less useful.

153

Strategies for day-trading

In intraday charts you often see long columns of Xs or Os. Your trading strategy should be designed to get you into the position on a Simple Buy or Sell, and then get you out either after a certain number of boxes have been filled or on the first reversal.

The Vodafone intraday chart below illustrates how crucial it is to protect profits by using strategies such as taking profits on the reversal, "10 up 3 down and out" or setting profit targets. On the last day, the open (at 120) and the close of the day (at 122) are highlighted. What you can see from the chart is that trading the intraday swings, in our case 120 to 123 to 118 and back to 122, would have been highly profitable for a day-trader only if strategies were used to take profits early. These strategies were covered earlier in this chapter but opposite is a brief reminder.

Chart 3.25 – Intraday, 06.01.03-10.01.03, Vodafone [VOD.L]

```
124.25    .........................124.25
124.00    ___X_____124.00
123.75    ...XO.....................123.75
123.50    ...XOX....................123.50
123.25    ...XOXO...................123.25
123.00    ...XOXOX.X.........X......123.00
122.75    ___XOXOXOXO_____XO_____122.75
122.50    ...XO.O.OXO........XO.....122.50
122.25    ...2....OXO........XO.....122.25
122.00    ...X....OXO........XOX....122.00
121.75    ...X....OXO........XOX....121.75
121.50    ___X____O_O_____XOX____121.50
121.25    ...X.....O........XOX.....121.25
121.00    ...X.....O........XOX.....121.00
120.75    ...X.....O........XOX.....120.75
120.50    ...X.....O........XOX.....120.50
120.25    ___X_____O_____XOX_____120.25
120.00    ...X.....O....X...XOX.....120.00
119.75    ...X.....3....X4..XOX.....119.75
119.50    .X.X.....OX...XO..XOX.....119.50
119.25    .XOX.....OXO..XO..XOX.....119.25
119.00    _XOX_____OXO_XO__XOX_____119.00
118.75    .XOX.....OXO..XO..XOX.....118.75
118.50    .XOX.....O.OX.XO..XOX.....118.50
118.25    .XOX.......OXOXO..XOX.....118.25
118.00    .XO........O.OXO..XO......118.00
117.75    _X_____OXO__5_____117.75
117.50    .1...........O.O..X......117.50
117.25    ................O..X......117.25
117.00    ................O..X......117.00
116.75    ................O..X......116.75
116.50    _____OX_X_____116.50
116.25    ..............OXOX.......116.25
116.00    ..............OXOX.......116.00
115.75    ..............OXOX.......115.75
115.50    ---------------O-O--------115.50
115.25    --------------------------115.25
```

Liquidating positions

- **Target number of boxes**. Liquidating a position after a certain number of boxes have been filled is a profitable strategy. The number of boxes is best derived from statistical analysis of historic tick data or by a visual estimation. It is obvious that you should watch the stocks you want to use for day-trading over quite some time and hence you should get an understanding of where and how to take profits.

- **Reversals**. Liquidating the position on a reversal is also a very simple concept which we have already spoken about in a previous chapter. Having entered into the position, you liquidate when the first reversal occurs. You also have to try not only to exit on reversals, but also to enter into positions on the reversals. If you have fast enough access to the market and very quick reactions, then that strategy is highly profitable.

Pyramiding and day-trading

As we see large columns in intraday data more often than in end-of-day data, we can be – in a liquid asset – aggressive in pyramiding.

What we mean is that you can increase your position on each new box in the column that is filled in the direction of your position. Pyramiding in day-trading is dependent on your access to the market and the liquidity. We can only suggest that you experiment and see if you can increase and later liquidate positions fast enough. We have run aggressive pyramiding strategies in the highly liquid currency markets where they work very well.

Real-time, manual P&F

The authors once got a group of traders to use manual p&f for futures scalping. The reason for doing it manually was that the programmers were so stressed and behind schedule that they were unable to create a special program. Although the charts can become quite big (because for scalping you use box sizes of one or two ticks), the manual charting worked beautifully!

What you have to be careful of in rapid manual charting is to keep precision. In futures scalping, manual p&f worked extremely well, because it kept the traders completely focused on the price movements. This was possible because only one asset was being traded per trader (in our case stock index futures). Manual charting is, however, impossible if you try to do high-frequency trading on several assets. Or if you try to do some testing involving a series of days' worth of data. If, for instance, you divide the high-frequency data into 5 minute intervals, you get a sample size of 120 per day in a market which is open for 10 hours. That is comparable to half a year of daily data! The challenge with high-frequency data is the sheer amount of data.

155

Software challenges

Integration of the data feed with the charting software

Because professional traders usually have custom software, which is connected to electronic trading platforms, the integration of a real-time feed (RTF) is normally structured in a customized way. Point-and-figure for intense trading works so well that no effort should be spared in a professional set-up to integrate it with the trading front-end.

As all software-developers are continuously improving their products, it is possible that by the time you read this book, the three software packages we recommend will have real-time p&f ready. We have seen real-time p&f with Updata Trader 2 and can recommend the product.

Storage

From the incoming data stream the individual quotes have to be extracted and appended in real-time to the data file which is used as input for the p&f charting program. Because storage these days is so cheap, we recommend that you keep all data and establish a good historical database. Professional trading facilities alrready have such real-time databases, which can be easily linked to the p&f program.

If you do not have access to a real-time database that can be linked to your p&f program, you will probably have to buy a software package like Updata, which performs real-time point-and-figure.

Historical tick data

Most exchanges provide historical tick data or time&sales. The LSE's service is good, but quite expensive for the private user. However, this should be seen in perspective: the cost of the LSE data will be a tiny fraction of your commission costs. Eurex tick data is good and relatively cheap. Third party data – on the other hand – is expensive, but normally it is processed and therefore erroneous or suspicious prices are eliminated.

Converting the data

The time&sales data provided by the exchange has to be converted into a data series in order to feed the point-and-figure application. Because point-and-figure is flexible whether you use a range of prices or one price, you can basically just extract the time-stamp and the price from such a time&sales file, and this is by far the easiest way to go about it.

Such files are delivered each day after market close. You split the files into the individual securities, throw the ones out that you do not need, and you then need to fuse the data of the individual securities for the day into one file that covers a sequence of days. This file is then used for doing the point-and-figure.

Due to the amount of data, this conversion of the data has to be done by a program. Probably the easiest is to program an Excel macro, whereby the entire file is imported and then the desired data is copied to a new sheet. To our knowledge, there are unfortunately no standard conversion scripts that can be downloaded from the internet, as the use of historic tick data is not very widespread.

The amount of data is enormous – a typical daily file from the LSE is 25MB. The downloadable file which is delivered in a compressed format only occupies about one tenth of that space, but in order to use the data on a computer you need to decompress it. You therefore need some serious disk space.

There are also some private companies such as Olsen and TickData (see Appendix 3 on page 249) which sell historical tick data. They allow you to choose formats which consume less space, such as 1 minute or 5 minute high, low, close formats.

Summary

Point-and-figure is ideally suited for fast trading styles.

The important points in the implementation are of a technical nature, namely computers and data feeds. If you trade either as a day-trader, scalper or market-maker and you have not tried point-and-figure, you might have been missing out on significant profits.

Extending point-and-figure to other markets

Up to now, our discussion has dealt almost exclusively with the charting of stocks, especially UK and European stocks. But p&f is much broader in scope. In addition to being an exceedingly effective tool for the analysis and forecasting of stock prices, it is applicable to all types of bonds, currencies, commodities, stock options, and market indices. In fact, almost anything that shows price fluctuations can be charted, including stamps, coins, real estate and art.

The techniques for drawing Xs and Os are no different for stocks, bonds or options than they are for futures contracts. Trend lines, price objectives and the long, short and stop-loss formations are also identical.

If you know how to chart stocks using the traditional three-box reversal method, recognize signals as they evolve, calculate vertical and horizontal price objectives, and draw trend lines, you have all the skills necessary for the successful charting and trading of *any* type of investment.

To illustrate this point, on the next two pages are charts of the Gold and Oil index, which are correlated to the price movements of the underlying commodities.

Chart 3.26 – Gold Index [.XAU]

```
XAU / 3 box rev, log3/ 1988.02.01 to 2001.07.02
157 ......|....|.........|........|.....|..........|........|......|........|........|..................|.......|....  157
152 ......|....|.........|........|.....|..........|.....X..|......|........|........|..................|.......|....  152
148 ......|....|.........|........|.....|..........|...23...|......|........|........|..................|.......|....  148
143 _____X_____XO_____  143
139 ......|....|.........|........|.....|......10......|......XO...|......|........|........|..................|.......|....  139
135 ......|....X.........|........|.....|.........XOX..X..|......X6...|......|........|........|..................|.......|....  135
131 ......|....X2........|........|.....|........B.XOX4..XA..|....7.XO....|........|........|..................|.......|....  131
127 ......|...C.XO.......|........|.....|......X.X.XOX2XO..XO..|....XO1O.X..|........|........|..................|.......|....  127
124 _____XOXO__X_____XOX8XOCOXOX_XO____X_6OCOX9XO_____  124
120 ......|...XO1O..XO...|........|.....|......7OXOXO|3.056XO..|..X5XOX78OBOX.......|........|..................|....  120
116 ......|...XO|0..XO...|........|.....|.......XOXOX.|..OXOXO..|..XOXAXO.O.OX3.....|........|..................|....  116
113 ......|...X.|3..XO...|........|.....|.....X.XO.OX.|..OXO9B..|..XOXOX....1XO......|........|..................|....  113
110 ..X...|...B.|OX.80...|........|.....|.....X6X..OA.|..OX7.OX|X.30.OX....OXO....X..|........|..................|....  110
107 ___X8____X_X__4X6X9_____XOX__9X____O__OX1XOX__B_____2_OX___XA_____  107
103 X.XO..|.9AX.|05O70...|........|.....|......XOX..OX.|.....OXOXOX...|.....OX6X.XO..|........|..................|....  103
100 X5XO..X.8OX.|O.OXA...|........|.....|.......5O...OX.|.....C.O.O2...|.....4XO89XO..|........|..................|....  100
98  3060X.2470..|..OXO..|........|.....|.......X...OX.|.....|.O....|....OXOXOXO.....|........|..................|....   98
95  XO.OXBXOX...|..OXO..X|....X...|.....|.......X...O..|........|.....|....O5OXOXO.....|........|..................|....   95
92  X__9AOXOX_____O_OX_X1__X_78_____X_____O_7XO_O___X_____X_____   92
89  X..O.OXO6...|....OXOXO...3OXO..|.......|....4.X.......|........|.....|...OX..O..|...X5.......|.........XOX..|....   89
87  2....C15....|....OBOXOX.XOXOX.|.X....|XOX.........|........|.....|...O..O..|..40..X..|.........XOXO.....|....   87
84  ....O|.....|....O.OXOXOXOXOXBX.78...|XOX.........|........|.....|...O.|.XO..XOX.|.........XOAO.......|....   84
82  ......|.....|....OXOXOX4XOXOX3XOX...|3O.........|........|.....|...B..|.XO..XOXO|.....X....XO.O.|....  82
79  _____C_2_O_O6OXOXO6OXA__X_____O___XO_AOXO_____XO___X_O_____  79
77  ......|.....|.......|....5.OAC1OXO9O.|X.........|........|.....|...O..|X.XO..XOBO|....5O...X..O.|....  77
75  ......|.....|.......|.......9.O|OXO.O.|X.........|........|.....|...OX|X2XO..XOXOX.....XO...X..O.|....  75
73  ......|.....|.......|.......|OX..BX|X.........|........|.....|...OX1XO36..XOXOXO....XO...X..OX|....  73
70  ......|.....|.......|.......|45..OX1X.........|........|.....|...CXOX__OXOXO_CXOX___XO__X9X__OXOXO_____  70
68  _____O____OXO2_____CXOX__OXOXO_CXOX___XO__X9X__OXOXO_____  68
66  ......|.....|........|.......OCO.........|........|.....|...OXOX..OXOX..OXOXOX.XOX.8OX..B.OXO.....|..X.  66
64  ......|.....|........|.......|O.........|........|.....|...O.OX..7XO..OXO2OXOXOX7XO....CXO.....|..XO  64
63  ......|.....|........|.......|.........|........|.....|...O...OX...O1O.O3OXOXOX.....12OX.X..|..XO  63
61  ......|.....|........|.......|.........|........|.....|...8X....O|..O.OXOXOX......O.OXOXO.|..XO  61
59  _____OX_____O4_6_O_____3X_O6O___XO_____  59
57  ......|.....|........|.......|.........|........|.....|...OX....|.....O..........|.050.O.|X.50  57
56  ......|.....|........|.......|.........|........|.....|...OX....|............|.4...7.|3OX6  56
54  ......|.....|........|.......|.........|........|.....|...OX....|...........O.|XOXO  54
52  ......|.....|........|.......|.........|........|.....|...OX....|............OX|XOX7  52
51  _____O9_____OX1XOX__  51
49  ......|.....|........|.......|.........|........|.....|...O......|..........|...9XOXOX.  49
48  ......|.....|........|.......|.........|........|.....|........|..........|...ACOXO4.  48
47  ......|.....|........|.......|.........|........|.....|........|..........|...OX2.O..  47
45  ......|.....|........|.......|.........|........|.....|........|..........|...OX|....  45
44  _____OB_____  44
43  ------8-----9---------9---------9------9---------9--------9------9----9---------9----------9---------------0-----0-0-----  43
41  ------9-----0---------1---------2------3---------4--------5------6----7---------8----------9---------------0-------1-----  41
```

The gold index – consisting of a portfolio of gold mining companies – is charted over a long time period, and shows once again the amount of information regarding trading levels which is packed into a p&f chart. You can clearly observe long-term trends and trend reversals. You can also see that the chart is bullish, as the last signal was a buy.

Chart 3.27 – Oil Index [.HUI]

```
HUI / 3 box rev, log3/ 1996.06.04 to 2003.01.31
205  6...|.......|..............|..........|........|..............|............|.......       205
199  O                                                                                        199
194  O...|.......|..............|..........|........|..............|............|.......       194
188  OX..|.......|..............|..........|........|..............|............|.......       188
183  7X9X|.......|..............|..........|........|..............|............|.......       183
177  O8OXCX......|..............|..........|........|..............|............|.......       177
172  O_OBOX3_____         172
167  ..A.OXO.....|..............|..........|........|..............|............|.......       167
162  ....OXO.....|..............|..........|........|..............|............|.......       162
157  ....124X...A|..............|..........|........|..............|............|.......       157
153  ....O.OX6..XO..............|..........|........|..............|.......X.........1.X..      153
148  _____O5OX_XO_____X_XO_____XOX_____     148
144  ....|.O..OX9XO.............|..........|........|..............|.XOXO.........XOX.....      144
140  ....|...780XO.............|...........|........|..............|.XO6OX..X......XO.....      140
136  ....|..O.O.O.............|............|........|..............|.XO.OXOXO..X...X......      136
132  ....|......O.............|............|........|..............|.X..OXOXO..90..X......      132
128  _____O_____X_OXOXO__XO_█_____      128
124  ....|......O..X..........|............|........|..............|.X..OX7.O..XOX.X......      124
121  ....|......O..X5.........|............|........|..............|.X..OX..O..XOXOX......      121
117  ....|......B..XO.........|............|........|..............|.5..O..O..XABOC..+....      117
114  ....|......O..40.........|............|........|..............|.X......O..80XO|.+....      114
110  _____O__XO_____X_____OX_XOX__+_____      110
107  ....|......XO............|............|........|..............|.X......OXOXOX.+......      107
104  ....|......O..XO.........|............|........|..............|.X.X....OXOXO.+|......      104
101  ....|......O2..X..........|...........X..............|.40X....O.OX.+.|.......      101
98   ....|......CXOX6.....XO..|..........X..XO..........|..............|.XOX.......OX+..|......      98
95   _____OXO3O_____XO_____XOXO_____XO_____O+_____      95
92   ....|......OXO..O...X.XOX.|.....XOXO..........|..............|.X.........+....|.......      92
90   ....|......1X..O...XOXOXO.|....XOAO..........|..............|.X.X................      90
87   ....OX..7..X.XOAOXO|....XO.O..........|..............|.XOX..............       87
85   ....|......O...O..XOXO.OXO|...X..X..O........|..............|.XO3...........|.......       85
82   _____OX_XOX__OBO____5O__X__OX_____XO_____         82
80   ....|......|..8XOXOX..O.OX..XO..X..OXO.......|..............|.X................       80
77   ....|......|..OXOXO.....CXO..XO..X..BXOX.......|..X.........2..............       77
75   ....|......|..OXO.......OXO..XOX.X..OXOXO......|..XO......X...............       75
73   _____OX_____OXOXOXO8OX_OXO_O_____XOX__XA_X_____         73
71   _____OX_____OXOXOXO8OX_OXO_O_____XOX__XA_X_____         71
69   ....|......|..OX.......OXO2OXOXOX..1X..OX.......|..XOXOX.XOX.X............       69
67   ....|......|..OX.......O1O.OXOX9X..O2..OXO......|..XOXOX9XOXOX..............       67
65   ....|......|..OX.......O|..3X6XO..O...3XO.......|..XO6OXOXOBOX............       65
63   ....|......|..09.......|..047.....|..OXOX......|..XO.780.O.O1............       63
61   _____O_____O_____O5OXO_____X_O_____O_____         61
59   ....|......|........|............|....4.060....|.X.X............|.......       59
58   ....|......|........|............|.......O.O...|.305.........|.......       58
56   ....|......|........|............|.......7...|.XOX.........|.......       56
54   ....|......|........|............|.......O...|.XOX.........|.......       54
53   _____OX_____XOX_____         53
51   ....|......|........|............|.......OXO..|.XOX.........|.......       51
50   ....|......|........|............|.......O9O..X.XOX.........|.......       50
48   ....|......|........|............|.......8.O..XOX4.........|.......       48
47   ....|......|........|............|.......O..XO2.........|.......       47
45   _____AX_XO_____         45
44   ....|......|........|............|.......OCOX............|.......       44
43   ....|......|........|............|.......OXOX............|.......       43
42   ....|......|........|............|.......OXO1............|.......       42
40   ....|......|........|............|.......OXO|............|.......       40
39   _____OX_____         39
38   ....|......|........|............|.......OX.............|.......       38
37   ....|......|........|............|.......BX.|...........|.......       37
36   ----9-------9--------------9----------0---------O--0-------------0----------------0-------   36
35   ----7-------8--------------9----------0-----------1-------------2------------------3-------   35
```

The oil index is a portfolio of oil companies. In its p&f chart you will observe a nice trendiness which tells us that it is attractive to trade. Moreover, we see that the chart is bullish (by the end of January 2003) as its last signal was a buy and as the prices are moving above a bullish support line.

Scaling for different markets

An important issue when using point-and-figure for all investments is the scaling (i.e. putting a value on the box size). It is easy to understand that a government bond has a much lower volatility than a stock and should therefore use a smaller box size. Otherwise price movements that would be relevant for a bond, would not show up in a chart scaled for stocks.

Below we list some recommended scales for: bonds, commodities and market indices. We have to insist that one has to try with different scales. We give our recommendations in the following, but again those values are indications only. In an exceptional case, like the famous attempt by the Hunt brothers to buy up all silver contracts (the 'Silver Corner') which lead to an explosion of the price, you would most probably have to adjust the scale by using a multiple of the original box size.

Table 3.2 – Scaling bonds

Bond price		Corporate	Government
from	to	(Box Size)	(Box Size)
6	14	0.02	0.01
14	29	0.05	0.02
29	60	0.1	0.05
60	140	0.2	0.1
140	290	0.5	0.2
290	600	1	0.5
600	1400	2	1

Table 3.3 – Scaling commodities

Commodity contract	Points
Corn, wheat, oats	1
Soybeans	2
Sugar	5
Crude oil	10
Cattle, hogs, bellies, cotton	20
Gasoline, NatGas, HeatOil	20
OJ, copper, coffee	50
Lumber, cocoa, soy oil	100
Palladium	50
Silver	100
Gold, platinum	2

Table 3.4 – Scaling market indexes

Index		LongTerm	MidTerm	ShortTerm
from	to	(Box Size)	(Box Size)	(Box Size)
14	29	0.5	0.2	0.1
29	60	1	0.5	0.25
60	140	2	1	0.5
140	290	5	2	1
290	600	10	5	2.5
600	1400	20	10	5
1400	2900	50	20	10
2900	6000	100	50	25
6000	14000	200	100	50
14000	29000	500	200	100
29000	60000	1000	500	250

For market indexes, the box size you use will depend on the time-span you want to cover with your chart. If you are interested in long-term charts – more than 5 years – use one scale and if you are interested in a chart covering only a few months which needs to depict smaller price moves, then you should use the box scales on the right of the table.

Summary

All markets are plotted in the same manner, except that box sizes will vary from one market to another. The scales can change depending upon the trading range of the security and its volatility.

Except for these minor cosmetic modifications, everything else remains the same. The techniques for determining trading formations, trend lines and price objectives are identical for stocks, bonds, commodity and currency futures, stock options and market indicators like the Dow Jones index family and commodity indices.

It is worth adding that the techniques which have been so successfully employed in the more conventional kinds of investment are just as applicable to works of art, stamps, coins, real estate or anything else which rises and falls in price over time.

As we have explained above, the fundamental property of point-and-figure is the *variable time-scale*, which is a terrific concept, and which can be used for all sorts of prices. Various academic studies have shown that point-and-figure is profitable for stocks and commodities. We can confirm this through our research. If you want to trade something which is not covered by this research, then hopefully you have access to some historical data so that you can figure out yourself (either with computer simulation or by trial-and-error) what sort of box size and reversal number should be applied. And if you can calculate the standard deviation of the price returns, then you should try to start with a figure we suggest in Tables 4.2 and 4.3 (pp 185-186) regarding correlations of volatilities and parameters. We show you how to do this in a later chapter.

About shorting, brokers and commissions

Shorting

In this section we briefly talk about positions. If you want, you can trade point-and-figure on the long side only, which means that you enter on a buy and liquidate on the sell. You do not have to trade short positions – entering on a sell and liquidating on the buy – and you may prefer not to, as shorting can sometimes be difficult for private investors.

However, if you want to profit from price moves in *both* directions you do have to look into the matter of shorting stocks.

In practice, due to the history of the markets, short selling of stocks is heavily regulated. This is a sensible precaution because you are selling stocks that you don't own, which, if conducted by an ignorant or dishonest investor, could damage the market.

Shorting can be done in a number of ways. As well as the traditional borrowing of stock and selling it, you can replicate short-stock positions with options, stock futures and other instruments. Other alternatives include CFDs and spread betting.

Education

If you are thinking of shorting, it is a good idea to discuss this first with your broker. Many of the online brokers have articles on their websites that explain how to short, i.e. profit from falling prices.

Bear in mind that shorting is no mystery, being simply the opposite of buying a stock, with some additional rules that have to be considered.

Choosing a broker

Choose a broker that you hear positive comments about. It is easy to open multiple trading accounts with different brokers – so open an account with a new one and try them out. The two main factors in choosing a broker are:

1. Trading costs (including commission, spreads, slippage, and tax)
2. Speed

Transaction costs

It is crucial that you compare the real transaction costs of the different alternatives. Reduction of transaction costs is very important – especially for active traders. Some brokers offer very low prices for certain contracts, such as CFDs.

If you trade cheaply, you can use p&f with parameters that generate many transactions. If your transactions costs are high, you should trade less frequently, using standard box sizes and probably 3 box reversals.

If you trade derivatives based on the chart of the underlying, we suggest that you trade with the less active parameter sets, in order that you avoid surprises due to sporadic small changes in the correlation between the derivative and the underlying in phases of high volatility. This advice applies, of course, only if you base your trading decisions on the chart of the underlying. If you chart the derivative, then you do not incur that problem.

Further references

Trade execution by brokers is a subject unto itself. For the UK investor the book by Stephen Eckett on *Online Investing* [3] is an excellent compilation of answers to frequently asked questions about the whole process of opening accounts, choosing brokers, etc. The title of the book is a bit misleading as it also answers all sorts of questions a non-online investor would have. For the other European markets no such compilation of questions and answers exists, at least to our knowledge. You could ask your broker, or the exchange themselves. Most continental exchanges have good information and educational material. We have provided a list of exchange websites in Appendix 3 on page 250.

---

[3] Stephen Eckett, *Stephen Eckett on Online Investing*, Harriman House, 2002

Tips from experienced traders

There are refinements as well as trading tips, drawn from the experiences of successful traders.

The tips are not meant to be hard and fast rules, but are simply ways in which some chartists have made the basic p&f system more applicable to their specific needs. Their use is purely optional. Adapt them to your own trading system if you wish, or totally ignore them in favour of the traditional method.

The modifications have the advantage of:

1. keeping **tighter stops**
2. **realising profits** more frequently.

But they have the disadvantage of increasing the number of trades as well as forcing more frequent changes in the open stop-loss orders held by the broker.

Take your charting seriously

Point-and-figure charting is a dynamic market technique which must be practised daily. A casual weekly review of the prior week's charts is simply not enough – the entire trend of a position can change in the span of a single day and the casual trader will never be aware of such changes.

Because of the speed of trend and signal changes, p&f charts can only serve as a useful trading tool if they are kept up to date each and every day. This is also vitally important since signals are anticipated through the placement of stop orders at the signal prices. However, since signal points change with every single reversal, the orders must be continually adjusted, and only through daily chart updating can the required adjustments be known.

Speeding up the process

Daily updating and analysing takes only a few minutes a day, but there are some tricks which will speed up the process, make it more effective, and provide better results:

- **Only analyse charts of securities or futures contracts which you are seriously considering for portfolio inclusion** and those in which you already hold a position. This sounds easy and logical, but many chartists who followed a certain position a few years ago when it was 'hot', religiously continue to maintain the chart long after the move is over, and long after concluding that they would never again trade the position.

- **Update and study your charts before the opening of the market** each day, since all signals are anticipated. It is no good learning that a buy signal will occur at 300 the day after it occurs. Prior to the market opening, your chart should contain all of the previous day's data so that you can correctly anticipate signals before they occur.

All the software products that we recommend in this book can be configured so that they collect market data after the daily close. Some even scan the charts of an entire portfolio automatically for break-outs or whatever signal you stipulate.

Keeping the size of losses to a minimum

The traditional point-and-figure technique calls for you to take a position when you receive a signal, but a variation on this approach can be used if you need to keep your immediate capital exposure small. The variation involves scanning the charts for favourable entry points where the risks are relatively small should the position be reversed and stopped out.

Example 3.8 – Limiting losses, silver

Chart 3.28 – Silver, small risk   Chart 3.29 – Silver, big risk

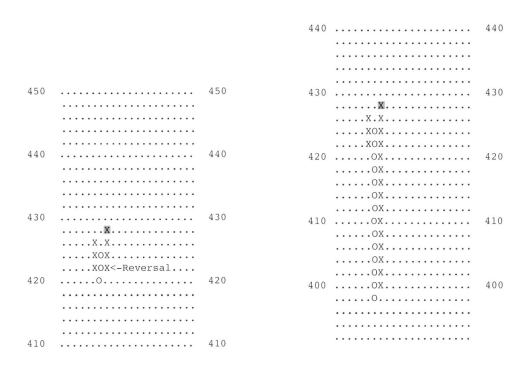

In the example above left, if silver with 200-point (2 cent) boxes and a three-box reversal chart gives a buy at 428, the minimum potential loss is the sell signal price which can never be less than five boxes away (three to create a reversal and two additional to trigger a sell). Thus the minimum loss would be 1,000 points or $500 (see chart above). But it could be considerably larger if the column of Xs was longer (see chart 3.29 on page 167), where the stop is sixteen boxes away.

Traders working with a very limited amount of capital should avoid taking a position on the original signal but instead they should attempt to take the position close to support where the risk exposure is considerably lower. This is basically waiting for a better entry point.

As a further proof of the logic of this technique, let us assume a trader has £5,000 to invest and that he is trading commodities requiring £2,500 in initial margin, or stocks selling at £25 per share. If he takes the original signals and loses £500 per trade he can sustain only five consecutive losses in a row and still remain in the market trying for the big winner. But if he takes positions close to the stop-loss point and thereby risks only £100 per trade, he can be wrong twenty-five times in a row. And we all know there are long strings of losses in trendless markets which must be absorbed while you patiently wait for the major money-making moves. Only if capital can be protected during these bad runs can a trader expect to profit in the long-run.

But this technique is not without its risks. There is the risk that the position shows a dramatic move in the direction of the breakout immediately after the signal, thus the position is never taken.

Unfortunately some chartists do what should never be done. They take the original signal but superimpose a stop within their risk parameters. For example, if the chart stop-loss point based upon taking the original signal is £1,000 away, yet they are willing to risk only £300, they take the signal but place a stop at such a level as to produce a loss of no more than the £300. There is absolutely no justification for this action, since it involves the selection of an arbitrary stop which lacks universal acceptance and thus is not self-validating. The point-and-figure system works well in the normal manner, but such modifications are not valid, have not been institutionalised into practice, and have not been optimised and, therefore, have a very limited chance of success.

Evaluating signals

Quite often a trader will find himself in a situation in which two or more different contracts are poised for signals, in which formation types, past profitability, and reliability figures are similar, and in which he must decide which one to take and which to ignore. With all major factors identical, the decision boils down to determining which has the closest stop-loss point as measured in pounds. If one has a stop £600 away, one £700 and one £1,000, the contract with the closest stop would be the one to enter on the signal.

Another common situation is that a trader will look at the three trading opportunities and say that the loss on all three is too large in relation to the size of his capital or in view of his personality makeup. If this is the case, the positions could be acquired on the pullback toward support following the initial signal or the trades could be passed completely. Hence the rule:

If the risk on a trade is too great, either pass the trade, or take a commitment only after a reversal which brings the price close to the stop-loss point and thus reduces the risk to a tolerable level.

And, as mentioned earlier, it is preferable to take a position on a positive reversal after the stop holds than closer to the stop during a move in the negative direction.

Taking profits early

Modern financial econometric analysis has shown that volatility is clustered, which simply means that after big moves you tend to get more big moves.

In the context of point-and-figure trading, this translates into the unpleasant experience of giving back open profits or, on the chart, of moving up one column and down the other because a stock or commodity moves a substantial distance after a signal with no reversal occurring during the move.

To prevent this from happening, we recommend that you establish levels at which you take open profits. Such a strategy – getting out of winners early – can significantly improve the returns on point-and-figure trading, especially in whippy markets.

As we explained in the chapter covering stop and limit orders, it is often better to take profits before an opposite signal occurs, and we showed there that you have three ways of taking profits early, namely:

1. Using the **tailing stop** at the level of the reversal

2. Using a **fixed profit target** (e.g. 12 boxes)

3. Using a **variable profit target**. (e.g. half the number of the boxes of the previous column)

We have shown the method for taking profits at the level of the reversal in a previous chapter. This method of protecting profits in a situation where a pole is formed is often called: *up 10, down 3 and out*, referring to the insertion of a trailing stop after a pole of at least 10 boxes in height is formed. The target height of 10 boxes for the pole can be altered, but should not be smaller than 2 times the reversal distance, i.e. 6 boxes. The use of such trailing stops is easy. One has just to find the hypothetical reversal level and use it as a level where profits would be realized. That's as easy as counting up to three!

Example 3.9 – Taking a profit early on a reversal in three occasions

Chart 3.30 – Profit targets, HBOS [HBOS.L]

```
HBOS.L / 3 box rev
  880   ....|................   880
  860   ....|................   860
  840   _____   840
  820   ....|................   820
  800   .B..|................   800
  780   .XOX|................   780
  760   OXOXO...............   760
  740   OXOXO_____   740
  720   OXOXO...............   720
  700   OXOXO...............   700
  680   OXO.O...............   680
  660   O...C...............   660
  640   _____1X_____X_   640
  620   ....OXO...........XO   620
  600   ....OXO..X.X.......XO   600
  590   ....O.OX.XOXO......XO   590
  580   ....|.OXOXOXO.....XO   580
  570   _____OXOXOXO_____XO   570
  560   ....|.OXOXOXOX.....XO   560
  550   ....|.O.OXOXOXO....XO   550
  540   ....|...O.OXOXO....XO   540
  530   ....|.....OXO2O....XO   530
  520   _____O_O_O__X_XO   520
  510   ....|........OX.XOXO   510
  500   ....|........OXOXOX.   500
  490   ....|........OXOXOX.   490
  480   ....|........OXOXOX.   480
  470                OXOXOX    470
```

The sequence of trades shown in the chart above is:

- Short at 510, taking a profit at 480
- A losing, or false, long at 520, covered with a loss at 450
- Simultaneously reversing the position to go short at 450, taking a profit at 440
- Long at 530, taking a profit at 590

For the use of non-trailing stops, however, one obviously needs a way to calculate or estimate the profit targets. This can be done either visually, by scrutinizing the long-term chart, trying horizontal and vertical counts, or by applying statistical methods.

We have also studied variable profit targets. We suggest an efficient though simple variable profit target, which works fine for most of the European blue-chip stocks:

Take a profit when it reaches a level equal to 1.5 times the average height of the preceding three columns.

The concept of profit targets is extended over several columns and is not only applied to a pole.

The following example illustrates early profit taking based on variable profit targets.

After a short-trade at 270 based on a Simple Sell, the variable profit target is calculated in order to introduce the stop-order enabling early profit taking.

The target is the average over three columns multiplied by 1.5, therefore being the sum of the last three column's boxes divided by three which equals 6, multiplied by 1.5 equalling 9. We keep this profit target until the nature of the chart changes – i.e. an opposite signal occurs – or until it is hit. In our example, it was hit at 180, therefore we liquidate the position with a profit and wait for the next signal, which occurs some time later, namely a buy at 240.

Example 3.10 – Profit target - variable, moving average type; at 1.5 times average preceding three columns

Chart 3.31 – Profit targets

```
360   ..........   360
350   ..........   350
340   X.X........   340
330   XOXO.......   330
320   XOXO.......   320
310   XOXO.......   310
300   XOXO.......   300
290   XOXO.......   290
280   .O.O.......   280
270   ...◼....X..   270
260   ...O....X..   260
250   ...O....X..   250
240   ...OX...X..   240
230   ...OXOX.X..   230
220   ...OXOXOX..   220
210   ...O.OXOX..   210
200   .....O.OX..   200
190   .......OX..   190
180   .......◼X..   180
170   .......OX..   170
160   .......O...   160
150   ..........   150
140   ..........   140
130   ..........   130
```

Explanation: a sell signal is generated at 270. The three preceding columns before the sell-signal average a box size of 6. The profit target is established by taking 1.5 times 6 which equals 9. Hence, the profit target is put 9 boxes below the level of the sell signal.

Example 3.11 – Profit targets, taking a profit early

Chart 3.32 – Profit target, HBOS [HBOS.L]

```
HBOS.L / 3 box rev,
 880    ....|................    880
 860    ....|................    860
 840    _____    840
 820    ....|................    820
 800    .B..|................    800
 780    .XOX|................    780
 760    OXOXO................    760
 740    OXOXO_____    740
 720    OXOXO................    720
 700    OXOXO................    700
 680    OXO.O................    680
 660    O...■................    660
 640    _____1X_____X_    640
 620    ....OXO...........XO    620
 600    ....OXO..X.X.......XO    600
 590    ....O.OX.XOXO......XO    590
 580    ....|.OXOXOXO......XO    580
 570    _____OXOXOXO_____XO    570
 560    ....|.OXOXOXOX.....XO    560
 550    ....|.O.OXOXOXO....XO    550
 540    ....|...O.OXOXO....XO    540
 530    ....|.....OXO2O....XO    530
 520    _____O_O_O__X_XO    520
 510    ....|........OX.XOXO    510
 500    ....|........OXOXOX.    500
 490    ....|........OXOXOX.    490
 480    ....|........OXOXOX.    480
 470    _____OXOXOX_    470
 460    ....|........OXO.OX.    460
 450    ....|........O...OX.    450
 440    ....|.........OX.    440
 430    ....|.........OX.    430
 420    _____OX_    420
 410    ----0------------0--    410
 400    ----0---------------    400
```

We went short at 660. We calculate the profit target, namely 1.5 times the average over the last three columns. The last three columns are highlighted. The average is 6 (the sum of 7+6+5 divided by three) multiplied by 1.5 equals 9. This target is hit nicely at 540, avoiding a liquidation through a buy at 600.

Trading the reversals

If you like to trade fast and have low trading costs, try the following: Get into the positions with the reversal, get out, either based on a set limit (i.e. 1 to 1.5 times average of last three columns to five columns) or on the next reversal.

This strategy is a very active trading strategy. You change positions every new column. The advantage is that you follow the minor swings very closely. As an example we use Shire Pharma.

Example 3.12– Getting in and out on reversals

Chart 3.33 – Shire Pharmaceuticals [SHP.L], generating profits in excess of 1200 points

```
SHP.L / 3 box rev,
 1450    ....|........X............................  1450
 1400                   XO                            1400
 1380    ....|........XO...........................  1380
 1360    ....|......X.XO...........................  1360
 1340    ....|......XOX■...........................  1340
 1320    ....|......XOXO...........................  1320
 1300              XOXO                             X 1300
 1280    ....|....X■XO....X.....................X.. X 1280
 1260    ....|......XOXO....XO..................... X 1260
 1240    ....|......XO■O....XO..................... X 1240
 1220    ....|......XOXO....XO..................... X 1220
 1200              XO_O____X■                        X 1200
 1180    ....|......X..O....XO.....X...........X.X 1180
 1160    ....|......X..O....XO......XO.........XOX 1160
 1140    ....|......X..O....XO......XO........X.XO■ 1140
 1120    ....|......X..O....XO......XO.......XOXO7 1120
 1100              X__OX_X_XO_____X■_____XOX■_ 1100
 1080    ....|......X..OXOXOXO.....XO........XOX.. 1080
 1060    ....|......3..OXOXOXO.....XO......X.X■X.. 1060
 1040    ....|......X..OXO4OXO.....XO..X..XOXOX.. 1040
 1020    ....|......X..OX■.■.O.....XOX.XO..XOXO... 1020
 1000              X__OX___O_____XOXOXOX_XOX____ 1000
  980    ....|......X..OX....OX.X...XOXOXOXOX■.....  980
  960    ....|......X..OX....OXOXO..XOXOX■XOX......  960
  940    ....|......X..OX....OXOXO..5OX■XO.OX......  940
  920    ....|....X.X..O.....OXOXO..XOXOX..■.......  920
  900              X_XOX_____OX■XO__XO_OX_____  900
  880    ....|..XOXOX........O.OXOX.X..OX..........  880
  860    ....|..XOXOX.........OXOXOX..OX..........  860
  840    ....|..XO.■X........OXOXOX..OX...........  840
  820    ....|..X■.2X.........OXOXO..O............  820
  800              X__OX_____OXOX■_____  800
  780    ....|..X..O...........OXOX................  780
  760    ....|..X..............OXOX................  760
  740    .X..|..X..............OXOX................  740
  720    .XO..|X.X.............OXOX................  720
  700    _CO__XOX_____OXO_____  700
  680    .BO..|XOX............OX..................  680
  660    .X■X|XO............O.................... 660
  640    .XOXOX■................................. 640
  620    .XOXOX..................................  620
  600    _XO_OX_____  600
  590    .X..■X.................................  590
  580    .A..O..................................  580
  570    .X..|..................................  570
  560    OX..|..................................  560
  550    OX_____  550
  540    OX..|..................................  540
  530    OX..|..................................  530
  520    O■..|..................................  520
  510    9X..|..................................  510
  500    O_____  500
  490    ....|..................................  490
  390    ....|..................................  390
  380    ....|..................................  380
  205    ----O----------------------------------  205
  200    ----O----------------------------------  200
```

The chart shows the trades produced by the strategy to simply trade the reversals. This strategy is a non-orthodox trading style which distances itself from classic point-and-figure as it ignores the formation of trading signals. For example, the Simple Buy or Sell signal is formed over three columns, whereas in trading the reversals on every column a trade takes place. It's advantage is the continuous realization of profits and its simplicity. It can be very profitable, but should be used with caution as it is very sensitive to the chosen box size.

Forget about the RSI

Many scholars of point-and-figure claim that they can improve its profitability by filtering signals based on RSI readings.

The RSI (Relative Strength Index), invented by the well-known technician J. Welles Wilder, is an oscillator defined by one variable (number-of-days), that measures the amount of daily up moves against the amount of daily down moves over a set period of time, which is usually set to 14, 10 or 5.

For example, if the time span is set to 10 days, then if the last five days had increasing closing prices (Day 10 higher than Day 9, Day 9 higher than Day 8 etc.) the RSI reading would be 100. If, on the other hand, the prices were decreasingly lower, then the RSI would be 0. And if over the 10 days the amount of the positive difference was equal to the amount of negative difference, then the RSI would be 50.

If the RSI filter did work, then false buy signals should be much more frequent where RSI indicates an over-bought situation and false-sell signals should be more frequent when the RSI shows low, over-sold readings. It would be possible to set an RSI level above which a buy signal should be ignored and a level below which a sell signal should be ignored. And using that filter, it would be possible to increase the profitability of point-and-figure.

Our rigorous statistical studies show, however, that the correlations between both false point-and-figure signals and RSI, and correct point-and-figure signals and RSI are insignificant. This means that filtering point-and-figure with RSI does not increase profitability. Based on our research we do not see any reason for combining the two. However, we do not dismiss the possibility that there could be ways of using functions of RSI readings, like differentials, in order to filter signals efficiently.

But in general, forget about the RSI.

But don't forget the big picture day-trading

If you day-trade stocks, always keep the end-of-day chart in mind. If the end-of-day chart has clearly defined channels or trend line break-throughs, keep that in mind and day-trade aggressively in the direction that the end-of-day chart indicates.

Thus, before you start your trading session, look at the end-of-day chart of the stock and define resistances, supports and direction. Then incorporate that information in your strategy for the day. Say you trade an index basket. Short heavily the stocks with bearish end-of-day charts and buy the index. Go long the stocks with bullish end-of-day charts and sell the index.

If you trade a currency on an intraday basis, then consider the long-term chart with the bigger box sizes. If the long-term chart is bullish, be more aggressive on the intraday buy signals than on the intraday sell signals.

Summary

In this chapter we have shown several modifications used by experienced traders.

Most important of all is taking the charting seriously and doing it with surgical precision. The techniques discussed involved:

1. Keeping the size of losses to a minimum by entering a position near a stop-loss price.

2. Evaluating signals by real money risks.

3. Using a reversal criterion for artificially placing a stop-loss point close to the market after a move of dramatic proportions.

4. Using price targets to liquidate profitable positions.

5. Trading the reversals.

These are just five of the techniques practised by successful chartists. They are not mandatory, but are simply ideas and suggestions which should be considered by each chartist. Those which make sense should be adopted, and those which don't, ignored.

Develop your own modifications

The list above is certainly not a comprehensive list of good ideas. After using the point-and-figure technique for a while, each chartist should modify it to fit their specific needs, desires, risk capital structure and personality. The implementation of modifications to personalize the system is half the fun of this technique. But before any modification is made, think through the logic of the change to make sure that it is in accord with the basic philosophy of support and resistance patterns, which is what p&f charts are all about.

4 New optimisation techniques

- Optimisation techniques — making the good better

- Optimisations and simulations

- Point-and-figure parameter sets for different volatilities

- Optimisation with a standard software package

- How to benefit from optimisations

Optimisation techniques — making the good better

Why optimise?

Point-and-figure charting with a reversal of 3 boxes works fine, but the question remains whether it can be made any better.

Let's be clear what we want to achieve: we want to find adjustments to the traditional p&f techniques which work with a higher profitability level in the future with a high level of confidence.

Optimisation fallacy

The one thing we want to avoid is the *optimisation fallacy*. When working with past data there is always the danger of finding trading systems that would have worked optimally in the past, but are not valid for the future.

If you optimise any trading strategy on the past data of FTSE stocks, say in the period 1995 to 2000, you will definitely come up with a parameter set that would have generated optimal results during that period. However, to be of any use, you would need to have known that parameter set in 1995! Or, put another way, for that parameter set to be of any use *in the future*, you need to test it on the 2000 to 2002 data to see if the results correlate.

Optimisation methodology

What we have to investigate first is whether optimisation is a valuable concept at all in the context of the current discussion. In order to assess that, we have carried out various analyses. What we have done first is split our data into segments of random length. Then we have run some brute-force optimisation on those segments and have used the found parameters in subsequent data.

As an example we have taken FTSE stock data for the years 1988 to 1991, optimised the parameters (box-size, minimum reversal, strategy) and used those parameters for the data 1992 to 2003. Then we have compared the result with the traditional 3 box reversal method.

We have also studied all sorts of statistical correlations between values generated by the optimisations and other statistical data regarding the stock data, like different types of volatility.

The results have been positive, and therefore we think it is worth explaining the concepts in a bit more detail.

But one thing should be clear from the start. **We mainly see the benefits of optimising for intraday applications. For end-of-day data analysis we actually prefer the traditional 3 box and standard-scaled chart.**

The familiarity of traditional parameters for end-of-day P&F

The reason we prefer the traditional parameter set for end-of-day is that the benefit from optimising is too small in comparison with the loss in familiarity with the charts. What we mean by this is that we have worked with the traditional 3 box reversal charts for such a long time that we are used to them and are able to compare different stocks and market conditions. And also, as we already know from the Davis Study, standard point-and-figure works well.

This point about familiarity will be easily understood by experienced traders or investors. In p&f charting, you want to compare different types of securities over different time spans, and so the parameters regarding minimum reversal value, box size and scaling should be the same. You cannot compare a Citigroup, logarithmic scale with 1% growth, 4 box reversal, with an HSBC, linear scale, 2 box reversal. And especially for trading arbitrage and spreads you need to compare several securities, which is best done with the 3 box reversal.

Optimisations and simulations

Overview

Optimisations and simulations are dealt with in the same chapter because they are both related to the testing of parameter sets with computers. In the optimisations we seek a set of parameters that works optimally for a given data series. In the simulation part we check whether the results calculated in the past would have worked for the data following the last data point of the data fed into the simulation.

Selection of data sets

You can run simulations on historic data or on generated data:

1. Either you take the optimised parameter set and use it on a **data sample of real historic prices**. That sample should not be included in the dataset you used to find the parameters.

2. Or you can generate **hypothetical prices** – normally via a Monte Carlo simulation – and use your parameters on those prices.

It is important to understand that optimisation and simulation have to be conducted on *different data series*; most logical is the use of successive data. For example, optimisation run on data from January 1995 to January 2000, which yields the new parameter set; simulation on the data with the new parameter set from February 2000 until February 2003.

The aim is for the simulation to be as close to the real trading as possible. Therefore, issues such as transaction costs (including commission, bid-ask spread) have to be modelled correctly.

Parameter-determination is done in the most straightforward way possible. All reasonable parameter sets are tested and their results scored. The parameter set with the best score is chosen and used in the simulation. This is only possible because point-and-figure charting is such a beautifully uncomplicated system defined by very few parameters.

The 'over-fitting' fallacy

We strongly warn against using point-and-figure in combination with other indicators, because such an approach leads to the *over-fitting fallacy*. This fallacy is best described as using different trading systems, say point-and-figure, and some oscillator or some index, and based on such a combination, creating complex trading rules, such as,

```
BUY IF point-figure buy signal AND RSI > SomeValue AND
oscillatorX < SomeOtherValue.
```

Such complex trading rules can – by tinkering with the parameters – be adapted to any past data series and generate great hypothetical profits. But again, they will not work in the real world with real data. Traders using backtesting software usually fall into this trap.

Be on your guard against authors or fund managers who claim to have improved point-and-figure by combining it with some other technical indicator. It probably won't work. The whole issue is described with lots of humour in the classic book *Fooled by Randomness*.[4]

Goal of optimisations and simulations

It is important to briefly discuss the goal of conducting optimisations and simulations.

It is indispensable for a trader to look at the charts of the securities he's trading. When we run optimisations, we basically try to find the point-and-figure chart that tells the story of the stock in the most convincing way. If you trade regularly or professionally, you know exactly what we mean. If not, let us explain. Every trader has a certain style of trading, be it risk arbitrage, scalping, day-trading or swing trading. The trader's mind gets coupled with the stock or whatever security he's trading. As a trader you will do two to three optimised charts and decide which one is closest to your own interpretation of a stock's behaviour. By trading in volume, market makers and other specialists develop an intense relationship with the product they are trading. They can use the point-and-figure efficiently, adjusting only two parameters, in order to get the best chart for their trading style. That is the essence of optimisation.

The optimised chart is a fingerprint of the stock.

Simulations give us the certainty that point-and-figure works. Not always, but with a high and constant probability. And that is the confidence we love to have when we trade. Due to the simplicity of its parameters and the ease of adjusting it to personal trading styles, we consider point-and-figure the best technical analysis tool ever used.

Parameters involved

The other beauty of p&f is the definition of the system by only two basic parameters:

1. box size
2. reversal-number

The *box size* is a function of the scaling algorithm and can be optimised further. We optimise based on three types of scaling and dozens of strategies. We leave the minimum *reversal number* close to three.

We have also worked extensively to correlate those parameters with inherent values of price data, especially *volatility*.

---

[4] Nassim Taleb, *Fooled by Randomness*, Texere 1999

The output of such optimisation runs are immense, often hundreds of printed pages. The results of all that research make it possible for us to talk with confidence about the subject.

Pole lengths

We also measure the frequency of the occurrence and the length of poles of the charts. That information helps us hammer out some strategies. The well known strategy *up 10, down 3 and out* can be geared to the expected value of the majority of poles. You can do this the most basic way by looking at the long-term chart, or the most sophisticated way by doing a Monte Carlo simulation and deriving most probable pole lengths. If you see that the majority of poles have a length of nine, then you would probably adapt the strategy to *up 9, down 3 and out*.

Strategies tested

Different trading styles exist and we try to model them with different strategies. Some traders prefer an *asymmetric approach* to entries and exits. For example, they enter on basic signal and exit on reversals/calculated stops.

Types of strategy:

- Some traders **do not enter positions on the simple buys or sells** (B1, S1). [*2 Strategies*]
- Some traders **take profits early** and get fast out of losing trades. [*4 Strategies*]
- Some traders use **reversals** to either enter into or exit positions or both. [*3 Strategies*]
- Some traders **pyramid** aggressively. [*2 Strategies*]
- Some traders **do not trade on trend line induced signals**, for some they are primordial. [*3 Strategies*]

Moreover, strategies are clearly dependant on one's cost of trading. Strategies which generate a lot of trades have normally – according to our research – a less volatile P&L. Therefore we model strategies with *different trading frequencies*. The most active strategy would be to use small box sizes and to trade every reversal. Such a strategy would generate, on average, a trade every two days. When defining strategies for day-trading, they have to be adapted to market-micro-structure limitations, such as bid-ask spreads and the estimated depth of the market.

All these different strategies are modelled by our software. The number of the resulting strategies is quite large because it represents a multiplication of the different alternatives, which are stipulated above in square brackets. For example, 2 x 4 x 3 x 2 x 3 equals 144 different strategies, however the set is reduced to 11 which have shown to be the most profitable over different time periods and instruments).

The table opposite lists the 11 strategies tested.

Table 4.1 – Strategies tested

Strategy	Description
1	Pyramiding, Entry (B1..B4,S..S4), Exit (B1..B4,S1..S4)
2	Pyramiding, Entry (B2..B4,S2..S4), Exit (B2..B4,S2..S4)
3	Pyramiding, Entry (B2..B4,S2..S4), Exit (B2..B4,S2..S4) and big Variable Price Target
4	Pyramiding, Entry (B2..B4,S2..S4), Exit (B2..B4,S2..S4) and small Variable Price Target
5	Pyramiding, Entry (B2..B4,S2..S4), Exit (B2..B4,S2..S4) and Trailing Stop
6	Pyramiding, Entry (B2..B4,S2..S4), Exit (B2..B4,S2..S4), big Variable Price Target and on Pole Trailing Stop
7	Pyramiding, Entry (B2..B4,S2..S4), Exit (B2..B4,S2..S4), small Variable Price Target and on Pole Trailing Stop
8	Pyramiding, Entry (B2..B4,S2..S4), Exit (B2..B4,S2..S4) and Reversal
9	Trade inside Trend-Channels (Parallel trend lines)
10	Trade Reversals, Exit also on Profit Target
11	Trade Reversals and Trend lines

Optimisations

As mentioned above, we use the brute force approach. We test all reasonable box size, reversal-distance, scaling and strategy combinations and rank them. The ranking can be done in many different ways, but here as well, we prefer simplicity. We like:

1. a good P&L
2. stable parameters
3. a minimum number of trades

We do not like parameter combinations that have made all the profits with just very few trades. Based on our experience we know that they usually do not perform in the simulations.

How to avoid over-fitting

In order to avoid the over-fitting of the data, we distil from the optimisation results a few parameter sets and strategies only, namely the parameter sets that work for the greatest amount of securities in a group. Such a group could be FTSE high beta stocks, FTSE low beta stocks, EURO stocks with a high average volatility, AA-bonds and so forth.

We do not optimise parameters for a single stock or security, so we avoid over-fitting.

Once again, over-fitting is the result of testing many trading rules and choosing the one which has worked best, ignoring the fact that it may have worked by pure luck. For any given stock one can use a random generator of trading strategies, test the randomly generated strategies and come up with a strategy that would have worked brilliantly in the tested data.

It is difficult to avoid that over-fitting problem. We try (as mentioned before) to alleviate it by the grouping of the data and therefore optimising over an entire portfolio and by studying the results carefully.

Simulations

During the simulation we take the parameters found in the past-data optimisation and apply them on data that is subsequent to the data used for the optimisation.

In order to study the optimised p&f approach, we shift the optimisation/simulation window from left to right, from older data to the most recent data.

It is also crucial not to change parameters too often. We recommend a cycle of not less than 1 year for end-of-day-trading and 10 days for high-frequency data.

Summary recommendations for optimising point-and-figure

We would like to summarize our recommendations for optimising point-and-figure:

1. Optimise the parameters over an entire group of securities.
2. Keep the reversal number close to three boxes.
3. Use realistic assumptions about transaction costs.
4. Use log scales for long-term simulations.
5. Simulate trading strategies that correspond to your trading style.

P&F parameter sets for different volatilities

We have studied the impact of volatilities on p&f parameters extensively. The studies showed clearly that the profitability of point-and-figure is enhanced if the parameters – scale and minimum reversal number – are adapted to the volatility of the security charted.

There are many ways to calculate volatility, but in order to make our results widely applicable, we have chosen one of the most simple methods. We calculate volatility as the annualised standard deviation of one year's price returns, calculating the returns – the differences from one day to the next in percentage points – based on the closing prices.

If you calculate this simple volatility yourself, take the closing prices of one year, calculate the change (return) from one day to the next, then calculate the standard deviation of those returns. The last step is to multiply the result with the square root of 252 trading days in order to annualise the volatility.

To recap, the standard deviation is calculated by firstly calculating the average return and secondly summing the squared differences between the average return and each individual return and thirdly to divide the sum of the squared differences by the number of days minus one.

Once you know the volatility of the underlying you are about to chart, we recommend that you use one of the suggestions found in Table 4.2 below or Table 4.3 overleaf.

If you can't adjust the scale then use Table 4.2 where different minimum reversal numbers are suggested in dependence of the volatility. If you can change the scale then use Table 4.3.

Table 4.2 – Minimum box reversal numbers

Volatility	Recommendation
Below 25%	Use 2 box reversal
Between 25% and 45%	Use standard 3 box reversal
Above 45%	Use 4 to 5 box reversal

Table 4.3 – Standard scale

Price *from*	*to*	0-10% Vol Box Size	10-20% Vol Box Size	20-50% Vol Box Size	50% + Vol Box Size
6	14	0.05	0.10	0.20	0.40
14	29	0.13	0.25	0.50	1.00
29	60	0.25	0.50	1.00	2.00
60	140	0.50	1.00	2.00	4.00
140	290	1.25	2.50	5.00	10.00
290	600	2.50	5.00	10.00	20.00
600	1400	5.00	10.00	20.00	40.00

Optimisation with a standard software package

As far as we know, no specific optimisation package for point-and-figure exists on the market. We programmed our own for that very reason, but also because we needed additional statistical functionalities for our academic studies.

If you do not have the patience to program your own specific p&f optimisation program, it is still possible to perform optimisations with the standard software packages we have already mentioned in this book. (They are listed for reference in Appendix 3 on page 249). What you would have to do is to chart your favoured stocks with different box sizes and reversal numbers.

Advice for doing your own testing:

1. First, make sure that your **data is correct** and up-to-date.
2. Choose a **limited number** of stocks and sector indices.
3. Use a **systematic approach** and write down your results. A journal of your optimisations will help you when you do the next optimisations some months later.
4. In your systematic approach, just **test a few combinations**. Consider also our volatility/parameter table.

A good start is to test reversals of 2, 3, 4 boxes and standard box sizes and half of the standard-size. That's all. Then as we mentioned above, you would choose the best combination of the two for your stock, and use the combination on subsequent data.

For example, you do your six combinations (3 reversals times 2 box sizes) on data spanning from 1996 to 2001, and then you choose the one you like most and apply it on the data from 2001 to 2003. You should also use the same parameter combination for a couple of related stocks and see whether the parameter combination works fine for the other stocks too.

Through that process you get the best combination of box size and reversal, and can then use it with confidence for your trading.

Most important of all, if you run those optimisations thoroughly you will get a good feeling for the behaviour of your tested stocks. You will see which parameters work through a quiet phase and which ones should be applied during a volatile phase. This type of information, as it becomes evident, should be written down in your journal, as it will help you to economize work on subsequent optimisations. It will also help you to adapt parameters quickly when the market climate changes.

All the software packages that we recommend allow you to do this. Sure, it is more tedious than using a specific program like we do, but it is absolutely feasible.

In the section which starts overleaf, we show charts used to visually analyse the parameters for trading BSKYB with Updata. What you have to do is to analyse the different charts in the context of your favourite trading strategy.

Example of a visual determination of an optimal parameter set

On the Updata charts you can see some filled dots, which represent the changes from one month to the next. Based on those dots it is obvious which parameter sets give frequent signals and which do not, as a chart with lots of dots is a chart that covers many months and is therefore condensing information and giving a small number of signals.

(As a quick reminder: the frequency of the signals increases – or, putting it the other way around, the compression of the price moves decreases – when the box size or the minimum-reversal numbers are decreased.)

The logarithmic scale used in the Updata example is similar to the standard scale, whereby the percentage number indicates the box size in percentage points. For example, in a 1% logarithmically-scaled p&f chart the box size is always 1%, which means that when the stock is trading at 10, the box size is 0.1, or when it is trading at 250 the box size is 2.5.

The charts shown are scaled logarithmically with a box size ranging from 1% to 3% and minimum reversal numbers from 2 to 5. What you can clearly see is that small numbers in both box size and minimum reversal number increase activity substantially.

When you do a graphic analysis of different parameter sets you first have to generate all the relevant charts and then take your time to study each of them and decide which parameter set results in a chart that you consider to represent the behaviour of the stock the optimal way. You would especially look at signal frequency and false signals.

Please note that the first four charts are bullish, the fifth is bearish – as the buy signal is not formed yet, and the last – which is very slow – is bullish again, as a preceding bearish signal was never generated.

Also, BSKYB moves quite a lot. For a less volatile stock, less compressing parameters would have to be used, like starting with a 2 box reversal with a log scale number of 0.5%.

Chart 4.1 – BSKYB [BSY.L], 2 box reversal, 1% log scaled

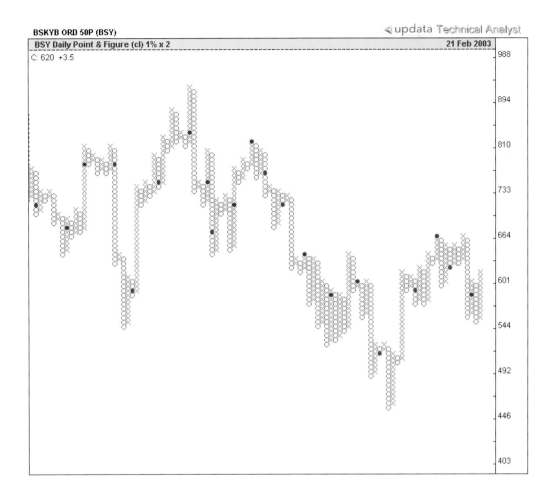

The above is too active for many investors. Small price moves generate signals. For instance, a Simple Buy could be generated by a reversal of only 18p, that is, 12p for the reversal plus 6 for the breakout.

The parameters used might, however, work better for a less volatile security, and might be acceptable to an active trader who pays low commissions.

Chart 4.2 – BSKYB [BSY.L], 3 box reversal, 1% log scaled

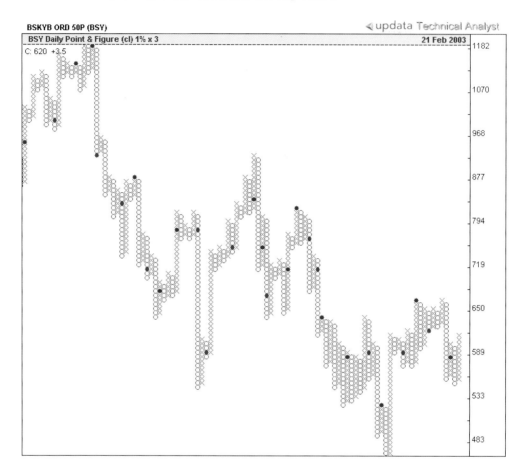

The combination 1% x 3 (3 box reversal, 1% logarithmic) is often used as a starting point, especially for stocks with a volatility in the mid-range. The resulting chart explains the price moves of BSY well and would be suited for an active investor or a stock analyst.

Chart 4.3 – BSKYB [BSY.L], 2 box reversal, 2% log scaled

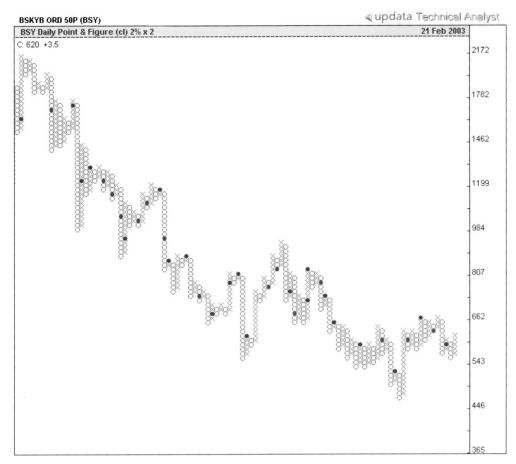

The combination 2% x 2 (2 box reversal, 2% logarithmic) is seldom used for stocks. We can see that in the above case the chart lacks some of the sharp definition of the 1% x 3 chart. This is due to the smaller minimum reversal number which allows for more frequent interruptions of a growing column. Such a combination would need a 6% move for a Simple Buy or sell signal to be generated. 6% equals 2% times 3 (2 minimum reversal plus 1 for the signal).

Chart 4.4 – BSKYB [BSY.L], 3 box reversal, 2% log scaled

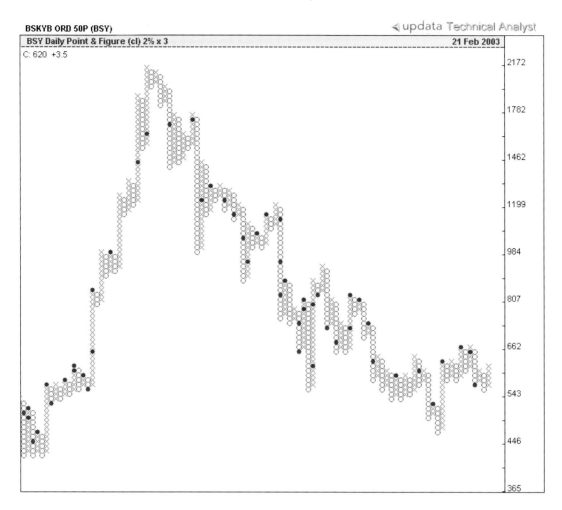

The combination 2% x 3 is classic for stocks and always a good starting point. Being 'slower' in the sense of less frequent signals or new columns, the chart compresses price information more than the former parameters and is therefore geared towards a longer investment time horizon.

Chart 4.5 – BSKYB [BSY.L], 3 box reversal, 3% log scaled

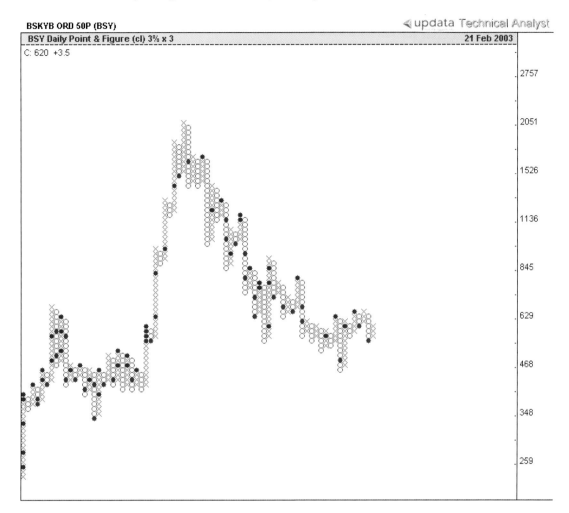

The slow combination of 3% x 3 results in a bearish chart. In contrast to the earlier charts the buy signal is not formed yet as it would need 4 more Xs to be added to the current column.

Chart 4.6 – BSKYB [BSY.L], 5 box reversal, 3% log scaled

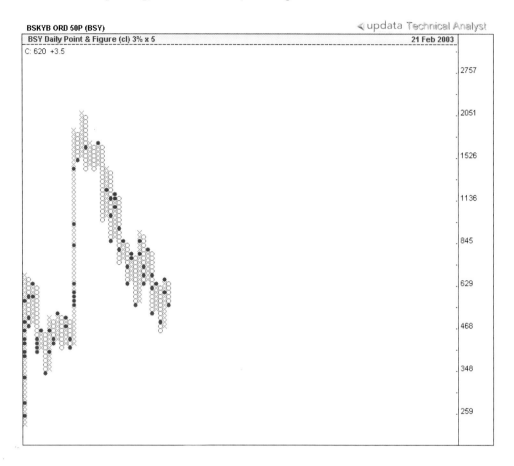

This extremely slow 3% x 5 is shown in order to give an idea of further compression of the price movements. In this chart, for example, the up-move from about 400 to about 1,800 is one single column formed over the period of 8 months. Such a slow parameter set would be used to analyse stocks over a very long time horizon.

How to benefit from optimisations

Trading ultimately comes down to making bets like –

'Is the economy going to grow or shrink?'

or

'If a war breaks out, given the political situation, should I bet on the increase of the price of some commodity?'

and so on. Optimisations tell you what sort of parameters are best in a specific market environment. **Standard three point reversal works and is the best way to chart price movements.**

If, on the other hand, you want to add bells and whistles, you can use optimised parameter sets. These parameter sets are optimised for certain market conditions. However – and this is crucial – you have to decide *when* and *which* optimised parameters to use.

This is very similar to what we experienced in many years of options trading. You can use the most sophisticated models to price options, but you have to be aware that they are parameterised, and ultimately you have to choose which model to use. At nearly every major options conference, new models for pricing some sort of options are presented. However, all these new models need input, be it the model defining the volatility, the probability distributions used or whatever.

This need for input or parameterisation means that there is never one 'best' model that exists for all. It is up to the option dealer to decide which model to apply for pricing a certain option.

Similarly, in the optimisation of point-and-figure parameters, the investor or trader has to make some fundamental choices, especially concerning which security to trade and whether that security follows a similar behaviour in the future as in the past.

We believe that the tables giving the different sets of parameters for different volatility scenarios (Tables 4.2, 4.3 on pages 185-186) are extremely useful in this respect. In order to benefit most from optimisations, you need to use common sense. Do your optimisations on reliable data and optimise over a price history that you expect to be similar to the future price history.

The point about reliable data is obvious. To illustrate the point about the price history, consider the following example: it would be wrong to use data in the period of the Iraq war to optimise point-and-figure parameters for charting and trading Crude Oil futures in the period after the war, because during the war the high amount of political, exogenous impacts to the price were untypical. Parameters found during the Iraq war should be employed during another similar highly volatile period.

Profitability analysis –
does p&f charting really work?

- Why p&f is a good trading system

- Introduction to the historical studies

- The profitability of p&f stock trading - the original research

- The profitability of p&f commodity futures trading - the original research

- Later commodity profitability research

- Profitability of p&f commodity trading 1996-1997

- Profitability of p&f stock trading 1994 -1996

- Weber-Zieg study on European stocks 1988-2002

Why P&F is a good trading system

The attributes of a good trading system are:

- ease of maintenance
- simplicity
- the ability to understand its functioning

and, of course

- profitability

Many believe that profitability is all that matters, and to some it is the only consideration. But the average trader would generally sacrifice a few percentage points of profit for the ability to fully understand the functioning of the system itself. There are many systems which perform well, but because of their complexity do not lend themselves to ready understanding. Their ingredients might include exponential weightings, non-linear relationships, probability experience factors, data smoothing, filtering algorithms, and the like. They require substantial computer capability, and few feel truly comfortable or are willing to put complete faith in a computer output, the derivation of which they only vaguely comprehend.

A good trading system must also involve the trader in the decision-making process. For, regardless of the lip service we give to satisfaction derived from the compound annual rate of capital appreciation, the thesis expressed by Adam Smith in *The Money Game* prevails – we really play for the fun as much as for the money. We must win on occasion, of course, to stay in the game. And we want to win as often as possible, for this is the measure of our skill at playing. But we need to be involved in the decision-making process if we are truly to enjoy the excitement of the game. We must feel that we are personally analysing the data, making a decision, and then entering the order. If the trade is a success, we take the credit for superior judgment and this makes the game worthwhile. If the trade turns sour, the whippy market is our scapegoat.

When a computer, programmed by another person, gives a signal and it is a success, we can take no part of the credit. This sophisticated trading game may be more profitable than a simple technique, but it certainly is not as much fun to play.

In this sense, point-and-figure charting provides the best of both worlds. It is simple to understand, costs virtually nothing to maintain, demands daily personal involvement, can serve as a scapegoat for bad trades, yields credit to the user for winning trades – and it is profitable.

Introduction to the historical studies

How well has point-and-figure charting performed over an extended period of time, and how well has it performed recently? These seem like questions for which it should be easy to obtain answers, as point-and-figure is one of the more popular charting techniques in use today. But just try to find the answer to these profitability questions! The answers are nowhere to be found.

Point-and-figure chartists have generally accepted the system on faith, and – having once accepted it – tend to follow it blindly without the need to rely upon constantly updated performance records. It seems that few empirical studies have ever been conducted.

Other than our own research and academic studies, the only historic profitability studies on p&f charting we have discovered are the research results of Robert E. Davis and Charles C. Thiel, Jr., published by Dunn and Hargitt in limited printings.

The profitability of P&F stock trading - the original research

In 1965, Davis authored *Profit and Probability*, which provided the results of an extensive test of traditional p&f techniques as applied to common stocks. The study covered two stocks for the period of 1914 through 1964, and 1,100 stocks representing all industrial groups for the period 1954-64.

In his study, Davis defined sixteen entry points – as discussed in detail on page 64. Eight of the sixteen entry points were used for closing short positions and establishing long positions; seven of the other eight formations were used for closing long positions and entering the market on the short side. Of the sixteen formations, all but the S-8, the Downside Breakout Below a Bearish Support Line, were analysed for profitability and reliability.

In this study Davis assumed that a position was taken on each appearance of a formation and the position was held until a stop was executed with a stop being defined as the first appearance of a simple signal, B-1 or S-1, on the other side. Thus regardless of what formations signalled a long position, the long would always be liquidated on the very first appearance of an S-1. Conversely, a short position would be covered on the first occurrence of a B-1.

The results of this research are interesting. For example, it was found that Ascending Triple Tops (B-4) represented 6.6% of all buy signals generated. Of the B-4s that occurred, 79.5% were profitable and 20.5% were losses. The average profit was 36.0% of the full cash investment (assuming no margin leverage) and was realized in 8.0 months. The average loss was 8.1% realized in 3.6 months.

Using the Breakout of a Triple Bottom (S-3) as an example of a short-sale formation, it was found that this formation represented 15.5% of all short-sale formations, was profitable 93.5% of the times that it occurred, and realized an average profit of 23.0% in 3.4 months. In the 6.5% of the occurrences which resulted in losses, the losses averaged 8.7% and were realized in 3.4 months.

But most importantly the often quoted frequency of occurrence of the point-and-figure signals was established in this study. We have cited the results before, but include them again:

Table 5.1 – The Davis Study: frequency of occurrence of buy and sell formations

Buys	Freq in %	Sells	Freq in %
B1	12.8	S1	13.5
B2	56.9	S2	56.4
B3	15.3	S3	15.5
B4	6.6	S4	8.4
B5	2.4	S5	1.6
B6	1.2	S6	2.6
B7	3.9	S7	1.4
B8	0.7		
	99.8		**99.4**

Davis has also published profitability numbers associated with the signals. We have looked in depth into his research and have found some questions regarding those numbers and prefer therefore not to quote them.

The profitability of P&F commodity futures trading — the original research

Upon completing this, the only comprehensive analysis of the profitability and reliability of the more complex point-and-figure formations applied to stocks, Davis's interest and research switched to commodity futures.

His next book, co-authored with Thiel, entitled *Point and Figure Commodity Trading: A Computer Evaluation,* was published in 1970. It was a brilliant research model designed to provide trading results for a variety of point-and-figure box sizes and reversal distances, in an attempt to determine the optimal box size and reversal distance for each commodity. Although the optimal box and reversal values seldom coincided with the values generally used by chartists today, the results are invaluable because for the period of 1960-69 they reveal, using two delivery months six months apart, the maximum results which would have been attained regardless of the box size or reversal distance. The returns using conventional box sizes and the standard three-box reversal value would naturally be lower, simply because this is not always the best set of rules by which to play.

The results show once again the profitability of point-and-figure: 53% of all 799 signals were profitable, and the average net profit on all trades (including both profitable and unprofitable ones) was $311 realized in an average of 49.8 days.

However, when Dr. Zieg came to the subject, he was disappointed to find that the Davis-Thiel research represented the complete universe of published research on the profitability of p&f charting. Furthermore, as good as this research was, it ended in 1969; and we as traders are interested in the here and now, in markets almost unrelated to those of the 1960s in terms of volume, volatility, and values. It was therefore imperative to continue the Davis and Davis-Thiel research and examine more modern markets.

Later commodity profitability research

In 1974, Dr. Zieg conducted his first research by analysing the profitability of commodity point-and-figure charting during late 1973 and early 1974.

Initially it seemed that all that would be necessary would be to view charts over a given period of time, assuming that a long position was taken at each buy signal, and at each sell signal the long was liquidated and a short position taken which remained in force until the next buy signal. When each position is closed and a new position of the opposite type is taken, the profit or loss on the closed trade is calculated, a commission is charged, and the results of all completed trades are added and then divided by the number of transactions.

But unfortunately the research study was not this simple.

Problems of research

1. **Trading gaps**

    Point-and-figure charts do not reveal gaps which, if occurring at a signal point, would mean that the transaction price would not coincide with the signal price, and that any analysis assuming an entry price equivalent to the signal price would bias the results in favour of the system. For example, if a potential buy signal occurred at 27.00, and if sugar had a daily high and closing price of 26.99 on one day, thus missing the signal, and opened at 27.99 the following day, all stop orders to buy at 27.00 would be filled at 27.99. Therefore, analysis based solely upon the chart and not taking into account actual trading data would show the system to be more profitable than it would actually have been. This is certainly one problem.

2. **Duration of trades**

    The next problem, and one of major interest to traders, involves the determination of the duration of the trades, meaning the length of time that each position is open. Since p&f charts are not keyed to time, making an analysis of the duration of positions from the charts themselves is impossible.

To overcome these two problems, it was necessary to computerise the *three-point reversal method of point-and-figure charting*, drawing on historic daily price data to determine realistic entry and exit points, and maintaining a file of the days of duration of each transaction.

First study

In the first study it was assumed that all entries and exits were on simple signals, B-1 and S-1. The study also assumed standard or non-optimised box values and reversal distances existing in 1974.

First study (Zieg 1974) summary

*   Analysis covered a period of only 135 trading days ending May 17, 1974.
*   During the period there were 375 signals generated in two delivery months of 22 commodities.
*   Of the 44 contract months analysed, 28 or 63.6% were profitable on a cumulative basis.
*   Of the 375 signals, 150 or 40% were profitable.
*   The average net profit after commissions per transaction was $306.48.
*   The average duration of a position was 12.4 days.
*   The total return was $114,930.71.
*   The minimum margin investment being $64,400.
*   The profit represented a 178.46% return on minimum margin (with minimum margin defined as 10% of the contract value).
*   The profit was realized in only 135 trading days, a period slightly over six months.

Second study

A second study was then conducted to review the profitability of the Simple Buy and Sell Signals using a slightly different calendar period (135 trading days ending June 28, 1974), 23 commodities, (cotton was added), and examining only one delivery month of each commodity, with the delivery month selected generally being different from those used in the earlier study. Furthermore, in this second study, like the first, no attempt was made to optimise the box sizes and reversal distances.

The results were very similar to the earlier study in terms of reliability, with the second study yielding 41% profitable trades compared with 40% in the first study. But in terms of profitability, the second study showed a 100% return on minimum margin, down from 178% earlier. The lower return on margin resulted primarily from the higher commodity prices and thus higher margins during the later period.

Third study

A third study was also undertaken to test the changes in profitability and reliability of the simple entry points by optimising the box sizes and reversal distances in a manner similar to, but more extensive than, that done by Davis and Thiel.

The contracts tested and the calendar period under review were held constant with the second study, while box sizes and reversal distances were changed to optimal values. This third study revealed that the profitability nearly doubled to 199% while the reliability increased by more than 50% to 66% meaning that two of every three trades were profitable.

The optimisation process and the resulting higher returns have been hailed by students and practitioners of the markets alike as a significant improvement in point-and-figure charting.

Table 5.2 – Summary of the 3 Zieg studies, P&F commodity trading profitability, 1974

Study	Profitability (%)	Reliability (%)	Notes
1	178	40	Non-optimised, 2 delivery months for 22 commodities
2	100	41	Non-optimised, 1 delivery month for 23 commodities
3	199	66	Optimised, [other parameters as Study 2]

Profitability of P&F commodity trading 1996-1997

To update all of the prior profitability research, several new studies were undertaken by Dr. Zieg for both commodities and stocks.

The first review dealt with commodity profitability for the 12 month period ending January 10th, 1997.

Study parameters

- Only one delivery month of each of 38 commodities including agricultural, industrial, precious metals, energy, currency, bond and index future contracts was examined.

- One contract position was established at all initial long and short signals.

- Commissions were set at $40 per round trip trade.

- Actual average initial margin rates in effect at the major discount commodity brokerage firm of Lind-Waldock was utilised to set investment capital requirements and for the calculation of return on investment.

Summary of study results

There were a total of 261 total trades during the 12 months.

- 120, or 45%, of the trades were profitable.

- The average commodity had nearly 7 trades for the year, for an average duration of 52 calendar days.

- The net profit per trade was $238.98, representing a 79% annual return on initial margin*.

* This net of $238.98 per trade is obtained after subtracting all commission costs and losses on bad or loss trades. Thus the trader made an average of $238.98 times the number of trades executed. Or stated differently, for this 12 month time period, had $78,008 in initial margin been employed, and every original B-1, B-2, S-1, and S-2 been acted upon in the one delivery month of the 38 commodities, a net profit of $62,375 would have been generated.

In all three time periods, point-and-figure trading of commodity futures contracts was extremely profitable.

The average profit per trade was $311 in 1960-69, $306 in 1974 and $239 in 1997. The reliability percentage (percentage of profitable trades to total trades) ranged from a high of 53% in 1960-69 to a low of 40% in 1974 and increased to 45% in 1997. Time duration was 49.8 days in 1960-69 and 52 days in 1997.

No matter how you view the results, it is obvious that p&f commodity trading is profitable.

Table 5.3 – Profitability analysis of commodity futures, for the 12 months ending January 10th, 1997

Commodity	Month	Total Trades	# Profitable Trades	Total Profit [1] (Loss) ($)	Margin [2] ($)	Total Return (%)	Reliability (%)
Cattle - live	apr-97	7	4	600	675	88	57
Cattle - feeder	mar-97	8	3	1,000	810	123	37
Cocoa	mar-97	12	3	(4,380)	700	-626	25
Coffee	mar-97	11	6	3,685	2,450	150	54
Copper	mar-97	6	2	1,265	1,600	78	33
Corn	mar-97	8	2	1,330	540	246	25
Cotton	mar-97	9	6	1,440	1,065	135	66
Crude Oil	mar-97	5	4	2,100	2,425	86	80
Gasoline	feb-97	4	2	(1,756)	2,425	-72	50
Gold	jun-97	1	1	6,960	1,013	687	100
Heating Oil	mar-97	7	3	(406)	2,425	-16	42
Hogs	mar-97	7	3	2,040	945	215	42
Lumber	mar-97	7	4	3,320	2,100	158	57
Natural Gas	feb-97	9	3	(930)	5,400	-17	33
Oats	mar-97	14	4	(1,060)	810	-130	28
Orange Juice	mar-97	9	3	1,440	1,275	112	33
Platinum	apr-97	1	1	1,516	1,215	124	100
Pork Bellies	mar-97	12	4	(1,420)	1,600	-88	33
Silver	mar-97	5	3	2,000	400	500	60
Soybeans	mar-97	9	3	2,540	1,350	188	33
Soybean Meal	mar-97	6	4	2,760	1,080	255	66
Soybean Oil	mar-97	10	3	(1,000)	540	185	30
Wheat	mar-97	11	5	560	1,080	51	45
Sugar - World	mar-97	12	8	24	560	4	66
T Bills	mar-97	1	1	585	550	106	100
T Bonds	mar-97	5	4	10,050	2,700	372	80
T Notes	mar-97	6	2	2,510	1,755	143	33
Muni Bonds	mar-97	4	4	3,027	2,295	131	100
S&P 500	mar-97	6	2	7,760	15,120	51	33
NYSE Composite	mar-97	9	3	(8,110)	7,800	-103	33
Australian Dollar	mar-97	5	2		1,325	0	40
British Pound	mar-97	4	3	5,715	1,900	300	75
Canadian Dollar	mar-97	5	3	2,000	675	296	60
Euro Dollar	mar-97	9	3	(2,360)	475	-496	33
German Mark	mar-97	9	3	1,265	1,350	93	33
Japanese Yen	mar-97	4	3	5,590	1,700	328	75
Mexican Peso	mar-97	2	2	4,420	4,125	107	100
Swiss Franc	mar-97	2	1	6,295	1,755	358	50
TOTAL		261	120	62,375	78,008	79	45

Average Trade Profit				238.98			
Average Trade Length		52 days					

1. Assumes commission of $40 per round trip trade
2. Average initial margin requirements existing during time period as charged by Lind-Waldock

Table 5.4 – Comparison of profitability research results for point-and-figure commodity trading techniques

Study	Time Period	No of Commodities	Holding Period (days)	Reliability (%)	Average Profit Per Trade ($)
Davis-Thiel	1960-69	15	50	53	311
Zieg	1974	22	12	40	306
Zieg	1997	38	52	45	234

Profitability of P&F stock trading 1994-1996

The next research study by Dr. Zieg involved analysing the profitability of point-and-figure trading in common stock.

First test

Study parameters

- The first evaluation covering calendar years 1994-96 examined the performance of 150 stocks selected at random for the universe on the New York Stock Exchange, American Stock Exchange and in the over-the-counter markets.

- Commission costs were set at $40 per 100 shares of stock.

- A round lot was traded at each initial signal.

Table 5.5 – Profitability analysis for randomly selected stocks, for the 3 years ending December 31st, 1996

Number of stocks analysed	150
Selection method	Random
Total number of trades	1730
Commission rate per 100 shares	$40
Total number of profitable trades (after commissions)	710
Reliability (profitable trades to total trades)	41%
Average stock price	$30.25
Average net profit per trade	$28.32
Average duration of trades	95 days
Average net profit per long position	$146.33
Reliability for long positions	52%
Average net profit (loss) per short position	($99.63)
Reliability for short positions	28%

Key points

- During the 36 months, 1730 trades were executed.

- 710, or 41%, of them were profitable.

- The average stock price was $30.25, or $3,025 per 100 shares.

- The average profit per trade was $28.32.

- Trades were open on average 95 days.

- This was only a 3% return on the invested capital.

The 1994-96 period was a very bullish time, but this first study assumed that all long and short trades were taken. Because the short sales in a rapidly rising market were big losers, the results of only taking buy (long) positions, and ignoring all short signals was examined. The results were much improved. The average net profit per long position was $146.33 or 9% annualised profit on a cash investment. Better, but still not a decent return.

The test group of 150 stocks were certainly not a real winner for this period. It seems highly unlikely that any investor or trader would randomly select such a portfolio of stocks. Hopefully, most would utilise some selection criteria to bias the portfolio toward stronger fundamental and technical issues. With this in mind, another test was undertaken.

Second test

In this new test, 20 stocks were selected at random each January from the list of 100 Value Line stocks ranked 1 (highest) for performance in the next 12 months as found in *The Value Line Investment Survey*.

The results are in the table opposite.

Results — long and short

Table 5.6 – Profitability analysis of point-and-figure charting for common stock with Value Line timely ranking 1 for the three years ending December 31, 1996

Number of stocks analysed - 20 per year	60
Selection method	Random 20 from VL ranking in January each year
Total number of trades	178
Commission rate per 100 shares	$40
Total number of profitable trades (after commissions)	82
Reliability (profitable trades to total trades)	46%
Average stock price	$24.25
Average net profit per trade	$129.10
Average duration of trades	123 days
Average annual profit per security taking all signals	$382.99
Annualized profit per security taking all signals (cash account)	15%
Average net profit per long position	$452.48
Reliability for long positions (take only long positions or out of market)	65%
Average annual profit per security	$648.55
Annualized profit per security taking only long positions (cash account)	26%

If all original long and short signals were selected for these 20 securities, the average profit per trade was $129.10 with a duration of 123 days. The average price of the selected stocks was $24.25. But this is a list of securities expected to perform well in the forthcoming year, so why go short on such potentially bullish stocks?

Results — only long

If only buy signals were selected, the average net profit per long position increased to $452.48. The average annual profit was $648.55, representing a 26% profit on a cash transaction. If 50% margin was employed, the annualised return jumps to a respectable 52%.

The selection criteria of the stocks was based on the rating by Value Line.

Third test — using support and resistance lines

An alternative strategy for the chartist is to employ the point-and-figure 45 degree support and resistance lines in addition to Simple Buy and Sell signals. Thus a study was undertaken to determine their impact on the profitability of the 150 randomly selected stock for the 3 years of 1994-96.

Using support and resistance lines makes p&f charting more complicated, but their implementation had a dramatic impact on the results. Many of the whippy or losing transactions were eliminated while keeping the trader in a winning position for the major portion of a trend.

Table 5.7 – Profitability analysis of point-and-figure charting for common stock utilizing support and resistance lines in conjunction with simple signals for the three years ending December 31, 1996

Number of stocks analysed	150
Selection method	Random
Total number of trades	1080
Commission rate per 100 shares	$40
Total number of profitable trades (after commissions)	507
Reliability (profitable trades to total trades)	47%
Average stock price	$30.25
Average net profit per trade	$261.38
Average duration of trades	152 Days
Average annual net profit per security	$627.65
Average annual net profit per security (cash account)	20%

Key points

- The results indicate that there were considerably fewer transactions (1080 versus 1730).
- Reliability (profitable trades as a percentage of total trades) increased from 41% to 47%.
- Average profit per trade showed a significant jump, increasing from $28.32 to $261.38.
- Duration of open trades increased from 95 to 152 days.
- The annualised return on an unleveraged or cash account also increased from 3% to 20%, or from 6% to 40% if a 50% margin were employed.

Fourth test — selection criteria plus trend lines

As in the third test, resistance and support lines were used. Additionally a selection criteria was introduced, namely the Value Line ranking as already explained in the second test. In comparison with the earlier tests, the results are positive, though the difference is small.

Table 5.8 – Profitability analysis for stocks with Value Line timely ranking 1 utilizing support and resistance lines in conjunction with simple signals for the 3 years ending December 31st, 1996

Number of stocks analysed	60
Selection method	Random 20 from VL ranking in January each year
Total number of trades	63
Commission rate per 100 shares	$40
Total number of profitable trades (after commissions)	37
Reliability (profitable trades to total trades)	58%
Average stock price	$24.25
Average net profit per trade	$651.36
Average duration of trades	323 Days
Average annual net profit per security	$677.41
Annualized profit per security (cash account)	27%

Weber-Zieg study on European stocks 1988-2002

When we, the authors, joined forces to run extensive studies on the European markets, we again tried to go a step further than in the previous studies. As explained in the chapter covering optimisations, we have implemented some concepts to make the tests as realistic as possible, such as optimising over entire portfolios and using subsequent data for the simulations.

We have also extended the strategies we have been analysing. We have applied the modern concepts of simulations normally used for the pricing of exotic derivative instruments. We have been looking at the influence of volatilities of the parameter sets, trying to answer the question,

'If we experience an increase of the volatility of the underlying, should we change the point-and-figure parameters?'

Summary of study results

Our studies show:

- Cyclical optimisation and simulation, as described above, is an excellent concept and it works. It clearly improves profitability.

- Distributions of signals on the European markets are different from the distributions found in the Davis Study. For example, one third of the signals are a Simple Buy or Simple Sell (B1, S1), whereas in the Davis Study they account for less then one seventh.

- The level of accuracy of the signals of recent price history of European stocks is well below the level of accuracy found in the original Davis Study.

- The performance of the parameter sets depend on the volatility of the stock or security. Davis did not take into account different levels of volatility of different stocks.

Strategies involving the early realisation of profits increase overall profitability

We have looked at the frequency of point-and-figure signals and we have examined whether they were wrong. The criteria for being wrong was established as generating the signal on the top or bottom of a column. We also checked the frequencies of the signals B1 to B4 and S1 to S4. The frequencies show to be different for the FTSE 100 stocks than for the US stock portfolio used in the Davis study.

Table 5.9 – FTSE 100 Signal Frequencies, 1988-2002

Total Signals	9,527	100%
Total False	2,715	28.50%
Total False Long	1,387	14.56%
Total False Short	1,328	13.94%
	Avg in %	*St Dev in %*
B1	34.54	7.01
B2	19.80	8.22
B3	19.80	7.24
B4	29.22	7.63
S1	35.42	7.51
S2	17.42	6.33
S3	17.54	7.64
S4	26.24	6.16

The results shown above are highly valuable and encouraging for the trader as the results clearly suggest that in more than 70% of the cases the point-and-figure signals are correct. Such a high number of accuracy has not been found – to the authors' knowledge – in any other technical trading system. Moreover, the time horizon of 15 years is very long and therefore the results are statistically relevant, which translates directly into higher confidence while applying the p&f method for your own account. The long-term analysis makes clear that a 70% chance exists to be correct entering a position based on a p&f signal.

Precise studies like the FTSE example obviously need clean price data and a fully automated process to calculate all relevant values. Such a computer-based approach was not common until the 1980s and it has to be said that the original studies of Prof. Davis still included a lot of manual work and therefore had a bigger probability of carrying errors. Today, once we have our data audited, no possible errors are imaginable. Parameters can be chosen differently, like commission rates, slippage, bid-ask spread etc. but the resulting figures will always be correct.

In order to conduct further research on the UK market, we have chosen a subset of the FTSE 100 Index as of 25 October 2002. The subset consists of the 80 stocks that have a price history of at least 6 years. Specifically the portfolio was as outlined in the table overleaf.

Table 5.10 – FTSE 100 test stocks

ABF.L	CBRY.L	JMAT.L	SDR.L
AHM.L	CPI.L	KGF.L	SDRt.L
ALLD.L	CS.L	LAND.L	SFW.L
ANL.L	CW.L	LGEN.L	SGE.L
AUN.L	DGE.L	LLOY.L	SHEL.L
AV.L	DMGOa.L	MKS.L	SHP.L
AVZ.L	DXNS.L	MRW.L	SMIN.L
AZN.L	EMG.L	NXT.L	SN.L
BA.L	EXL.L	PRU.L	SPW.L
BAA.L	GAA.L	PSON.L	SSE.L
BARC.L	GKN.L	RB.L	STAN.L
BATS.L	GSK.L	REL.L	SVT.L
BG.L	GUS.L	REX.L	SXC.L
BLND.L	HAS.L	RIO.	TOMK.L
BNZL.L	HG.L	RR.L	TSCO.L
BOC.L	HNS.L	RSA.L	ULVR.L
BOOT.L	HSBA.L	RTO.L	UU.L
BP.L	ICI.L	RTR.L	VOD.L
BSY.L	III.L	SBRY.L	WOS.L
BT.L	ISYS.L	SCTN.L	WPP.L

We have used this portfolio – which we call FTSE_6year – for several simulations. What we have seen is that:

the approach to optimise parameters repetitively increases the profitability significantly.

We have seen that over the most simple optimisation/simulation cycle, (whereby the new setting of parameters was done once a year, always January 1, and only 4 basic strategies were tested), we achieved an increase of profitability over the traditional 3 box reversal system, and a very high percentage of gainers.

The first optimisation was done over the period beginning 1995 to end 1996, and the first trading simulation – based on the parameters found during the first optimisation – was conducted on the subsequent year, 1997. Then this cycle was repeated 6 times, the last optimisation being from the beginning of 2000 to the end of 2001 and the last simulation 2002. The result was very satisfactory. In 69% of all stocks the approach worked and showed profitability. This result is very promising, because the sample size is big, calculated as 480 trading years, being 80 stocks times 6 years, and therefore the result is statistically relevant.

This optimisation was done exactly as it could be done with a standard software package.

(We continuously do optimisations/simulations on many model portfolios. Whether sectors or national markets. The detailed results of the studies will be published soon.)

The main conclusions from this most recent research are:

1. Run optimisation / simulation cycles periodically.

2. Volatility matters, however, it is taken into account with each optimisation cycle.

3. Use a portfolio of at least 3 stocks in order to reduce the risk of 31% (100% *less* 69%) that the stock does not perform.

4. Be patient during sequences of whippy trades, chances are high that the P&L of the stocks recuperate.

5. There is no better or more scientific way to improve technical analysis than to run optimisation / simulation cycles. The timing of such runs is probably a field which could be investigated in order to find optimal criteria to decide upon the timing of new optimisations.

Summary

Research period: 1914-1964

It has been shown historically for the period of 1914 through 1964 that the traditional point-and-figure charting technique is an extremely reliable and profitable method for trading stocks on both the long and short sides. Typically, over 80% of all transactions were profitable, and profits averaged in the mid-20% range. Losses were rare, occurring less than 20% of the time, were small, generally around 15%, and were realised quickly in a matter of several months.

Research period: 1961-1969

It was also shown that for the period of 1961 through 1969, using optimal values for box sizes and reversal distances, the point-and-figure technique as applied to commodities was profitable 53% of the time, the average profit per transaction was $311, and the average duration of trades was 49.8 days.

Research period: 1974

The later studies of profitability results covering a period of 135 trading days ending May 17, 1974, using non-optimised box and reversal values (the generally accepted box sizes and the three-box reversal criterion in use during the study period), showed that 40.0% of all commodity trades were profitable, trades remained open for an average of 12.4 days, the average profit per transaction was $306.48, and the net return was a healthy 178.46% earned in just over six months.

Still later, a 1974 research has revealed that while sizable commodity returns were possible by taking positions on simple signals using the non-optimised approach, even larger returns and higher reliability occurred when an optimised technique was employed.

Research period: 1997

Subsequent research for both futures and stocks show a continuation of profitability for point-and-figure trading. For the 12 months ending January 10, 1997, trading in just one delivery month of 38 commodities, 45% of all trades were profitable, the average duration was 52 days and the average per trade profit was $238.98. This represents a 79% annual return on retail brokerage initial margin requirements. These figures are very similar to those found in all of the previous research studies.

Research period: 1994-96

Stock profitability of a randomly selected portfolio for the 3 years 1994-96 showed a small annual profit of 3% on cash. When support and resistance lines were utilized in addition to Simple Buy and Sell signals, the profit increased to 20% on a cash investment. Where portfolio selection techniques were employed, such as randomly selecting stocks from the list of Value Line's most timely stocks, and only simple signals were used, the annualised profit on cash was 26% if only long positions were traded, and 15% if all signals were employed. If 50% margin was employed, the returns increased to 52% and 30% respectively.

The Davis, Davis-Thiel, and the Zieg studies covered different time spans, different securities or commodities and employed different research methodologies, but the conclusions are obvious. Point-and-figure charting is a profitable trading tool, yielding a substantial return per transaction while permitting the users the satisfaction of understanding and participating in the decision-making process.

Research period: 1988-2003

During 2003, Zieg and Weber conducted extensive studies on European stock portfolios, using volatility as the major indicator to choose parameter sets. Once again, point-and-figure was shown to be an excellent approach to orchestrate one's trading. Over a large sample size, 15 years, false trading signals averaged below 30% of the total number of signals.

The conclusion is that few, if any, trading systems are so inexpensive to maintain, require so little time to keep current, are so readily comprehensible, provide such personal satisfaction, use so little mathematics and are so profitable as point-and-figure.

Table 5.11 – Summary of major P&F research

Study	Underlying	Optimized	Profitability
Davis 1914-1964	US-Stocks	No	Excellent
Davis-Thiel 1961-1969	Commodities	Yes	Good
Zieg 1974	Commodities	No	Fair
Zieg 1994-1996	US-Stocks	No	Fair
Zieg 1997	Commodities	No	Fair
Weber-Zieg 1988-2003	UK-Stocks	Yes	Good

Technical notes

- The conflict between technical analysis and academic research

- More about scaling

- Description of the program environment used

The conflict between technical analysis and academic research

Introduction

It is common knowledge that the financial industry devotes considerable resources to the study of technical analysis. At the same time there is a respected academic theory called the *Efficient Market Theory* which rejects the entire basis of technical analysis. We would like to comment on this obvious conflict and long-standing paradox.

History of quantitative finance

Quantitative finance and financial econometrics has come a long way since its beginning. Its history could be defined by this list of groundbreaking ideas:

1938 – Macaulay: theoretical problems regarding price movements
1959 – Markowitz: portfolio selection
1965 – Fama: behaviour of stock prices
1973 – Black, Scholes, Merton: option pricing
1976 – Box-Jenkins: ARIMA models for time-series analysis
1977 – Boyle: Monte Carlo approach to value options
1986 – Bollerslev: GARCH, a forecasting method for volatilities

From 1986 onwards there has been an explosion of quantitative finance and financial econometrics. Only time will tell which theories work and will be regarded as outstanding in the future. If you want a detailed synthesis of the latest developments, we strongly recommend Paul Wilmott's book, *Paul Wilmott on Quantitative Finance.*

In quantitative finance many statistical parameters can be calculated, always based on certain assumptions. The cornerstone of the discipline is the calculation of risks based on assumed probabilities and correlations. The original ideas of *random walk* and *normally distributed stock prices* that ignited the animosity between followers of technical analysis and theoretical finance have now been replaced.

The micro-structure of markets

Today we study the micro-structure of the markets, including technical levels and micro squeezes. Volatility clustering has become an accepted feature of the behaviour of asset prices.

Volatility clustering means that after violent moves, there follow violent moves. Leptokurtosis, or so-called *fat tail behaviour,* of the return distributions are scientifically described. These concepts have been used for a long time by market technicians. They just called the phenomenon by a different name – *break-outs.* What we also know from science – behavioural economics – is that technical analysis works because a high percentage of market participants use it. The majority of traders base their daily trading decisions fully or partly on technical analysis. Technical levels are continuously scrutinized and when they break, moves get amplified and thus make them significant and therefore give a justification to technical analysis.

Today we are in a situation where technical analysis has lost its flavour of astrology and gained acceptance in the scientific world. This acceptance is highly important. The crucial problem is a certain misunderstanding between the two worlds of technical analysis and theoretical finance.

Technical analysis and subjectivity

In technical analysis we look at charts and interpret them. There is always some subjectiveness to this interpretation which is hard to model.

Mathematical finance tries to model market behaviour, calculates risks based on given return distributions, and estimates derivatives prices based on simulated asset paths. These are all excellent tasks for mathematicians. However, even the most straightforward trading systems, such as point-and-figure, are difficult to value from the perspective of mathematics.

Let us tell you why: point-and-figure is adapted by traders to individual trading styles and is used like a map in order to find the way to a location, and not like an autopilot. Mathematics, however, can only evaluate autopilots, systems that totally exclude human interaction.

Technical analysis has not been popular within the academic world. Why? Because it always included and *will* always include a lot of subjectivity. Relationships in technical analysis are far too complex to be described with calculus. Technical analysis is furthermore not based on a scientific methodology and is therefore often difficult to grasp. We are convinced, though, that quantitative or econometric finance and technical analysis are both important.

Technical analysis catalogues repeating patterns in price moves, whereas quantitative finance models the behaviour of price moves. Both have a strong *raison d'être.*

Today, the situation in a trading room is usually as follows: the trader makes his decisions based on technical analysis, incorporates obviously important fundamentals, and uses quantitative models to help value the derivative instruments that he has decided to buy. Later, the risk managers will use quantitative models to parameterise the risks the trader has taken.

We think that this explanation of the intertwining of both schools of thought makes clear that quantitative methods are not a threat to technical analysis, but complement it.

Quantitative finance

Quantitative finance, roughly speaking, started off with the model of the random walk of asset prices and the arbitrage-free world. Traders always knew that stock returns are not normally distributed and that arbitrage exists. Today, after a couple of decades of intensive research, we have seen quantitative finance maturing. The research in high-frequency data, especially, shows non-random behaviour as well as the development of the various GARCH models which demonstrate a certain predictability of the variation of returns as opposed to the concept of random walk.

Specific applications from Artificial Intelligence, so called *artificial neural networks*, being considered the state-of-art in econometrics, are used to predict future prices. Such artificial neural networks are searching for patterns in the price history of one or several financial values (stock-prices, interest-rates, economic growth etc), test those patterns on the past and once validated, use them for forecasts or trading decision support. This process which, from a global view, resembles classic technical analysis and especially the way we propose to optimise point-and-figure.

What we like in the scientific approach of quantitative analysis is that the researchers have the courage to abandon concepts which are shown to be erroneous and work on new ones. And, as in all science, the drive is towards better, more realistic, models and not towards defending an established concept.

Both technical analysis and quantitative finance have profited a lot from the decrease in the price of computing power. In quantitative finance, particularly, the calculation performance of modern computers has shifted the focus on simulations. In quantitative finance the most complicated derivatives can now be priced in simulations. Difficult stochastic integrals can be resolved the same way. Huge amounts of high-frequency data can be analysed.

But one thing always remains the same: the data input is the market data. And markets move by greed and fear, two of the most prominent characteristics of human behaviour. We know that human behaviour leads to markets which are complex chaotic systems, still very far from being modelled by even the most sophisticated calculus.

We are convinced that in the near future more and more research will give credit to technical analysis, and therefore to point-and-figure, its most aesthetic representative in our opinion. And books like this one will give it more and more credibility as well.

But again, in both schools it is important to understand what one is doing. A trader should never get carried away by backtracking software, nor should he sub-estimate the fat-tails of an asset-return-distribution.

The understanding of each others' endeavours is really crucial in order to advance this subject. Even today, it is often difficult for an engineer to understand an econometrician, as they use 'regress' and mean 'approximate', or 'error' and mean 'difference between calculation and observation'. The difficulty experienced by an engineer talking to a technical analyst is maximal. Hopefully, it will be possible to develop a common language for all people, whether practitioners or academics, interested in forecasting prices and risks.

We are also aware of the fact that so far technical analysis lacks a structured scientific approach and thus allows charlatans into its ranks, who harm the serious scholar of technical analysis. Some concepts are very helpful. Others dangerous. We urge the reader to use logical concepts such as point-and-figure. We warn the reader against systems that are a cocktail of various indicators so complex that they are impossible to understand and most importantly without a logical background. What we mean, if you take the same time series, and based on it you do all sorts of arithmetic or geometric operations (oscillators, indicators, fans, angles), you have simply over-analysed the same time series over and over again. It is then obvious that one of the myriad of combinations of technical indicators lead to a terrific past performance. However, such a combination is so closely fitted to the time series that it is not much more than stating that over the sample period it would always have been wonderful to buy before an up-move and sell before a down move. Unfortunately, in the media there are loud proponents of such a wrong and over-simplistic concept, and the result is that they harm the serious technician while making this method an easy target for scientific attacks.

We are convinced that a system using more than five parameters applied to the same data-series should be looked at very critically and most probably avoided.

We include good arguments for the use and concept of the best of all technical analysis methodologies – point-and-figure – in order to bridge a gap between quantitative finance and technical analysis. And again point-and-figure does not only work but is a mature and coherent philosophy about how to interpret price moves. Science is an art, the most progressive ideas have always sprung from creative processes. It is the same with point-and-figure, science and art.

More about scaling

Summarising what we have already explained:

•   the point-and-figure chart is drawn on a structure of squares
•   each square on the chart represents a unit of price
•   the values of the boxes change based on the price of the security being tracked

The Classic Scale

A steady evolution of the system has led to the traditional scale for US stocks, which we call the *classic scale*. The classic scale works the following way: for prices under $5.00 per share each box represents $0.25 or one quarter of a point. Between $5 and $20, each box is $0.50 or a half a point. Above $20 and below $100, a box has a one-point value, and above $100, boxes are 2 points each.

In order to develop extensions and adjustments to the original scale one needs to take a brief look into the history of point-and-figure. When you do this, it becomes clear that during the development of the system – when the majority of stocks traded between 15 and 60 dollars – the chartists did the only logical thing, namely to approximate a logarithmic scale, without complicating the charting excessively. The result is the original classic scale, as described above and shown in the table below:

Table 6.1 – the US classic scale for stocks

From		to	Box Size
0	–	5	0.25
5	–	20	0.5
20	–	100	1
100	–	>100	2

The scaling for the early point-and-figure traders was finding the balance between mathematical robustness and fast calculability. The same principle is applied in order to produce a similar staggered scale as the original scale for stocks and stock indices trading between 0.50 (an unfortunate Dotcom) and 40,000 (a Nikkei during its glory days). We call this *standard scaling*.

We have also seen that classical US box sizes work well for Continental European stocks, denominated in Euros. UK stocks which trade in the hundreds of pence can be – however cumbersome – scaled with the same scale, box sizes being simply adjusted by a division. This means that for manual charting one can simply divide the UK price in pence by ten and use the US scale. In this manner you would treat a 615p stock like a $61.5 stock, therefore transforming the $1 box into a 10p box. Then, just to make the point clear, if the stock fell to 150p you would use a 5p box size as the US system implies 50 cents a point.

Logarithmic point-and-figure charts

The idea of using smaller box sizes for prices in lower ranges and bigger boxes for prices in higher ranges is correct and logical. But any scaling system that is different from a real logarithmic scale has arbitrarily chosen levels where box sizes change, box sizes which are not proportional and generate therefore discontinuities. This is best described by the following example, based on the US scale.

A stock which trades in the range of $21 to $25 has box sizes of about 5% in contrast to a stock that trades in the $95 range which has a box size of about 1%. The three box reversal of the $21 stock would need a move of 15%, whereas the reversal for the $95 stock would need only a 3% move. In order to resolve that problem, mathematically correct logarithmic scaling was introduced. Nowadays, thanks to computer technology, it is easy to produce logarithmic scaled charts, and because the technique is so simple and accurate, most analysts use them. In the logarithmic p&f chart the reversals are always defined by the same percentage move, irrespective of the actual price level of the stock.

Modifying box-sizes

Last but not least, you can modify box sizes to cater for different levels of volatility or different types of securities. We have done a lot of research on the subject of scaling p&f charts and we are confident about our recommendations. One could obviously complicate the issue of scaling a lot. But what we want to present in this book are the results of our research and experience in the most comprehensive and pragmatic way.

The standard system which we use – that is, an extension to the US classic scaling – is a good approximation to a mathematically perfect logarithmic scaling. It is shown in the table overleaf, with two types of box size, one for stocks with a normal volatility and one for stocks with a low volatility.

Table 6.2 – Standard scaling

| Standard | | Normal Volatility | Low Volatility |
from	to	Box Size	Box Size
1	1.4	0.02	0.01
1.4	2.9	0.05	0.02
2.9	6	0.1	0.05
6	14	0.2	0.1
14	29	0.5	0.2
29	60	1	0.5
60	140	2	1
140	290	5	2
290	600	10	5
600	1400	20	10
1400	2900	50	20
2900	6000	100	50
6000	14000	200	100

The standard system has quite a few advantages, but most of all it is *easy to apply*. Used in the way that we use it, it comes quite close to the mathematical correctness of logarithmic scaling, but has the advantage of generating user-friendly price levels.

When using other than constant box sizes from a standard p&f software package you have to make sure that you understand the general concept of how the computer calculates them. It may give you some reassurance to know that we have invested quite a lot of time testing the scaling done by the software packages we recommend. Be aware – some software or chart services use linear percentage charts, whereby they simply divide the trading range into equal boxes. That is of course the easiest way to scale with a computer, but it is fundamentally flawed and most importantly, it means that each and every time the stock makes a new high or low the box sizes change, which makes such charts unusable in the long run.

In the two following examples you will see the difficulties of charting securities with a big span in prices. Big price intervals are typical for long-term charts or volatile stocks (like the technology sector). But even an index of a mature stock market, like the Hang Seng in our example, can have price moves that make the application of increasing box sizes a must.

Chart 6.1 – Scaling of the Hang Seng [HIS]

```
^HSI / 3 box rev, / 1997.01.02 to 2002.01.07
18000  .....................|...................|..................|..3.X.X...|..........|18000
17500  .....................|...................|..................|X.XOX4X9..|..........|17500
17000  _____X_XOXOXO7O_____ 17000
16500  .........8...........|...................|................X1XOXO.OXO..|..........|16500
16000  .........XO..........|...................|.............COXO...OXOX.1...|..........|16000
15500  .........70..........|...................|............XO2....OXOXOX3...|..........|15500
15000  ......6.XOX..........|...................|...........XO.....O6OBOXO........|..........|15000
14500  _____XOXOXA_____7_____X_____5XA_OCO_____ 14500
14000  .X.....XOX9XO........|...................|.......XO...X.X|.....OX..O|O..........|14000
13800  .XOX...XO.OXO........|...................|.......XO..X.XOX|.....OX...|O..5.X....|13800
13600  .XOXOX.X..OXO........|...................|....X.X.XOX.X9XOX|.....O....|O..XOXO...|13600
13400  .XO2OX3X..OXO........|...................|....XOXOXOXOXOXOB|..........|O..XO6O....|13400
13200  1_O_OXOX__OXO_____XO5OXOXOXOXO_OX_____O__XO_O____ 13200
13000  ....0.05..0.0........|...................|..X.XO.OXO8OX..OX|..........|OX.X..O...|13000
12800  ......OX....O........|...................|.XOX..OXO.OX..OX|..........|OX4X..O...|12800
12600  ......OX....O........|...................|.XOX..OX..O..AX|..........|OXOX..7...|12600
12400  ......OX....O........|...................|.XO...OX.....OX|..........|O.OX..O...|12400
12200  _____4X____O_____X____O6____O_____O__O_____ 12200
12000  ......O.....O........|...................|.X....O........|..........|.....8....|12000
11800  ......O.....X..|.........X..............|.X.............|..........|.....O..X.X11800
11600  ......O....X.XO.|.........3.X4.........|.X.............|..........|.....O..COX11600
11400  ......O....XOXO.|.........XOXO.........|.X.............|..........|.....O..XO111400
11200  _____O___XOXO_____XOXO_____4_____O__XO_11200
11000  .........OX...XOXO.|....X.X.XOXO.........|..X............|..........|.....9..X.|11000
10800  .........OXO..BOCOX|....XOXOXO.O........X..|X.X...........|..........|.....O..X.|10800
10600  .........OXOX.XOXOX1...XOXOX..O.........XC.|XOX...........|..........|....OX.B.|10600
10400  .........OXOXOXOXOXO....XOXO...O........B.XOX|XOX...........|..........|....OXOX.|10400
10200  _____OXOXOXOXO_O____XOX____5_____XOXOX1XOX_____OXOX_10200
10000  ...........OXOXO.OX..O...XO.....O.......XOXOXOXO3.........|..........|....OAOX.|10000
 9800  .............O.OX..OX..O....X.......O.......XO.O.O.OX.........|..........|....OXO..|9800
 9600  .........OX..O...O..X.X......O........X....|.OX............|..........|....OX...|9600
 9400  .........OX....O..XOX......O.......X....|.OX............|..........|....OX...|9400
 9200  _____OX____OX_XOX____O_____X____2_____OX____9200
 9000  ...........OX.....OXOXO2....O......X...|..............|..........|.....O....|9000
 8800  .............O......OXOXO.......67....X...|..............|..........|..........|8800
 8600  .............OXO.....OXOX....X...|..............|..........|..........|8600
 8400  .............OX.........OXOXO....X...|..............|..........|..........|8400
 8200  _____OX_____OXOXO__X_A_____ 8200
 8000  .............O........OXO.O..XOX....|..............|..........|..........|8000
 7800  ...............|......OX..OX.XOX....|..............|..........|..........|7800
 7600  ...............|......OX..8X9XOX....|..............|..........|..........|7600
 7400  ...............|......O...OXOXOX....|..............|..........|..........|7400
 7200  _____|_____OXOXO_____ 7200
 7000  ...............|......OXO.......|..............|..........|..........|7000
       --------------------9-------------OX-------9--------------0---------0----------0
       --------------------8-------------O--------9--------------0---------1----------2
```

In the Hang Seng example we use the standard scale and therefore use box sizes of 200 between 6,000 and 14,000, and box sizes of 500 above 14,000.

Chart 6.2 – Scaling of the THUS Group: log 5%!

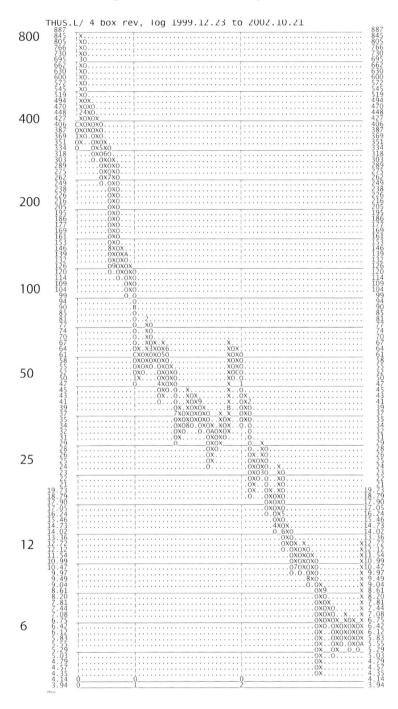

The example of Thus is extreme. The price crashes from a high of 840 to a low of 4.50. Such stocks are best charted with a logarithmic scale, using a high growth rate such as 5%.

Summary

What are the possibilities when scaling my chart?

1. **Standard** – recommended for most stocks and other tradable assets.

2. **Percentage linear** – flaws charting, to be avoided.

3. **Logarithmic** – recommended for volatile stocks, mathematically sound.
    (*Hint*: always first try with 2%)

Why does logarithmic scaling make a lot of sense?

Logarithmic or standard scaling – which is an approximation to logarithmic scaling – has the property that reversals have the same percentage value irrespectively of the price charted. It is clear that security price moves, or returns, have to be compared on a relative basis. That means a 2% move of BARC.L with a 2% move of stock HSBA.L.

Or, explained the other way round, a 100 point down move on the Dow at 1,200 is something totally different than a 100 point at 8500: one represents a 8.3% crash and the other a 1.2% slight correction.

A major argument in favour of logarithmic scaling, therefore, is the *comparability of log-scaled charts*. There are many other advantages, but our conclusion is that, especially for testing trading strategies over the long run and long-term charts, log scaling is a must. Moreover, long-term trend lines only work on log-scaled charts, a fact which becomes especially evident when you look at 'heaven and hell' tech stocks, where during the aggressive up-moves the bullish support lines on non-log scales lose all meaning.

How can I do a logarithmic scale with only a calculator?

You can do this very easily. It's a piece of cake!

Even the most simple calculator will do. You take the last closing price of the stock you want to chart (let's say it was 98.5), round it to the next good looking number (obviously 100). Then you decide what multiplication factor you want to use. Use growth rates between 0.5% to 5%, but let's assume that you choose 3%. Then you just take 100, multiply it by 1.03 and get the next box limit. Then you take that number and multiply it again with the same 1.03. That way you get the boxes above 100. For the boxes below 100, you simply divide the number by 1.03, again and again.

No logarithm table required!

Description of the program environment used

Computer programs and hardware

Overview

Optimisations and simulations are a very delicate matter and therefore you have to be cautious in the choices you make. One thing is whether the purpose is to run statistical studies of trading systems, and the other whether money is involved.

Conducting an academic study is intellectually rewarding and its main purpose, even if it is not fulfilled very often, is to describe something new. As a result, there is no shortage of new financial research, which is good, but often it lacks precision and robustness, both of which are needed if the results are to be used for trading. In academia what counts is the concept. The same is basically true for financial analysts. They can base research reports on the latest findings and facts, issue a recommendation and in the end include some word of caution to soften up the recommendation.

Trading is different.

Either you buy or you sell. Trading systems generate signals, which are acted upon. Starting to feel ill at ease with trading signals is often the beginning of the end of a trader's career. This is because the trader starts to interpret and judge such signals subjectively. He will start to use some, but not all. He will increasingly rely on gut-feeling to decide which ones to use and which ones to ignore. After a while, he has shifted completely from a systematic approach to a gut-feeling approach, which will eventually ruin him.

If you want to do optimisations and analysis of data for real trading purposes with real money, you have to be extremely confident about the programs used, because the results will have a direct impact on the profit & loss in your trading account. P&L is the essence of any trading activity and it is consequently important to use a program that you really understand and know exactly what it does.

How many unsuccessful traders have we seen who use a myriad of parameters, oscillators, indicators and combinations of them, without actually knowing their formula and sensitivity to chosen parameters? The successful trader needs to understand the long-term performance of his system in different market conditions, and what happens when he fiddles around with the input parameters of a formula.

We think it is crucial that the reader conceptually understands both the stability of parameters and that optimisations wrongly done can easily fool investors.

We strongly advise against an amateurish approach to using computers. The *dilettante* uses the computer to back-test all sorts of trading signals, tinkering with parameters and trying to imagine patterns where there are none. Then he does some paper trading, sees that the system he previously thought terrific does not work, and begins all over again.

By contrast, the serious trader understands what makes his system tick. The serious trader understands the stability of the parameters and has a clear expectation of what a technical trading system can do and what its limitations are.

MatLab

We have been careful to choose a programming language which is known for not generating errors in arithmetic and is transparent, so that the code can easily be tested and its quality enhanced. Also the programming language should be of a very high level, which means the written code is easily understood.

For this reason we use the *MatLab* programming environment. This is a software package that is the standard used in mathematics, engineering and finance. Unfortunately without prior knowledge in programming, this tool is cumbersome to use; however, one learns quickly. It is basically an intuitive program language that is used to write one's own code. It can be written fast – once the basics are understood – because there exists a big library of already programmed functions. One could probably also use other highly-regarded mathematical or statistical programming environments that are known for their precision, such as *Mathematica*.

Incidentally, we are not associated with MatLab. We just write about it because it is our choice as the software environment.

MatLab is an interpreter and therefore much more convenient to use than a compiler. An interpreter processes the program code as it is being written. Therefore all variables are convenient to track and the program code can be modified instantaneously. A compiler translates the code first into a faster low-level code. This procedure makes the testing of the program and its quality more difficult.

MatLab is a program one can trust because it is proven to be precise. The code for charting, trading simulation and optimisation is written by ourselves in the MatLab M-language and therefore we know exactly what the program does and that the results are correct and applicable in real trading.

A potential risk of off-the-shelf charting and analysis software could be that errors, even if tiny, survive undetected. As we cannot inspect the program code of such off-the-shelf trading software, it is impossible to find and repair any errors. An additional problem could be the reduced flexibility. Having your own code means you can adapt it to all sorts of special situations or you can link it to an existing trading front-end. Because we have extensive experience with trading software development, we prefer to have control over the code and run our own programs.

In stating our preference for MatLab we would not wish you to infer that we think there are flaws in any of the off-the-shelf charting software products we have already mentioned. We do not! We have tested all the software products recommended in the book. All of them work, and can be used without any concern. From our point of view, having the source code and being able to analyse it and integrate it with other applications is a big advantage, but our program, we must emphasise, is not as user-friendly as the commercial software. It does not produce such beautiful charts, and the loading of the data is manual.

As far as hardware is concerned, as we explained at the beginning of the book, we would simply state the bigger the better. This is especially so for optimisations/simulations, where a powerful computer produces a real and noticeable reduction in the time taken to get the results. In our case, the optimisations used to take about 4 hours on an old portable computer; now, with the new machine, they take about 45 minutes.

Pros and cons of using MatLab

Obviously one could program what we have done in another environment, too, such as C or VisualBasic. Our experience has shown that those programming environments are useful to create fast code with handy graphical user interfaces. The drawback is that much more code has to be written than in MatLab, which has many built-in functions for charting and finance. In MatLab, the code can easily be linked to other existing financial applications, such as the *Financial Toolbox*, *Neural Network Toolbox* or the *GARCH Toolbox*. The combination with the Neural Network Toolbox, especially, made it possible to combine point-and-figure with an artificial neural network that learns and tests p&f patterns and in context with a different neural network can use p&f charts as explicative variables for volatility and short-term price forecasting.

The other big advantage is that MatLab is an entire programming environment designed for fast prototyping. Therefore a technical analysis application can be written in a much shorter time than with a normal high level language, like C or Basic. But it is fair to say that the latest versions of C, C++ environments come very close to the concept of software like MatLab. The crucial point is that because the other languages have a less mathematics-oriented purpose, their code often hides calculation errors and other possible traps.

The biggest advantage for the purpose of this book is that MatLab's M-language is clear and easy to understand. Even if you are not accustomed to MatLab, you will see that it is true, and the code is really easy to read.

The disadvantage of a system like MatLab is the speed. An interpreted program is much slower than a compiled one. We would estimate this to a factor of 20. Doing an extensive analysis of the 100 FTSE stocks takes close to 1 hour with interpreted MatLab. Had we written the code in compiled C we would probably need 3 minutes. Waiting for your output for a whole hour can be unnerving.

Advantages of do-it-yourself programming

You might think that we are perverse: first we talk about do-it-yourself charting with pencil and paper. And now we propose do-it-yourself programming. But we have to stress the fact that we are trading for our own account and that we are therefore highly aware of the importance of the quality of the charts and trading signals. Trading is complicated and stressful enough. One should not make it worse by the use of input – charts/signals – that one doubts. Or by using programs or data sources which are not extensively tested. Knowing that we are using high quality data and knowing what happens inside the computer gives us a lot of confidence. And to be confident entering a position or exiting it makes trading a much better experience.

Thus the advantages of do-it-yourself programming are:

1. In-depth understanding of the methodology.

2. In-depth understanding of the computer output.

3. Possibility to view and alter the code if a suspicion of an error occurs.

4. Independence of the charting software vendor.

5. Independence of new releases in the software or operating systems.

6. Only real possibility to perform automatic optimisation / simulation cycles.

The data

It goes without saying that the data is the essence for running a computerized trading system, which is expressed very well in the classic statistics lemma *trash in, trash out*. The lemma applied to technical trading means, of course, that if one uses data with many errors, a lot of false trading signals are generated. We therefore recommend using data which is completely trustworthy. There are many sources of data and normally the data found on the websites of the exchanges themselves is of very high quality. Data providers also adjust the data for stock splits and dividends. In the case of futures – because the contracts expire – the data providers fuse the data of the individual contracts. Databases can easily be tested for problematic errors and then they can be repaired if needed.

How data providers adjust the data for stocks in the case of splits and dividends, and how to do this yourself

When you download data from one of the recommended services you must be aware that stock data is adjusted for splits and dividends. It is also important for you to know about these procedures if you use a database that is updated manually.

Splits

Companies often split stocks, and recently there have been instances of reverse splits. The concept of the split is straightforward: for each share owned, the shareholder gets a number of new shares. In order to keep the data usable for charting or simulating, one just has to multiply the price data with the split factor and the volume with the reverse of the split factor. Say the split is 1 to 2; all of the before-split data would be multiplied by 0.5. And all of the before-split volume by 2.

Dividends

Dividends are a bit more complicated than splits. The stock that pays a dividend reduces a part of its value during that process. The stock ex-dividend has a lower value than the cum-dividend. Normally data providers keep the most recent data correct and therefore you reduce all of the pre-dividend price data by the entire dividend. Volume stays unaffected. The reduction can be done in two ways, either by subtraction or division.

If you need to conduct large studies of profitability, you want the data to be manipulated by subtraction. The reason is that in this way the real amount of trading profits stays intact. The disadvantage is that over very long time series, due to the effect of absolute growth of dividends, stock prices can become negative towards the beginning of the time series.

On the other hand, if you hate to deal with negative stock prices, you would prefer to use a division instead of a subtraction, whereby the pre-dividend data is adjusted in percentage terms, i.e. proportionally. That is the normal procedure applied by the data providers. However such data does not serve for long-range testing of the profitability of a trading system. Because the data is in a way multiplied down towards the left – the beginning of the data series – the P&L towards the left is weighted too little. This could mean that a trading system which is thought in the historic simulation to have made a lot of losses in the early years and more profits in the later years is wrongly given a good overall profitability. If you ran the same system with adjusted price data, the P&L would be much worse. Our conclusion is this:

For charts, use proportionally-adjusted data, and for trading simulations, use subtraction-adjusted data.

How data providers adjust the data for futures, and how to do this yourself

With futures contracts we get into a situation whereby the data series of individual futures contracts have to be merged into one continuous file without distorting the data with the difference in time value. Normally one uses the data of the most traded contract, normally the front month, and uses that data up to the point in the past where another contract traded with more volume. At that point the data is substituted by the data of the higher-volume contract.

The difference of time value has to be determined, by simple differencing, and all data towards the left has to be adjusted with that difference. As in each expiration some quantity is – normally – subtracted, we have to deal with negative prices when we use long data samples.

Data format used

In order to make things simple, we use Excel as our data editor. Because we handle quite a number of data series, as we are active traders, we need a way to handle our data conveniently. Excel is a really user-friendly program and everybody can perform the basic procedures needed in the context of this book. An additional advantage of the Excel spreadsheet is that it is so widely distributed, because it often comes pre-installed on new computers.

We store the data as a space-delimited text file of the format: *date open high low close volume*

How to control the quality of the data and repair it if needed

There are several ways to check the quality of the data.

1 **Spikes**
   The fastest one is to make a simple bar chart and control whether there are any suspicious spikes. Normally, when data is erroneous, it is easily spotted, because errors are mostly in factors greater then 10, meaning that for example a singular data point of the value 5,000 occurs in a data series of a stock that trades normally in the 100s. Such errors are easily detected. Errors on the right side of the decimal point are rare, but will probably stay hidden. However, since they are so small, they are not really a problem.

2 **Missing dates**
   The second quick test is to see if all dates are present. If a date is missing, it is either an error or a date where the specific asset did not trade.

We recommend conducting only those two checks. Except of course if you work with an asset that is notorious for being erroneously reported. The two checks, for spikes and dates, can be done in a minimum of time. In our experience we have hardly seen any errors, especially in the last few years, in the downloaded data from the sources we have listed above.

Where a date is missing or a spike is detected, you can either try to get the data from an alternative source, or, which is much faster, interpolate the missing or erroneous price. We believe that a simple linear interpolation is good enough. That means that in the case of a data series of closing prices of 101, 5000, 103, we would simply substitute the 5000 with 102, which is the mean between 101 and 103. The same would apply to all parts of the data record, i.e. open, high, low, volume.

It should also be noted that if several days are missing or are believed to include errors, then interpolation should only be applied as a last resort rather than a first resort. Before attempting an interpolation, you should check with all possible data sources to see if the missing data can be found and introduced into the database. The trouble nowadays is that databases are checked and crosschecked by the data providers themselves, so your chances of getting the missing or erroneous data from those sources are remote.

It cannot be stressed enough that the data used has to be clean. This is achieved fairly simply for daily data. Using tick or minute-by-minute data generates a much more complex situation. Here we stress the importance of using a high-quality source, such as Tickdata (www.tickdata.com), which guarantees that the data is as good as it possibly can be. Companies like Tickdata are at great pains to clean the data and to make sure that it is error-free. Obviously if one would detect an unnatural spike, one should eliminate it, but not much more can be done with high-frequency data.

How to program point-and-figure

Using a grid

Point-and-figure is best programmed using a grid in exactly the same manner as one uses a sheet of paper with squares. We stress that it is important to have done some charts *manually* in order to really grasp the concept and understand the proposed program.

In the program we use a matrix called grid. Its rows are the box or price levels and the columns also have the same meaning as on the paper grid used for manual charting. As default we use a grid with the size of 400 rows and 600 columns. Those values have been chosen in order that we can generate some massive charts.

We use one grid (`grid`) where we store the relevant price information and a second grid (`mgrid`) where we store miscellaneous information regarding the chart such as trend lines and year and month separations.

In the individual boxes of the grid we store not only Xs or Os, but we actually the record number of the data-point within time series that caused the box to be filled. We indicate X or O with either a positive or negative sign. Storing the record number allows us to retrieve the exact data when using the chart for simulated trading.

To use such immense grids is of course a waste of memory. One could also use a pointer-structure and actually use much less memory. But as memory is so generously available we went for the much more transparent grid-based solution.

Automatic trend lines

It is crucial that the program does the 45 degree diagonal trend lines for you. This is important because computerized trend lines are correct, precise and never overlooked. Everybody that has used bar-chart programs with a trend line facility understands problems regarding ambiguous breaks of trend lines, definition of a trend line and the difficulty in drawing it in presence of outliers.

Our approach to computerized trend lines is straightforward. We define the minimum length for the bullish support and the bearish resistance andd a minimum length for the bullish resistance and the bearish support. Then we have the computer draw all trend lines possible that fulfil the conditions of the defined minimum length. We store the trend lines in the second grid structure we mentioned above. It is important to store the trend lines in a format that allows you easily to test their existence while running strategies that use trend lines.

We choose those minimums in order to maximize clarity of the chart and avoid an overpopulation by minor trend lines. The settings we use are:

*   minimum length for the *bullish support* and *bearish resistance* in the range of **5 to 10**
*   minimum length for the *bullish resistance* and *bearish support* in the range of **8 to 16**.

We draw the bullish support and the bearish resistance lines starting 3 columns left to the relevant high or low and we always draw the trend lines to as much to the right as possible.

Stability of parameters

If you run an optimisation/simulation program you must avoid the trap of over-fitting.

As mentioned before we do this by optimising data over entire portfolios, by filtering the output and by excluding suspicious parameter-sets. What we mean is that we like the optimisation if a gradual change of a variable results in increases and decreases of the simulated P&L without wild fluctuations. We do not like situations where a singular parameter-set generates extraordinary results.

A singular parameter set is normally a parameter set which generates a low number of trades, but for whatever reason, had one or two excellent trades on the price-data tested. When you do computerised optimisations you have to incorporate a way of filtering out such solutions. If you do it manually – using one of the software packages we recommend – then you also have to check to see if a parameter set made all its profits in very few – normally 1 to 3 per year – trades and dismiss it, if that were the case.

Summary

We recommend software packages and data vendors. We run for the optimisations/simulations and charting our own program. The reason is that we like to do quite sophisticated simulations, which is beyond the scope of commercial software. Refer to this book's website (described in the Preface) for updates on our optimisations results.

If you have the knowledge to program yourself, we suggest that you program your own simulation/optimisation software.

- We believe that the approach to work with a grid to store the XO columns and a grid to store the trend lines is reasonable.

Appendices

Appendix 1

Quick reference guide to buy and sell signals

Buy signals	Sell signals

B1   Double Top, or Simple Bullish Buy
B2   Simple Bullish Buy with Rising Bottom
B3   Triple Top
B4   Ascending Triple Top
B5   Spread Triple Top
B6   Upside Bullish Triangle Breakout
B7   Upside Breakout Above a Bullish Resistance Line
B8   Upside Breakout of a Bearish Resistance Line

S1   Simple Sell
S2   Simple Sell with Declining Top
S3   Triple Bottom Breakout
S4   Descending Triple Bottom
S5   Spread Triple Bottom
S6   Downside Bearish Triangle Breakout
S7   Downside Breakout Below a Bullish Support Line
S8   Downside Breakout of a Bearish Support Line

Summary of buy signals

```
630  B1...B2....B3.....B4.....B5.......B6........B7........+B8............. 630
620  ...................................+...................+............. 620
610  ..............................+...................X+............. 610
600  .............................X+...................XO+............ 600
590  ..X.....X.....X.....X.......X...XO+.X...........X+..XOX+.......... 590
580  X.X..X..X..X.X..X..X...X..X..X..X...XOX+X...........X..XOXO+.X..... 580
570  XOX..OXOX..XOXOX..X.XOX..XOXOX.X..XOXOX...........+X...OXOX+X..... 570
560  XOX..OXOX..XOXOX..XOXOX..XOXOXOX...XOXOX+.......+OX...OXOXOX...... 560
550  .O....OXO....O.O...XOXO....OXOXOX...XOXO+.+..O...+.OX....OXOXOX+...... 550
540  .....O.........O.....O.O.O..X.XOX+.....O..+.XOX....O.O.O......... 540
530  ............................XOXO+......O.+.OXOX............. 530
520  ............................XOX+......O+.XOXOX............. 520
510  ...........................O+.......OX.XO.O............. 510
500  ...........................+.......OXOXO............. 500
490  ...........................OXO............. 490
480  ...........................O.O............. 480
470  ......................................................... 470
```

Summary of sell signals

```
470  S1...S2....S3.....S4......S5......S6........S7...........S8............ 470
460  ...................................+............................ 460
450  ..............................X+........X.X............. 450
440  .....X.........X...X...OXO.....XOXO............. 440
430  .X...XOX...X.X..OXOX...XOXOXO..OXOX+.....XOXOX.........X.X.... 430
420  OXO..XOXO..OXOXO..OXOXO..OXOXOXO..O.OXO+.....XO.OXOX......XOXOX........ 420
410  OXO..XOXO..OXOXO..OXOXO..OXOXO.O....OXOX+....X+.OXOXO.....XOXOXO.+..... 410
400  O.O...O.O..O.O.O....O.O..O.O...O....OXOXO+..X.+O.OXO,....XOXOXO+...... 400
390  ..O.....O.....O.....O.....O...OXOXO....X..+.O.O.....XOXOXO....... 390
380  ...........................OXO+.X....X...+..O....XOXO+O......... 380
370  ...........................OX+......X....+.O....OXOX+..O........ 370
360  ...........................O+.............+O....OXO+...... 360
350  ...........................+.............O....OX+...... 350
340  ...........................+.............O+...O+.......... 340
330  ...........................................+............. 330
```

Appendix 2

Glossary of terms used in point-and-figure charting

Accumulation channel

A rectangular pattern formed on a point-and-figure chart before the start of a bullish market (cf. distribution).

Backtesting

The process of testing a trading strategy – or whatever hypothesis – on past data.

Bar chart

The most widely used method to depict price moves graphically. A bar, or vertical line, is drawn between the high and the low of the price range. Often the open is marked with a tick on the left side of the bar and the close is marked with a tick on the right.

Base

Formed by a sequence of point-and-figure columns around the same price levels. A characteristic base would look like a square or rectangle. Bases are used to forecast future price targets via the horizontal count method.

Bearish

i) In general terms, a price trend to lower levels, or investors' pessimistic outlook.

ii) In point-and-figure charting, a chart whose last signal was a sell signal.

Bearish channel

A price move confined by parallel bearish trend lines, on the upper side a bearish resistance line and on the lower side a bearish support line.

Bearish resistance line

A 45 degree, or diagonal, falling line that confines the upper level of a downward price trend.

Bearish support line

A 45 degree, or diagonal, falling line that confines the lower level of a downward price trend.

Box

The base unit of a point-and-figure chart. The name box stems from the squares on the typical paper sheets used for manual charting. Each box is defined by a price level and the size of the box is given by the scale applied. A box can either be filled with an X or an O, or in some cases with a symbol that indicates a time step, usually a new month.

Box size

The distance between one box and the next. It can be fixed or variable and is defined by the scale.

Bullish

i) In general terms a price trend to higher levels, or investor's optimistic outlook.

ii) In point-and-figure charting, a chart whose last signal was a buy signal.

Bullish channel

A price move confined by parallel bullish trend lines, on the upper side a bullish resistance line and on the lower side a bullish support line.

Bullish resistance line

A 45 degree, or diagonal, rising line that confines the upper side of an upward price trend.

Bullish support line

A 45 degree, or diagonal, rising line that confines the lower side of a upward price trend.

Buy signal

A signal or pattern observed on a point-and-figure chart which forecasts further up-moves and which suggests that long positions should be established and/or short positions closed out.

Candlestick chart

A traditional Japanese charting method, which instead of bars (cf. bar chart) uses rectangles which are either filled white if the close is higher than the open or black if the close is lower than the open. Many patterns are described and used for forecasting.

Classic scale

The traditional scale used to define the box sizes for US stocks.

Complex signals

The buy or sell signals that are different from the Simple Buy or Simple Sell.

Day-trading

An active trading style that involves buying and selling the same security within the same day. Usually the position risks are largely reduced by end of each day.

Distribution channel

A rectangular area on a point-and-figure chart that is normally seen as a precursor to a down trend.

End-of-day data

Price information that is collected once the trading has terminated at the end of the day. Normally it is arranged in the following format: Date, Open, High, Low, Close, Volume.

Fixed profit target

A profit target which establishes where the profit on a profitable position is taken. It is called fixed because it is defined by a fixed number of boxes. For example, 12 boxes. (Cf. Variable profit target).

Fundamental analysis

The art of analysing and forecasting prices based on an assessment of the state of (1) a company as represented by the balance sheet and the market, or (2) an entire economy based on economic figures such as growth, unemployment, currency flows etc.

High-frequency data

Price data of liquid instruments that is recorded transaction per transaction.

Historical data

Past price or fundamental information.

Horizontal counts

The point-and-figure method of predicting future price levels based on an accumulation or distribution pattern, i.e. a sequence of similar sized columns forming a rectangle.

Hypothetical reversal level

The price on a point-and-figure chart which, when reached, would generate a reversal. (Cf. price reversal).

Kagi chart

A Japanese chart that has many similarities to a point-and-figure chart.

Line chart

A chart that is drawn by connecting data points on a line. It is the usual format for intraday charts, but seldom used for daily charts, where the closing prices would be connected to obtain the chart.

Logarithmic box size scale

A scale where the box sizes always represent the same return regarding a price. For example, 10 boxes up means plus 100% (value doubled) and 10 boxes down 50% (value halved). They are used to draw long-term and comparable point-and-figure charts.

Long; or long position

Defined (for stocks and bonds) by the ownership of securities; generally a portfolio that gains in value if the market goes up.

Optimisation

The process of finding the parameters that give the best result. In point-and-figure charting it refers to finding the best combination of box size and reversal number in order to obtain the best trading signals.

Optimisation fallacy

The false belief that one can optimise a trading strategy on past data – in-sample-data – and get as good results for future trades or the out-of-sample data.

Over-fitting fallacy

The error of designing an over-complex trading strategy with too many parameters that performs well on the in-sample-data, but is actually no more than a close description of the past data. This is a problem often encountered in time-series analysis and modelling.

Point-and-figure chart

A charting methodology that can be directly applied as a trading system, since it delivers clear entry / exit points and crystal clear trend lines. It is drawn by filling boxes either with Xs for rising prices and Os for falling prices.

Pole

A long column of either Xs or Os.

Price discretization

The method of dividing financial data according to a price scale in contrast to the widely used division according a time scale.

Price objective

The price level that is anticipated.

Price reversal

The reversal of the price trend that is recorded on a point-and-figure chart, once the criteria – defined by the minimal reversal number and box size – are fulfilled. This results in a new column to the right of the last column and a switch from X to O or O to X. (Cf. Three Box Reversal Method.)

Pyramiding

An asset allocation methodology that increases the profitability of winning positions.

Real-time data

Price information that is delivered with the minimal possible delay.

Resistance

A level that seems to impede prices from moving higher. The more often this level is touched, but not broken, the stronger it gets. (Cf. support.)

Risk

The amount of money one could lose if one's position reaches the estimated worst case.

RSI

The abbreviation of Relative Strength Index that is sometimes used by technical analysts to detect overbought/oversold conditions.

Scaling

The way of calculating the box sizes. It can be linear (e.g. each box measures €2), classic (Cf. classic scale), standard (cf. standard scale), logarithmic (Cf. logarithmic scale) or any other clear defined function that determines clearly how to fill the boxes on a point-and-figure chart.

Standard scaling

The traditional scale used for all point-and-figure charts.

Sell signal

A signal observed on the point-and-figure chart which forecasts further down-moves and suggests that action should be taken to close long positions and establish a short position.

Short

A position that makes money if the price goes down

Simple buy

(See: Buy signal)

Simulation

The process of mimicking real trading. Normally, it refers to the testing of trading strategies on historical data without the benefit of information after the start of the strategy in order to make the results of such tests as realistic as possible. For example, a trading strategy might be defined based on the data history spanning 1995 to 2000, and then this strategy would be tested over the years 2001-2002.

Stop order

An order that is not placed at the current price level, which becomes a market order – i.e. an order to perform a transaction after the specified level is reached. Buy stop orders are placed above, and sell stop orders are placed below, the current market price.

Stop-limit order

This is similar to a stop order, whereby the order becomes a limit order once the specified price is touched.

Stop-loss order

A stop order used to close positions.

Support

A price level that holds on a down-move and is therefore not broken. The more often this level is touched, but not broken, the stronger the support gets.

Swing trading

The art of trading the mid-term cycles of a financial instrument, using both long and short positions.

Technical analysis

The concept of forecasting price moves based on observed patterns on a chart, following the lemma that all information is in the price.

Three-box reversal method

The most widely used point-and-figure chart that has a defined minimal reversal count of three, meaning that a new opposite column can be drawn if and only if the existing last column can not be continued and the price move does allow three boxes in the opposite direction to be filled.

Tick data

Price data which is reported on a transaction by transaction basis. It is used in point-and-figure to draw intraday charts.

Trend lines

Lines that confine or seem to confine price moves. In point-and-figure charting they are always either 45% upwards (bullish) or 45% downwards (bearish).

Variable profit target

A calculated, and therefore price-dependant, price target at which an open and profitable position will be closed and profits taken.

Vertical counts

An approximate forecast of the target of future price moves based on past observations of major up or down-moves on the point-and-figure chart.

Volatility

The variability of the price data series. Historical volatility refers to the standard deviation of the historic returns or differences of prices from one day to the next. Implied volatility is the volatility defined by the quoted options prices, therefore it can be explained as the expected future variability of the prices.

Volume

The number of stocks/bonds/futures/other instruments traded.

Whipsawing

Results from a string of wrong trading signals generating a considerable loss through the accumulation of small losses through the frequent change of positions.

Appendix 3

Recommended websites

Point-and-figure software

We recommend any of the following programmes (in alphabetical order):

- MetaStock (www.equis.com), for very basic point-and-figure. We include this software in our list because as it is the most popular it is possible that the reader has access to a licence.

- PFScan (www.pfscan.com), a software boutique's outstanding application with unique features for scanning markets.

- Updata (www.updata.co.uk), probably the world's best point-and-figure charts.

For any readers who are interested in our proprietary software, we suggest that you contact us through this book's web site: www.harriman-house.com/pointandfigure

Data providers

- ADVFN (www.advfn.com)
- Downloadquotes (www.downloadquotes.com)
- Hemscott (www.hemscott.net)
- LSE (www.londonstockexchange.com)
- MetaStock with Reuters Data Link (www.equis.com
- Olsen, for tick data (www.olsen.ch)
- Paritech (www.paritech.co.uk)
- Sharescope (www.sharescope.co.uk)
- TickData, for US tick data (www.tickdata.com)
- Updata Trader II Professional's own data feed (www.updata.co.uk)
- Yahoo (finance.yahoo.com)

Subscription charts

- Chartcraft (www.chartcraft.com)
- Stockcube (www.stockcube.co.uk)

Exchanges

- CBOE (www.cboe.com)
- CME (www.cme.com)
- Eurex (www.eurexchange.com), excellent tick data available from www.deutsche-boerse.com
- Island (www.island.com)
- LIFFE (www.liffe.com)
- LSE (www.londonstockexchange.com)
- Virt-X (www.virt-x.com)

Appendix 4

Bibliography

The All New Guide to the Three-Point Reversal Method of Point & Figure Charting
Michael L. Burke
Chartcraft, 1993

Stephen Eckett on Online Investing
Stephen Eckett
Harriman House, 2002

Fooled by Randomness: The Hidden Role of Chance in the Markets and in Life
Nassim Taleb
Texere, 2001

The Money Game
Adam Smith
Random House Trade Paperbacks, 1976

Paul Wilmott on Quantitative Finance
Paul Wilmott
John Wiley, 2001

Point & Figure Commodity & Stock Trading Techniques
Kermit C. Zieg
Traders Press, 1997

All the above books can be bought from the Global-Investor Bookshop

http://www.global-investor.com

tel. +44 (0)1730 233870

Index

About Harriman House

Harriman House is a UK-based publisher which specialises in publishing books about money – how to make it, how to keep it, how to live with it, how to live without it. Our catalogue covers:

- Personal finance
- Stock market investing
- Short-term trading
- Biographies
- Property investment

Harriman House also runs online financial bookshops under the 'Global-Investor' brand. Our online shop stocks titles from over 200 other publishers, and is *the* specialist in the UK. Whichever book you want, we can get it, and usually offer it at a discount to the published price.

To see our range, visit:

http://books.global-investor.com

or ring +44 (0)1730 233870, or email info@harriman-house.com to ask for a free copy of our printed catalogue.

Harriman House Ltd, 43 Chapel Street, Petersfield, Hampshire, GU32 3DY

Some of Harriman House's books

500 of the Most Witty, Acerbic & Erudite Things Ever Said About Investing
A slim but wickedly entertaining collection of the most memorable quotes on money, wealth, investment, and success. Drawn from writings and speeches of celebrated investors, financiers, journalists, wits, comedians and social historians. Superb conversational ammunition!
2002, pb, 64pp, £4.99, Code 14896

Stephen Eckett on Online Investing
by Stephen Eckett
If you use the internet for investing, you have a choice: do all the work yourself and learn the ropes the hard way. Or hit the ground running with this collection of 200 tips, short-cuts and problem-solving hints. There is so much advice and information in this book, that it repays its cost many times over in saved time and hassle. An essential ongoing reference work.
2002, pb, 276pp, £12.99, Code 14434

The Book of Investing Rules

Global-Investor's acclaimed collection of 'rules' from 150 famous investors, traders, and writers. Reviewed in *The Sunday Telegraph* as *"Almost certainly the most useful financial book published all year"*, it is broad yet focused, serious-minded yet entertaining, a vast tapestry of intelligent thought and comment on how to make money in markets.
2002, pb, 502pp, £19.99, Code 14870

Marc Rivalland on Swing Trading
by Marc Rivalland

Marc Rivalland's unique approach to identifying swings in stock and index prices, using charting methods based on Gann, with four important modifications.

"Having recently purchased your book on swing trading I would just like to say - 'absolutely outstanding'. After 3 years of studying the main indices and indicators in an attempt to find a successful method of short-term trading, and also driving myself half mad in the process, not to mention near bankrupt, I have now glimpsed the light at the end of a very dark tunnel, thanks to your excellent book." M.D.
2002, pb, 224pp, £39.00, Code 14705

The Midas Touch – *The Stategies that Have Made Warren Buffett the World's Most Successful Investor*
by John Train

Warren Buffett is the most successful investor alive – the only member of the Forbes 400 to have earned his fortune entirely through investing. Bestselling author John Train analyses the strategies, based on the value approach, that have guided Buffett in his remarkable career, and summarises the 'rules' which private investors can use in their own investing.

> 'If you had put $10,000 in Buffett's original investing partnership at its inception in 1956, you would have collected about $293,738 by the time he dissolved it at the end of 1969. He had never suffered a down year, even in the severe bear markets of 1957, 1962, 1966, and 1969. When the partnership was wound up, you could have elected to stay with Buffett as a shareholder of Berkshire Hathaway, Inc., which was spun off from the partnership and became Buffett's investing vehicle. In that event, your $10,000 would by the end of 1986 have turned into well over $5 million.'

So, John Train introduces the remarkable story of Warren Buffett in his classic text, The Midas Touch. First published in 1987, The Midas Touch

was one of the first books to recognise Warren Buffett's spectacular record, and to attempt to explain how he achieved his success. It is short, lucid and written with style and wit. A worthy testimony to its remarkable subject.
2003, hb, 208pp, £14.00, Code 15842

Andrew McHattie on Covered Warrants
by Andrew McHattie

The UK's leading warrants expert explains what covered warrants are, how their price moves in relation to their underlying stock or index, the differences and similarities with spread bets and CFDs, and the proven strategies you can use to make profits.
2002, pb, 184pp, £21.99, Code 14709

December 2003

How to Analyse Company Accounts
10 Crunch Questions to Ask Before Buying Shares
by Robert Leach

Many investors ignore company accounts because they think they are too difficult. But, as Peter Lynch said *"Investing without looking at the numbers is like playing bridge without looking at the cards."* The mission of this book is to explain to ordinary investors, with no accounting knowledge, what to look for in a set of accounts and how to interpret what you find – so that you have an accurate 'health check' on a company in 10 simple steps. Robert Leach considers the entire subject from an investor's point of view, by asking, and then answering, the questions which matter most:

• Is the company growing?
• Are costs under control?
• Does it make a profit?
• How much cash does it have?
• Is its market value supported by assets?
• Is it using debt wisely?
• Are there any hidden nasties?
• Is management good enough?
• Can I expect a reliable income?
• Are there any threats to my interests?

He also looks at the techniques which companies use to flatter their accounts, and shows how accounts for companies in different sectors have to be looked at differently.

Due December 2003, pb, £19.99, Code 15717